THE JEWS AND JUDAISM DURING THE GREEK PERIOD:

THE BACKGROUND OF CHRISTIANITY

By

W. O. E. OESTERLEY

D.D., Litt.D.

LONDON
SOCIETY FOR PROMOTING
CHRISTIAN KNOWLEDGE
NORTHUMBERLAND AVENUE, W.C.2
NEW YORK: THE MACMILLAN COMPANY

First published 1941

MADE IN GREAT BRITAIN

THE JEWS AND JUDAISM DURING THE GREEK PERIOD

PREFATORY NOTE

THE importance of the study of Judaism—*i.e.*, the Jewish religion as developed during and after the Exile, and especially the forms it assumed during the Greek period—needs no insisting on. Christianity was born of Judaism, the study of which is a necessary preliminary to the understanding of much that we read in the New Testament. In many respects Judaism was, under divine providence, a preparation for Christianity. To illustrate this is the main object of the present volume. It will be found that there are a large number of passages quoted from Jewish writings belonging to the Greek Period. We have given many quotations in preference to merely indicating references, because the editions of the writings in question are not always easily available to the general reader. It must be emphasized that this book is not intended for specialists in the subject; rather, it is written for those who may be interested in the somewhat intricate investigation, but who are unable to find the time to study the sources and the various works of authoritative writers, English, American, German, and French, who have done so much to further information and knowledge, and to whom the present writer is much indebted.

Our object is to deal with the more outstanding and fundamental subjects; various subsidiary matters are, therefore, omitted. The illustrative material could have been greatly increased; but we felt that that was not necessary; to be exhaustive in this would be wearisome. It will be found that here and there some repetitions occur, but these could not well be avoided.

Warm thanks are due to Dr. Rowley, who has most kindly read through the manuscript, and made some valuable suggestions.

W. O. E. OESTERLEY.

CONTENTS

PART III
THE THEOLOGY OF EARLY JUDAISM

PART V
TEACHERS

PART VI
BELIEF IN INTERMEDIATE SUPERNATURAL BEINGS

PART I: HISTORICAL INTRODUCTION

CHAPTER I

GENERAL HISTORICAL SURVEY

WHILE our main concern is with the history of the Jews, a brief reference to the outstanding events of world-history during approximately the last three pre-Christian centuries is demanded; for it need hardly be said that in various ways, sometimes directly, at other times indirectly, the Jews were affected by the world of their surroundings. This was a period during which, as a result of the conquests of Alexander the Great (he died in 323 B.C.), the world underwent some remarkable changes in almost every sphere. Of these changes, those in which we are here more particularly interested were: (1) the intermingling of peoples of different nations, with a consequent universalistic tendency among certain circles of the Jews; (2) the use of Greek as an international language, whereby the interchange of thought among the nations was facilitated; (3) the influx of oriental influences, the result of which was that religious beliefs were affected in various degrees. These far-reaching consequences, arising out of Alexander's conquests, were not affected by the ultimate break-up of the world-empire which he founded.

I

THE CONQUEST OF PERSIA TO THE DEATH OF ALEXANDER THE GREAT

It was in the year 334 B.C. that Alexander's advance eastwards began. In this year was fought the battle of Granicus (the name of a river in Bithynia), which, as Diodorus (*Hist.* xvii. 19, 21) says, shook the edifice of the Persian empire to its foundations. Although the Persian forces under Darius iii Codomannus greatly preponderated, he suffered a very

I

severe defeat.   Other blows followed : the fall of Halicarnassus,
and the surrender to Alexander of the whole of Lycia and
Pamphylia; similarly, Paphlagonia submitted to him.   But
Darius had not given up the struggle.   There followed the
battle of Issus in Cilicia (October 333 B.C.), at which the
Persians were again badly beaten.   Darius retired into Mesopotamia, where, for the present, he was safe.   Alexander now
turned southwards, his initial purpose being to take possession
of the Phœnician coast-cities, for the Phœnician ships had
constituted the main part of the Persian fleet, the destruction
of which was essential.   Moreover, he could not prosecute
his chief object, the invasion of Egypt, while leaving hostile
cities in his rear.   In addition, he needed the wealth to be
obtained in Egypt before continuing his campaigns.   The
leading Phœnician city at this time was Tyre; other cities
had submitted, but Tyre refused to receive Alexander.   It
was, therefore, necessary for the city to be subdued.   The
siege began in January 332, but it was not until July or August
that the city fell.   On his entry into Tyre, Alexander, we are
told, offered sacrifice to Melkart, the god of the city (identified
with the Greek Heracles).   The only other city that offered
any resistance during his further advance southwards was
Gaza, which held out for two months before it was captured.[1]
The whole coastland of Syria, Phœnicia, and Philistia was
thus mastered by Alexander, and he was now free to advance
upon Egypt.   Here he was hailed as a deliverer.   The
Egyptians had suffered severe humiliation under the yoke of
Artaxerxes iii Ochus (359–338 B.C.), and the Persians were
hateful to them.   So far from desecrating their temples, as
the Persian ruler had done, Alexander showed all reverence
for the Egyptian gods; in Memphis he sacrificed to Apis,
and was recognized as Pharaoh of Upper and Lower Egypt.
After a stay in Egypt till the spring of 331, Alexander left for
Tyre, where he spent some time organizing the territories he
had conquered.   In the meantime, efforts had been made by
the Persians in getting together an army for attacking Alexander.   At the beginning of October 331 battle was joined
in the plain of Gaugamela, on the east of the Tigris; the

---

[1] For Alexander's entry into Jerusalem (Josephus, *Antiq.* xi. 325 ff.) see
the next chapter, p. 16.

Persians were again decisively beaten, and, as a result, the Persian empire was a thing of the past. Syria, Egypt, and Mesopotamia were now all incorporated in the empire of Alexander the Great. These are the lands with which we shall be mainly concerned; it will not, therefore, be necessary for our present purposes to deal with Alexander's conquests farther east.

In the summer of 325 B.C. Alexander turned westwards again; activities of many kinds occupied him, and he did not arrive back in Babylon until the spring of 323. But the tremendous physical and mental strain, undergone incessantly year-in, year-out, had told upon him only too ominously. In the early summer of this year symptoms of malarial fever, so easily caught owing to the marshy surroundings of Babylon, began to manifest themselves in him, and his vitality quickly wasted away. In the evening of the 13th of June 323 he died. He was not yet thirty-three years old, and had reigned for twelve years and eight months.[1]

II

FROM THE DEATH OF ALEXANDER THE GREAT TO THE
CONQUEST OF CŒLE-SYRIA BY ANTIOCHUS III

On the death of Alexander the question of his successor raised grave issues.[2] His half-brother Philip, or his posthumous son Alexander, by his wife Roxana, might, either of them, be regarded as his lawful heir. Each was at first supported by one or other of the dead monarch's generals. But loyalty to the memory of Alexander gave way to personal ambition; and the long struggle which now followed had not as its object the continuance of his dynasty, but the striving for world-power on the part of these generals, who had been the governors of different provinces. Each aspirant to power was faced by a coalition of his rivals; and most of them met with a violent death. It is not necessary to follow out the details

[1] For Alexander's conquest of Persia see the interesting account in Rogers' *A History of Ancient Persia*, pp. 268–370 (1929); and for his love of Greek culture see Wilcken, *Alexander the Great* (transl. by G. C. Richards, 1932), pp. 256 ff.

[2] For details see Bevan, *A History of Egypt under the Ptolemaïc Dynasty*, pp. 18 ff. (1927).

of this struggle; the climax was reached at the battle of Ipsus, in Phrygia (301 B.C.). This was fought between four of those who had been Alexander's generals, namely, Lysimachus, who ruled the province of Thrace, Seleucus, that of Babylonia, and Cassander, that of Macedonia, against Antigonus, who ruled over Pamphylia, Lycia, and Phrygia, being thus master of all Asia Minor. The victory was gained by the allies, and Antigonus lost his life; his Asiatic empire thus came to an end. But his son, Demetrius Poliorcetes, was able to retain Macedonia and the Phœnician coast-land of Syria. Here it must be pointed out that Ptolemy Lagi, the satrap of Egypt, who had joined the allies, did not support them in the battle of Ipsus, as he was engaged in invading Cœle-Syria (Palestine). It had been agreed before the battle that this land should be assigned to Ptolemy, but as a result of his failure to appear at Ipsus, the original agreement was declared void by Seleucus and the two other allies. This was destined to have serious consequences later; but as Ptolemy was now in possession of Cœle-Syria, no action was taken against him. Diodorus (xxi. 5) quotes Seleucus as saying that " with regard to Cœle-Syria, he would not for the present, for the sake of their friendship, take any action. Later on he would consider the best way of treating friends who tried to grasp more than was their right."

Alexander's empire, though theoretically one and fundamentally Greek throughout, was then divided up into various parts. Of these the three most important were: (1) Syria, including the bulk of what had been the Persian empire in Asia, as well as some parts of Asia Minor; here Seleucus founded the Seleucid dynasty; (2) Egypt, where Ptolemy Lagi founded the Ptolemaïc dynasty; and (3) Macedonia, including Greece, where the dynasty of the Antigonidæ was established. During the third century B.C. these three powers, bordering on the eastern Mediterranean, play the leading part in world-history. Our main concern is, however, with the first two.

The outstanding fact in the state of affairs to be noted during this period is the alliance of the Seleucids and the Antigonids against the house of Ptolemy. Egypt had become a great naval power, and as such it was always a source of

potential menace to the coastal lands within the domains of
the two other powers respectively. As Bevan remarks: " A
power which created a sea-empire, spreading its influence
over all the coasts and islands of the Levant, and interfering
in the politics of Greece and Ionia, was not a power which
either Seleucid or Antigonid could tranquilly behold." [1]
Nevertheless, the years which followed the battle of Ipsus
were comparatively peaceful. Seleucus was at first mainly
occupied with the internal development of his empire; but
in later years he penetrated into the West, and ultimately
gained, with the exception of Egypt, the whole of what had
been the realm of Alexander the Great from Greece [2] to
Central Asia and India. He was murdered in 281 B.C.
Ptolemy, however, was not again engaged in war; he died
peacefully in 282 B.C. The two kings were succeeded, respectively, by their sons, Antiochus i, Soter, and Ptolemy ii,
Philadelphus. From now on the hostility, just mentioned,
of the Seleucid and Antigonid powers against the house of
Ptolemy continued almost incessantly; with one or other of
them Egypt, before very long, was again and again at war.
Our main concern is with the struggles between Syria and
Egypt. True, for some years the relations between them were
friendly. It is a little difficult to decide what was the actual
cause of the war between the two powers which broke out in
274 B.C. There was, of course, the initial bone of contention
regarding the Cœle-Syrian question, mentioned above. But
apart from that, the continued efforts of Ptolemy ii to extend
his power over-seas may well have aroused more pronounced
hostility on the part of Antiochus i. Circumstances arose,
moreover, which were utilized by the latter to curb the power
of Egypt. When his son-in-law, Magas, viceroy of the province
of Cyrene, repudiated Egyptian overlordship, and took up a
hostile attitude towards Ptolemy ii, he was supported by
Antiochus i, and war was declared by them against Egypt.
From this it would appear that the war which now broke out
was due to the initiative of Antiochus i. On the other hand—
and this shows the difficulties presented by the records in

---

[1] *The House of Seleucus*, i. 146 (1902).
[2] After the battle of Corupedion and the death of Lysimachus, Greece
lay open to Seleucus, but before actually entering into possession he was
murdered.

obtaining any clear and reliable guide regarding the course of events at this time—a Babylonian cuneiform text refers to the outbreak of war at a somewhat earlier date.[1] According to this, Ptolemy invaded Syria as early as the spring of 276; this would suggest that he feared a hostile attack on Egypt. The Babylonian text in question says that the army of Ptolemy was routed in Syria. However this may be, the war continued, and it was not until 272/1 that Antiochus i made peace, leaving Egypt, on the whole, with the balance of gain. During the remainder of his reign Antiochus i was occupied with affairs in the western part of his empire. He died while fighting against Eumenes i of Pergamum, in 261, and was succeeded by his son Antiochus ii, Theos. Soon after his accession this king sought to extend his power in Syria, and war broke out again with Egypt. Very little is known about the details of this conflict, but what is certain is that Cœle-Syria and Phœnicia remained in possession of Ptolemy ii. Peace was made in 252, and the two royal houses became allied by marriage, Antiochus ii taking Berenice, the daughter of Ptolemy, to wife. In 246 Antiochus died; he was succeeded by his son Seleucus ii, Callinicus. Shortly after, in 245, Ptolemy ii also died; his son, now Ptolemy iii, Euergetes, had already, in 247, been appointed joint-ruler with his father.

And now, once again, war broke out between Egypt and Syria. The cause of this was as follows: Antiochus ii had married his half-sister Laodice, the daughter of Antiochus i, by whom he had two sons; but when the peace, in 252, was made between him and Ptolemy ii, he had agreed to take Berenice, Ptolemy's daughter, as his wife, and to repudiate Laodice; the latter was banished to Ephesus with her two sons. For this Laodice was later terribly avenged. After some years, in 246, she induced Antiochus to come back to her, in Ephesus. Here Antiochus suddenly died, whether poisoned at the instance of Laodice or not is uncertain, though suspicion fell on her. Thereupon she sent emissaries to Antioch who put Berenice and her infant son to death. Laodice's son, Seleucus, was then proclaimed king. The murder of Ptolemy's daughter and his grandson was an intoler-

---

[1] Sidney Smith, *Babylonian Historical Texts*, p. 152 (1924).

able outrage on the honour of the house of Ptolemy. As a result, the third war, called the "Laodicean War", broke out between Syria and Egypt.

At first Ptolemy iii was victorious, and conquered the whole of northern Syria; but on his being called back to Egypt on account of internal unrest, the conquered territories were regained by Seleucus ii. The Syrian king, as he now was, then sought to take possession of Palestine, but he was defeated, and had to retire to his own land. Peace was concluded in 240, and for a considerable period fighting ceased between the two countries. Seleucus ii died in 226, and was succeeded by his son Seleucus iii; but he reigned only for a few years, when he was poisoned, 223. His younger brother, Antiochus iii, the Great, then became king. In Egypt, Ptolemy iii died in 221, and was succeeded by his son, Ptolemy iv, Philopator, who was only twenty-three years of age; but Antiochus was still younger, having but reached the age of eighteen years. Owing to his youth—"almost a boy", as Polybius says—Antiochus seems to have been entirely under the influence of Hermeias, who had been at the head of the government in the time of Seleucus iii. It was on his advice that Antiochus determined to attempt the conquest of Syria 221 B.C. The first attempt, however, failed; for the efficient state of the Lebanon fortresses withstood the assaults of the Seleucid army. Antiochus had, for the present, to give up all further thoughts of advance owing to troubles in Babylonia, where his presence was demanded. For the time being no further attack was undertaken. But towards the end of the year 220, Antiochus, having satisfactorily quieted the symptoms of unrest in Babylonia, determined upon a renewed attempt to conquer Cœle-Syria. A good opportunity had, moreover, now presented itself, for Ptolemy iv, Philopator, had come to the Egyptian throne, a weak and self-indulgent ruler, "inattentive to business", as Polybius tells us, "and difficult of approach, and treating with entire negligence and indifference the agents charged with the conduct of affairs outside of Egypt." [1] As a first step, Seleucia in Pieria, on the coast, which had previously been conquered by Ptolemy iii, Euergetes, was captured. Then the invasion proper of the

[1] *Histories* v. 34.

B

land began. And this time Antiochus was, in the end, successful. Especially helpful to him was the action of Theodotus, the Governor of Cœle-Syria. Polybius records, in reference to him, as follows: " Holding the king (i.e. of Egypt) in contempt owing to his debauched life and general conduct . . . he now formed the project of entering into communication with Antiochus, and of handing over to him the cities of Cœle-Syria." [1] The important cities of Ptolemaïs and Tyre were soon occupied. Antiochus was then held up for a brief space by the Egyptian general Nicolaus, who withstood him in the fortress of Dora, south of Mount Carmel. He then retired into winter quarters,[2] leaving Theodotus in charge of the territories so far conquered. This, however, gave time to Sosibius, the Egyptian commander-in-chief, to reorganize his army in expectation of further attack. And this took place early in the year 218. The Egyptians, under Nicolaus, were stationed at Gaza. Nicolaus advanced northwards in order to intercept the Syrians in the Lebanon district. At first he had the advantage on account of the strong position of his forces entrenched on the slopes of the Libanus; but then, as Polybius records, " when Theodotus had forced back the enemy at the foot of the mountain, and then charged from higher ground, Nicolaus and his whole force turned, and fled precipitately " (v. 69). The remnant of the routed Egyptian army retreated to Sidon. After a short, but ineffectual, siege, Antiochus proceeded along the coast southwards, bent on more important conquests. On reaching Ptolemaïs he turned inland and captured Philoteria, on the Lake of Galilee; then, crossing the Jordan, he got possession of the eastern districts, and turning southwards, he captured Gadara, Philadelphia (Rabbath-Ammon), and other strong cities. Leaving sufficient forces in these parts, Antiochus returned to Ptolemaïs and took up winter quarters. In the spring of the next year (217), Polybius goes on to relate, " Antiochus and Ptolemy had completed their preparations, and were determined on deciding the fate of the Syrian expedition by a battle " (v. 79). This followed soon afterwards at Raphia. Polybius gives us a detailed description of this battle; the Syrian army suffered a disastrous defeat, and the whole of

---

[1] *Histories* v. 40.   [2] *Ibid.* v. 29.

southern Syria, Phœnicia, and Palestine, were once more firmly in Egyptian possession. " Such was the result ", says Polybius, " of the battle of Raphia fought by the kings for the possession of Cœle-Syria. After paying the last honours to the dead, Antiochus returned to his own kingdom with his army, and Ptolemy took without resistance Raphia and the other towns, each community endeavouring to anticipate its neighbours in going over to him and resuming its allegiance " (v. 86). Ptolemy, according to Polybius, regarded the victory as an " unexpected success "; and as the regaining of the possession of Cœle-Syria " surpassed his expectations ", he was glad to fall in with Antiochus' request for peace. After the victory, he tells us further, Ptolemy " remained three months in Syria and Phœnicia setting things in order in the cities ". It was during these months that, according to *iii Macc.* i. 9, Ptolemy came to Jerusalem, and " sacrificed to the Most High God, and offered thank-offerings, acting in some measure according to what was fitting to the place ".[1] This is likely enough to be historical, but what follows about the king's attempt to enter into the Holy of Holies, and the consequences following thereon, suggest the play of the imaginative powers of some devout Jew rather than historical reality. On the other hand, we have an important and reliable reference to the battle of Raphia, and what followed, in *Dan.* xi. 11 ff.: " And the king of the south (i.e. Ptolemy iv) shall be moved with choler, and shall come forth and fight with him, even the king of the north (i.e. Antiochus iii), and he shall send forth a great multitude, but the multitude shall be given into his hand (i.e. that of Ptolemy). And the multitude shall be carried away and his heart shall be exalted, and he shall cast down tens of thousands, but he shall not prevail (in reference to the final issue). And the king of the north shall return . . . and cast up a mount, and take defenced cities; and the arms of the south shall not withstand, neither his chosen people, neither shall there be any strength to withstand." These last words refer to the victory which Antiochus ultimately gained. To this we shall come presently. After

---

[1] This apologetic work belongs to about 100 B.C.; while it contains much that is unhistorical, it may well have been indebted to earlier sources for some historical details.

the battle of Raphia, Antiochus was too much taken up with
matters in various parts of his widespread empire to entertain,
for the present, further projects for the conquest of Cœle-
Syria.   Nevertheless, he had no intention of abandoning what
was the traditional aim of the Seleucids.   Years elapsed before
Antiochus felt free to turn his attention to Egypt; it was not
until 203 B.C. that the opportunity presented itself for the
new attempt.   In this year Ptolemy iv died, and his four-
year-old son, Ptolemy v, Epiphanes, came to the Egyptian
throne.   Rival factions at court and unrest among the native
Egyptian populations ensued, and Antiochus was not slow
to seize the opportunity thus offered.   Some preliminary
and indecisive fighting took place at first.   But in 201/200 B.C.
the battle of Panion (at the sources of the Jordan) was fought,
and Antiochus gained an overwhelming victory over Scopas,
the Egyptian general.   Scopas fled with the remnant of his
army to Sidon, where Antiochus besieged him by land and
sea.   The siege lasted till the spring of 199 B.C.; by then the
garrison was starved out, and Scopas surrendered; both he
and his troops were permitted to withdraw.   The victory of
Antiochus resulted in the whole of Syria being incorporated
in his empire.   The peace which followed was cemented by
the betrothal of his daughter Cleopatra to Ptolemy v, Epiphanes; the actual marriage took place in 196.   The remainder
of the reign of Antiochus iii was taken up with his war with
Rome.   The indemnity he had to pay took many years to
raise, and was the cause of the severe taxation imposed on
the Seleucid dominions, including Palestine, and also the
spoliation of temples.   The greater oppressiveness of Seleucid
rule, due in part to this cause, was one of the reasons which
led to the Maccabæan revolt.   For many factors entered into
that revolt.   Again, Antiochus had to leave a hostage in
Rome until the indemnity should be paid.   Antiochus
Epiphanes spent some time in Rome as the hostage, and
there learned that respect for Roman power which made him
hesitate when Rome's envoy met him in Egypt.   Still more
important, when Seleucus iv was murdered by Heliodorus,
the true heir to the throne was then the hostage in Rome.
Hence Antiochus Epiphanes was a usurper, and this fact made
his rule the more intolerable to subjects who had other grounds

for disaffection. When at last peace was made with Rome
Antiochus iii went into the East, and the Mediterranean lands
never saw him again. " The tidings came back to Antiochus
(Epiphanes) that he had adventured himself with a body of
troops in the Elymæan hills (the modern Luristan), where the
temple of some native god promised great spoil of silver and
gold, and had been overwhelmed by the fierce tribesmen.
That was the generally received version of his end." [1]

III

FROM THE DEATH OF ANTIOCHUS III TO THE DOWNFALL OF THE SYRIAN KINGDOM

Antiochus iii was succeeded by his son Seleucus iv, Philopator; but of his reign there is nothing of importance to
record for our purposes; he was murdered by Heliodorus,
the chief minister, in a conspiracy formed against him (175 B.C.).
His brother, Antiochus iv, Epiphanes, though not the rightful
heir, for Seleucus iv had children, usurped the Syrian throne.
In reference to him it is said in *Dan.* xi. 21–25: " And in his
(i.e. Seleucus iv's) place shall stand up a contemptible person,
upon whom had not been bestowed the honour of the kingdom (i.e. he had usurped it); but he shall come in time of
security (i.e. shall take them unawares), and shall obtain the
kingdom by flatteries (i.e. by guile). And armies shall be
utterly swept away from before him (i.e. the armies of Heliodorus and other domestic enemies), and shall be broken; yea,
also the prince of the covenant (i.e. the High-priest Onias iii).
And from the time that they shall make a league with him
he shall work deceitfully. He shall take the field and become
strong with a small force. And in time of security he shall
attack the fattest places of the province (i.e. Palestine); and
he shall do that which his fathers have not done, nor his
fathers' fathers; he shall scatter among them (i.e. his adherents) prey, and spoil, and substance; yea, he shall devise his
devices against the strongholds, even for a time (i.e. the time
fixed in the counsels of God)." [2] This bears out what we
know of him from other sources. Whatever better *traits* of

[1] Bevan, *The House of Seleucus,* ii. 119 f.
[2] Charles' translation in his *Commentary on Daniel* (1929).

character Antiochus iv may have possessed, there is no doubt
that he was by nature crafty, cruel, and utterly devoid of any
sense of honour. Indeed, the description of him as " a contemptible person " is comparatively charitable. More will
have to be said about him when we come to deal with the
history of the Jews. As in our general survey of world-
history we are mainly concerned with its repercussions on the
Jews, there is no need to follow out the details of the relations
between Antiochus iv and other nations. He died, according
to i Macc. vi. 12, 13, tortured with qualms of conscience (see,
further, Josephus, Antiq. xii. 357–359), in 164 B.C., and was
succeeded by his son, Antiochus v, Eupator, a boy only
nine years old. The administration of the kingdom was left
to Philip; he was, however, ousted from his position by
Lysias, who had previously received the rank of Kinsman.
But Antiochus v was not the rightful heir to the throne, for,
as we have seen, his father Antiochus iv Epiphanes, had usurped
the throne; at that time it was the son of Seleucus iv, his brother,
who was the rightful heir; his name was Demetrius, and he had
been sent as a hostage to Rome in place of his uncle, who had
gone as hostage for his father Antiochus iii. Demetrius was
at this time twenty-three years of age, and thoroughly attached
to Rome. That he should have looked to Rome to gain his
inheritance was in the nature of things; and it obviously fell
in with Roman desires, one would think, to have on the
Syrian throne one whom they could trust. Nevertheless, the
Senate refused to let him go. Demetrius thereupon took
things into his own hands, and managed to escape. He was
welcomed by the people of Syria; with his connivance the
boy-king, Antiochus v, and Lysias were put to death, and
Demetrius i, Soter, ruled 162 B.C. His relations with the
Jews we shall deal with later. He was slain in battle in
150 B.C.[1]

Alexander Balas, the pretended son of Antiochus iv, now
usurped the Syrian throne; he was supported in this by
Ptolemy vi Philometor; but not long after, for reasons which
are not altogether clear, Ptolemy was at war with Alexander
Balas, overcame him and placed Demetrius ii, Nicator, the
son of Demetrius i, on the throne (145 B.C.), but claimed

[1] See further the present writer's A History of Israel, ii. pp. 250 f. (1934).

Cœle-Syria as part of the kingdom of Egypt. Events soon arose, however, which baulked him of this prize. No sooner was Demetrius ii recognized as king, than his claim was disputed by Trypho, representing the son of Alexander Balas, named Antiochus vi, Epiphanes. But this was merely a subterfuge; for Trypho aimed at the throne himself. Within three years he had Antiochus vi assassinated, and proclaimed himself king. In the meantime the real king, namely Demetrius ii, had undertaken a campaign against the Parthians; this fell out unfortunately for him, for he was defeated, and taken prisoner (138 B.C.); for ten years he remained in the hands of the Parthians. Now Demetrius had a brother, Antiochus, who lived in the city of Side, in Pamphylia. On hearing of his brother's captivity, Antiochus came to Seleucia, and, as Josephus records, " his forces increased every day, and he marched to fight Trypho; and having beaten him in battle, he ejected him out of upper Syria into Phœnicia, and pursued him thither, and besieged him in Dora. . . . But Trypho fled from Dora to Apamæa, where he was taken during the siege, and put to death, when he had reigned three years " (*Antiq.* xiii 223 f.); according to Strabo (xiv. 668), he was made to commit suicide. The Syrian throne was thereupon occupied by Antiochus vii, Sidetes; and as long as the real king, Demetrius ii, was held in captivity by the Parthians, Antiochus vii continued as undisputed ruler. But this latter, in 130 B.C., undertook a campaign against the Parthians, who promptly released Demetrius, so that, when he resumed his rightful claim in Syria, Antiochus would be compelled to return thither. After some years, however, he fell in battle against the Parthians (129 B.C.). For his relations with the Jews, see below, p. 35. Thus Demetrius ii was once more king of Syria. But the remainder of his reign was destined to be troubled and of short duration. No sooner was he seated on the throne than the Egyptian king, Ptolemy vii, Physcon, set up a rival to him in the person of Alexander Zabinas, the reputed son of Alexander Balas. Not long after, Demetrius ii was put to death (125 B.C.); a similar fate befell his son, Seleucus v, in the same year, who was murdered by his own mother, Cleopatra, one of the wives of the Ptolemy just mentioned. The brother of Seleucus, Antiochus viii,

Grypus, thereupon attacked Alexander Zabinas, conquered him, and became king. After he had reigned for about eleven years, he was driven out by his cousin, Antiochus ix, Cyzicenus, who for two years remained in undisturbed possession of the throne. But in 111 B.C. Antiochus Grypus again appeared upon the scene; and for a number of years there were two rival kings of Syria between whom there was incessant war. Ultimately, in 96 B.C., Antiochus Grypus died. His son, Seleucus vi, Epiphanes Nicator, immediately attacked the rival king and defeated him. In order to avoid being imprisoned, Antiochus Cyzicenus committed suicide. But peace was farther off than ever. Seleucus vi had four brothers, and for about twelve years there was almost incessant fighting between all these brothers for possession of the Syrian throne. The hopeless condition of the country can be imagined. This dreadful state of affairs was at last put an end to by the Armenian king, Tigranes, who annexed the kingdom of Syria, and ruled over it for fourteen years (83–69 B.C.). In this latter year the Roman consul Lucullus inflicted a severe defeat on Tigranes; he placed on the Syrian throne a son of Antiochus Eusebes, one of the five brothers just mentioned, who went by the title of Antiochus Asiaticus, and reigned 69–65 B.C. In this latter year the Roman general, Pompey, who had been given entire control over the East, conquered all that was left of the Syrian kingdom; and Syria, including of course Palestine, became a province of the Roman empire.

Roman history prior to this affected Palestine and the Jews only indirectly. With the conquest of Carthage (201 B.C.), Rome had entered into close relations with the Hellenistic empires; but it is not necessary to discuss here the tangled and intricate affairs of the international politics of these Hellenistic powers into which Rome was drawn. The main object which Rome had in view throughout was to prevent the rise of any Eastern power which might involve danger to herself. This at times had its repercussions in Palestine; but it did not affect the Jews to any appreciable extent. It was only from the time that Syria was incorporated in the Roman empire that the relations between Rome and the Jews became close. With this we shall be occupied in the next chapter.

This historical survey is offered merely for the purpose of presenting a general picture of the world-history as this developed in the surrounding countries of Palestine; for this bears both directly and indirectly on Jewish conditions in every sphere; and it is with these, above all that which concerns the religious sphere, that we are to be occupied in the following chapters.

CHAPTER II

THE HISTORY OF THE JEWS DURING THE LAST THREE PRE-CHRISTIAN CENTURIES

THE brief outline of world-history given in the preceding chapter must now be followed by a survey of Jewish history during the same period before we come to our main subject, viz. the religion of the Jews as this appears during the three centuries under consideration.

I

JEWISH HISTORY DURING THE THIRD CENTURY B.C.

Up to the last quarter we have but the scantiest knowledge of the history of the Jews during this century. While of the two preceding centuries some of the Biblical books give us a good deal of information, and while of the centuries which followed our knowledge is abundant, the third century is, from the point of view of Jewish history, a dark period for the most part.[1] A few facts, however, emerge; and these may be briefly referred to, for from them some important deductions can be drawn.

Here we may mention, first, an interesting episode related by Josephus about Alexander the Great, and his attitude towards the Jews. We have referred above to Alexander's capture of Gaza during his advance upon Egypt (this was in 332 B.C.). Josephus tells us (*Antiq.* xi. 325 ff.) that on leaving Gaza, Alexander went to Jerusalem, and after reverently saluting the High-priest, entered the Temple, and offered sacrifice to God. The account is full of fantastic details, but it is just possible that it may have some basis in fact. In proceeding southwards towards the Egyptian frontier Alexander would not have been far distant from Jerusalem, of which he would certainly have heard. His entry into the

[1] The whole subject is well dealt with by Causse, *Les Dispersés d'Israël* . . . (1929).

Temple and offering sacrifice would be paralleled by similar
action in Tyre, as well as by what he was presently to do in
Egypt. The episode is mentioned in the *Midrash*, on *Lev.* xi. 1,
where the High-priest at the time is said to have been Simon
the Just, showing that the account is independent of that of
Josephus, who speaks of Jaddua as the High-priest at the
time. In each case the mention of these is unhistorical, for
both of them lived later. Nevertheless, to rule out the whole
episode as imaginary fiction, a view held by some,[1] strikes us
as a little too drastic. In any case, Jewish traditions about
Alexander represent him as favourable to the Jews. There
is, further, no reason to doubt the truth of the words of
Hecatæus of Abdera, who lived under Ptolemy i, Soter
(305–282 B.C.), quoted by Josephus (*Contra Ap.* ii. 43) to the
effect that, " for the equity and fidelity which the Jews had
exhibited to him (i.e. Alexander), he permitted them to hold
the country of Samaria free from tribute." [2] He also speaks
of the number of Jews who had enlisted in Alexander's army
(*ibid.* i. 192). These references to Alexander's relations with
the Jews are, it is true, but slight; it cannot be doubted,
however, that, as the great apostle of Hellenism and the prime
instrument of its introduction into Syria, his influence upon
the Jews and Judaism, though indirect, was nevertheless of
importance.

As to the constitution of the Jewish State, and its general
conditions, the High-priest was the political, as well as the
religious, head; he was supported by a Council of Elders,
the *Gerousia*. The Jewish Government, though subject to
Ptolemaïc rule, enjoyed a large measure of independent action,
and so far as internal affairs among their own people were
concerned, the rulers were left entirely free. Indeed, as to
the attitude of the suzerain power, there is every reason to
believe that the Egyptian kings were kindly disposed towards
their Jewish subjects. There was certainly no interference
with religious observances.[3]

[1] E.g. Tarn, *Hellenistic Civilization*, p. 181 (1930), holds that Alexander
" never visited Jerusalem ". On the other hand, see Abrahams' *Campaigns
in Palestine*, Lect. I (1922).

[2] This, as Schlatter points out, is an overstatement; the reference must
be to those villages in Samaria that had attached themselves to Judæa
(*Geschichte Israels von Alexander dem Grossen bis Hadrian*, p. 10 (1925)).

[3] What Josephus says in *Antiq.* xii. 4 reads strangely in view of *Contra*

Jewish territory was restricted to the province of Judæa, i.e., the land to the south of Samaria, but excluding all the coast cities, which were to a great extent inhabited by Gentiles; moreover, no part of the land east of Jordan was included in the Jewish State.

But the circumscribed area which constituted the Jewish State as a political entity was by no means the only centre in which Jews lived; for many of them were settled in other parts of Palestine, and in the trans-Jordan districts. And here a fact of far-reaching importance must be noted. From the time of Alexander the Great the founding of Greek cities in Palestine had gone on apace, while those cities already in existence became largely populated by Greek-speaking peoples. Of these latter the first to be hellenized was Samaria. Alexander had sent an official there to govern the city, but he was burned by the Samaritans; in consequence, the entire population was either put to death or banished; the city was transformed into a military colony, but its original name was retained. In somewhat later times, however, showing the trend of things, the traditional names of cities were changed to Greek names. Thus Bethshean was called Scythopolis, though, in this case, the old name continued to be used together with the new one; Acco, on the coast, received the name of Ptolemaïs; and similarly in the case of other Jewish cities. Then, further, of new Greek cities founded we have, for example, Anthedon, Apollonia, Straton's tower, Philoteria, Panion, Philadelphia, and many others. With regard to this last-mentioned city, situated in the Ammonite country east of Jordan (called by the Greeks Ammanitis), one of the Zeno papyri [1] speaks of a certain Tubias (the Hebrew form is Tobiah) as commander of a cavalry corps belonging to the Egyptian army. " It seems likely ", says Bevan, taking all the evidence into consideration, " that Ptolemy's cavalry commander was the head of a powerful local family, which had its seat in Ammanitis, and, being linked with the priestly aristocracy in Jerusalem, had become half-Jews. Tobiah the Ammonite of the book of Nehemiah who had married a

---

Ap. ii. 44; in any case what is said in the former is an isolated act. For the Ptolemaïc attitude to the Jews, see, further, *Contra. Ap.* ii. 45–47.

[1] C. C. Edgar, in *Annales* xviii and following vols. (1919 . . .), Pap. 13.

daughter of the Jewish High-priest, and whom Nehemiah roughly chased out of Jerusalem, was probably an ancestor of the Ptolemaïc Tubias." [1] That is an interesting point, and illustrates the close contact between Jews and Greeks, to which we must now draw more particular attention.

II

HELLENISTIC INFLUENCE UPON THE JEWS [2]

It was during the period of comparative peace, so far as Palestine was concerned, which resulted from the battle of Ipsus (301 B.C.), that Hellenistic influence upon the Jews became marked; an influence which was furthered through the considerate treatment accorded them by their Egyptian suzerains. The founding during this and the next century of Greek cities contributed, of course, immensely to the spread of this influence; for, as we have seen, these Greek cities sprang up in Palestine, as well as elsewhere; they had not merely a strategic, but also a cultural, purpose. The intercourse in regard to every-day affairs demanded the speaking of the Greek world-language, as it had now become.[3] This applies especially to trade and industry; but intercourse of this kind brought with it assimilation in various directions, customs and habits of Greek type were adopted, even down to fashions and the wearing of ornaments. Thus the stamp of the Greek spirit impressed itself upon the ordinary affairs of life. But far more important was the influence of Hellenism in the higher spheres; and here, too, Palestinian Jewry with its Greek environment was not unaffected; municipal organization, legislation, the administration of justice, the arrangements for public welfare, and so on, all were in one way or another indebted to the higher culture of the Greeks. Then, as to the most important sphere of all, religious belief, it must be noted that, prior to the Maccabæan wars many Jews had grown lax both in religious practice as well as in tradi-

---

[1] *The Ptolemaïc Dynasty*, p. 72 (1927).

[2] For details regarding the influence of Hellenism on the Jews we would refer especially to Schürer, *Geschichte des Jüdischen Volkes*, i. pp. 187 ff. (1901), ii. pp. 27–89 (1907); Wendland, *Die Hellenistisch-Römische Kultur . . .*, pp. 187–211 (1912); Tarn, *Hellenistic Civilization*, pp. 181–208 (1930).

[3] " Greek might take a man from Marseilles to India, from the Caspian to the Cataracts " (Tarn, *op. cit.*, p. 3).

tional belief; the evidence of the books of the Maccabees
makes this clear,[1] and it is further substantiated by the words
of Hecatæus of Abdera[2] (306–283 B.C.), to the effect that
" under the dominations which were established in later
times (he has been writing about the time of Moses), namely,
that of the Persians, and that of the Macedonians, who over-
threw the Persian rule, the Jews greatly altered the ordinances
of their forefathers " (πολλὰ τῶν πατρίων τοῖς 'Ιουδαίοις νομίμων
ἐκινήθη). This applies, however, only to a certain section
of the Jews; in its fundamental beliefs orthodox Judaism
remained firm.

Among the Jews of the Dispersion things were, as we should
expect, somewhat different, though here, too, the bulk clung,
in the main, to the externals of the traditional faith. Not
only did they pay the annual half-shekel to the Temple
authorities for the benefit of the priesthood and the main-
tenance of the sacrificial system, but, generally speaking, the
rite of circumcision was practised, and the sanctity of the
Sabbath was observed; moreover, the great festivals were
regularly celebrated, great numbers making pilgrimages to
Jerusalem on the occasion of the feasts of Tabernacles, Pass-
over, and Weeks.[3] But in various other respects traditional
Judaism among great numbers of the Dispersion Jews became
transformed, especially among the more cultured classes.
Hellenism had absorbed many oriental elements of belief
which were not without fascination for certain types of Jews.
They looked upon the larger world of their surroundings with
interest and sympathy, very different from the intolerant
attitude of rigid Pharisaic orthodoxy. Their religious interests
were not so entirely absorbed by what they considered true
that they could not appreciate the excellencies of Greek
thought and philosophy; they were ready to accept what
they felt to be true, even if taught in non-Jewish systems.
The outstanding figure of Philo of Alexandria is evidence of
this; but it must be emphasized that Philo was a more or
less unique phenomenon. The Dispersion Jew was a Jew at
heart, but not according to the Pharisaic standard; and

[1] See the quotation on p. 23.
[2] Quoted by Reinach, *Textes d'auteurs Grecs et Romains relatifs au Judaïsme*,
pp. 19 f. (1895).
[3] Cp. Josephus, *War* vi. 420–422, though this refers to a later time.

though convinced of the superiority of his own faith, he was ready to do justice to the opinions and convictions of others. In the *Letter of Aristeas*, 121, 122 we have the following interesting evidence of this: " Regarding discussions and explanations of the Law they possessed great aptitude. They struck just the right balance, for they discarded the hard literalness of the letter and were modest with regard to their own wisdom, and were ready to hold argument, to listen to the opinions of others, and to consider thoroughly every question that might be raised." The result of their general attitude was twofold; for while, on the one hand, there was the conviction of the superiority of Judaism, there was, on the other, the desire to commend it to Gentiles, with the frequent result that it was presented with such modifications that it could hardly be called genuine Judaism. In one important respect, on the other hand, however, Jewish teaching had a marked influence on Gentile thinkers. Dodd gives ample evidence to show that " the Jewish religion drew attention to itself in an age in which may religions sought to commend their teaching to the public, and there is a good deal of evidence of widespread curiosity about it. The Jewish insistence upon one supreme God, completely other than man, worshipped without images, in a temple where His presence was symbolized by darkness and silence, appealed to the best thought of the time, which was all moving, along different lines, towards Monotheism." [1] Many of those who became converts did no more than keep the dietary laws and observe the Sabbath, and this was acquiesced in. A spurious form of Judaism, so far as practice was concerned, thus sprang up in centres of the Dispersion which was looked upon askance by the orthodox in Palestine.

III

THE HISTORY TO THE EVE OF THE MACCABÆAN REVOLT

The Jews under Ptolemaïc sovereignty were, as we have said, treated with consideration. Apart from the paying of tribute, they had little to complain of, and, for the most part, they were permitted to control their own internal affairs.

---

[1] *The Bible and the Greeks*, p. 243 (1935). As to monotheistic tendencies, cp. the belief in Tyche, " Fate ", the one supreme over-ruling power.

This benevolent attitude is well illustrated by the kindly treatment accorded to the Jews living in Egypt, and especially in Alexandria. Josephus has much to say about this (*Contra Ap.* ii. 45–47). He also tells us of the translation of the Hebrew Scriptures into Greek (the Septuagint),[1] encouraged by Ptolemy ii, Philadelphus (285–246 B.C.), for the benefit of the Greek-speaking Jews in Egypt. Doubtless, the narrative of this, especially as developed in the *Letter of Aristeas* (see also Josephus, *Antiq.* xii. 11 ff.), is exaggerated and embellished; but there may well be a basis of truth underlying it. The probability is that the Pentateuch was translated under the auspices of this king; but the translation of the whole of the Old Testament is of later date. It was, at any rate, completed by the time of Ben-Sira's grandson, who wrote the Prologue to *Ecclesiasticus* in 132 B.C. The coming into existence of the Septuagint was an event of high importance for the Jews of the Dispersion.[2]

Further evidence of the friendly relationship existing between Egypt and the Jews is afforded by what Josephus relates about Ptolemy iii, Euergetes, who, "when he had got possession of all Syria by force (i.e. after he had defeated Seleucus ii), did not offer his thank-offerings to the Egyptian gods for his victory, but came to Jerusalem, and according to our own laws offered many sacrifices to God, and dedicated to Him such gifts as were suitable to such a victory" (*Contra Ap.* ii. 48).

Conditions among the Jews underwent a great change when the sovereignty over Cœle-Syria passed from Egypt to Syria. The conquest of Antiochus iii soon brought about a serious rift among the Jews which had grievous consequences for them. Hitherto the High-priesthood had been vested in the house of Onias; but now opposition arose on the part of the house of Tobias. The development of this party strife is recorded by Josephus in his *Jewish War* i. 31, 32: "At that time Antiochus, who is called Epiphanes (i.e. the successor of Seleucus iv who reigned after Antiochus iii), had a quarrel with Ptolemy vi about his right to the whole country of Syria; a great strife arose among the men of power in Judæa; for they had a contention about obtaining the government; for each of those who occupied a position of dignity could not endure to

[1] See further on this pp. 46 ff.   [2] See further below, p. 47.

be subject to his equals. Onias, however, one of the High-
priests, got the better, and drove the sons of Tobias out of
the city. These fled to Antiochus, and besought him to use
them as his guides, and to make an expedition into Judæa.
The king, long since disposed to do so, came against the Jews
with a great army, took the city by storm, and slew a great
multitude of those who favoured Ptolemy, and suffered his
soldiers to plunder them without mercy. He himself robbed
the Temple, and put a stop to the regular practice of offering
a daily sacrifice of expiation for three years and six months."
It is not necessary to go into the details of this strife, which
are very involved and impossible to trace out accurately.[1]
Subsidiary causes, such as possession of the office of *prostates*
(probably the official who administered the Temple treasury)
and the control of tax-gathering, which was a source of
wealth, had much to do with the antagonism between the
two houses; but more fundamental and far-reaching was the
politico-religious cause. The pro-Egyptian house of Onias
championed the orthodox Jews who clung to the faith and
practice of their religion as handed down, while the house of
Tobias, looking to Syria for support, represented the hellenistic
Jews. This is well illustrated by what is said in *i Macc.* i.
11–15: " In those days (i.e. of Antiochus Epiphancs) came
there forth out of Israel transgressors of the Law, and persuaded many, saying, Let us go and make a covenant with
the Gentiles that are round about us; for since we were
parted from them many evils have befallen us. And the
saying was good in their eyes. And certain of the people
were forward herein, and went to the king, and he gave
them licence to do after the ordinances of the Gentiles. And
they built a place of exercise in Jerusalem according to the
laws of the Gentiles; and they made themselves uncircumcized, and forsook the holy covenant, and joined themselves
to the Gentiles and sold themselves to do evil."

This passage shows clearly enough the powerful influence
wielded by the hellenizing Jews; and it was, in the first
instance, owing to them that the step, presently to be taken

---

[1] The classical work on the subject is Büchler's *Die Tobiaden und die
Oniaden im ii Makkabäerbuche* . . . (1899) ; but many scholars do not agree
with all his conclusions.

C

by Antiochus Epiphanes, was prompted. First to be noted is the arbitrary action of the king in deposing Onias iii from the High-priesthood. In *ii Macc.* iv. 7, 8 we read that when " Antiochus who was called Epiphanes, had succeeded to the kingdom, Jason, the brother of Onias, supplanted him in the High-priesthood, having promised the king, at an audience, three hundred and sixty talents of silver, and from another public revenue eighty talents ".[1] What would further have commended him to Antiochus was the fact that, as the context to this passage shows, Jason was a leader of the pro-Syrian party. Doubtless, Antiochus, as suzerain, would claim the right to appoint whom he would to positions of authority within his domains; the office of High-priest was to him nothing more than a local governor of a district. Naturally enough, from the orthodox Jewish point of view the action of the king was wholly unjustified. The High-priest, as divinely appointed, could not be deposed by man, however exalted his position. Jason was, therefore, an usurper; Onias was the legitimate High-priest. However, for the time being the Jewish opposition was passive. So far as Jason was concerned, he felt secure so long as he was supported by the royal favour. For three years he occupied his position of authority. The sordid means whereby this holy office could be obtained is seen by what is said in *ii Macc.* iv. 23, 24, where we are told that Menelaus " being commended to the king, and having glorified him (i.e. the king) as one in authority, got the High-priesthood for himself, outbidding Jason by three hundred talents of silver ". Jason belonged to the High-priestly family; but not so Menelaus, who was a Benjamite. This appointment, therefore, was bitterly resented by the law-loving Jews; and their resentment was greatly increased by the fact that through Menelaus' instrumentality the true High-priest, Onias iii, was murdered (*ii Macc.* iv. 32–34). In the meantime, Jason had fled, and remained in hiding. But on hearing that Antiochus was dead—a false rumour—he drove out Menelaus, and was recognized as High-priest by the Jews. In reference to this

[1] Of this nothing is said in *i. Macc.* i. 11 ff. nor in Josephus, *Antiq.* xii. 237 ff. On the differences in our sources here see Büchler, *op. cit.*, pp. 10 ff.

deposition of Menelaus, we read in *ii Macc.* v. 11 ff. that
" when tidings came to the king concerning that which was
done, he thought that Judæa was in revolt . . ."; and
thereupon Antiochus inflicted terrible reprisals for what he
regarded as an act of rebellion (*i Macc.* i. 24, *ii Macc.* v. 12–14),
and Menelaus was confirmed in the High-priesthood (*ii Macc.*
v. 23).

It is likely enough that the flouting of royal authority may
have been a contributory cause to the action which Antiochus
was soon to take. But there can be no doubt that, as an
ardent Hellenist, Antiochus aimed at enforcing the acceptance
of hellenistic religion and culture among all the peoples
within his empire. Thus, in *i Macc.* i. 41–50, we read: " And
the king wrote to his whole kingdom that all should be one
people, and that each should forsake its own laws. And all
the nations agreed according to the word of the king." How
strong hellenistic religious tendencies were among a large
section of the Jews is seen by the words which follow: " And
many of Israel were favourable to his worship, and sacrificed
to the idols, and profaned the sabbath." The intention of
the king to root out altogether the Jewish religion is then
clearly set forth: " And the king sent letters by the hand of
messengers unto Jerusalem and the cities of Judah, that they
should follow ordinances alien to the land, and should forbid
(the offering of) whole burnt-offerings, and sacrifice, and
drink-offerings, in the sanctuary; and should profane the
sabbaths and feasts, and pollute the sanctuary, and them that
were holy; that they should build high-places, and idol-
shrines, and sacrifice swine and unclean beasts; and that
they should leave their sons uncircumcized, and make their
souls abominable with all manner of uncleanness and profanation, so that they might forget the law and change all
the ordinances. And whosoever should not do according to
the word of the king should die." Emissaries were sent into
Judæa to see that these enactments were carried out. The
way in which this was done demands another quotation,
i Macc. i. 54–61: " And on the fifteenth day of Chislev, in the
one hundredth and forty-fifth year (= 168 B.C.) they built a desolating abomination (i.e. a heathen altar, see below) upon the
altar, and in the cities of Judæa on every side they constructed

high-places. And at the doors of the houses and in the streets they burned incense. And the books of the law which they found, they rent in pieces, and burned them in the fire. And wheresoever was found a book of the covenant in anyone's possession, and if anyone conformed to the law, the king's sentence delivered him to death. In their might they acted thus in Israel with those who were found in the (various) cities, month by month. And on the twenty-fifth day of the month they sacrificed upon the altar (i.e. the " desolating abomination ") which was on the altar (i.e. of burnt-offering). And the women who had caused their children to be circumcized they put to death, according to the commandment (i.e. of the king)—hanging their babes about their necks—together with their families and those who had circumcized them (i.e. the babes)."

We have thought it well to give these quotations in full because they help us to realize how desperate and bitter must have been the feelings of the law-abiding Jews against their oppressors. The result was inevitable, and rightly so, for no right-minded nation can submit to tyranny and oppression, least of all when its most sacred and cherished convictions are trampled on. Doubtless many Jews, true to their faith, set themselves against their oppressors, even at the cost of their lives (see *i Macc.* i. 62, 63); but the first effective resistance was initiated by Mattathias of Modein. This brings us to the era of the Maccabæan struggle.

IV

THE MACCABÆAN REVOLT. THE HASMONÆAN HIGH-PRIESTHOOD

Mattathias, whose home was in Modein, a small city situated in the hilly country between Joppa and Jerusalem, was the head of the family of Hasmon. Nothing is known of the origin of this family, but in later Jewish literature the descendants of Mattathias are called the Hasmonæans, after their early ancestor.

When the king's officers came to Modein to carry out the royal commands, a renegade Jew proceeded to the altar that had been erected, to offer sacrifice. But Mattathias, it is related, " ran and slew him upon the altar " and cried:

" Whosoever is zealous for the law, and maintaineth the
covenant, let him come forth after me " (*i Macc.* ii. 24, 27).
The standard of revolt was thus raised. Among the earliest
of those by whom Mattathias was supported were the *Chasidim*,
the " godly ones "; the mention of them without any word
of explanation shows that they were well known. They
appear here as a definite section among the people; but their
origin must be sought in much earlier times, see *Mic.* vii. 2,
Prov. ii. 28, *ii Chron.* vi. 41, and often in the *Psalms.*[1] They
had long been the most ardent upholders of the Jewish faith
against those who sought to introduce innovations contrary
to traditional belief and practice. They are spoken of in
i Macc. ii. 42 as " mighty men of Israel, every one that offered
himself willingly for the law ".

Mattathias was, however, advanced in years; his death is
recorded in *i Macc.* ii. 69, after he had exhorted his sons to
follow in his steps. Of these he designated Judas " who was
called Maccabæus "[2] (*i Macc.* ii. 4) as " captain " of the
people. And now the war against the Syrian oppressors
begins in earnest. At first the warfare consisted of encounters
between Jewish guerilla bands and small bodies of Syrian
troops, in which Judas was victorious largely owing to the
nature of the hill-country with which the Jews were familiar.
More serious battles soon followed. According to *i Macc.*
iii. 32, the king, Antiochus iv, Epiphanes, who was on the
point of going to the eastern parts of his empire, appointed
Lysias (see above, p. 12) as regent during his absence. It
was, therefore, left to Lysias to quell the revolt of the Jews.
Both in what has just been said and in the accounts of what
now follows, our three main sources, the two books of the
Maccabees and Josephus, are not always in agreement as to
details; but the general course of events seems clear enough.
Lysias despatched three generals to Palestine—Ptolemy,
Nicanor, and Gorgias—with considerable forces. The last
of these began operations by attacking Judas with his army
in the neighbourhood of Emmaus; the Syrian army was
routed, and Judas gained a signal victory (165 B.C.). In the

---

[1] See the present writer's *The Psalms*, I. chap. viii. (1939).
[2] The meaning of the word is uncertain, either the " hammerer " or
the one " marked off ".

following year Lysias himself came with a more formidable force; again Judas was victorious, and Lysias fled back to Antioch. It was after this second victory that the cleansing of the Temple took place, and the inauguration of the feast of *Chanukkah* (" Dedication ") ; for details see *i Macc.* iv. 36–59, *ii Macc.* x. 1–8, Josephus, *Antiq.* xii. 316–325. For about a year and a half the Jews were left in peace, the Syrian forces being required elsewhere. The interval was employed by Judas in extending his authority over the neighbouring districts, partly in order to succour the Jews living there, and also to subdue the Gentiles opposed to him; Edomites, Bæanites, Ammonites, Gileadites, and the Gentiles in Galilee, are all mentioned in *i Macc.* v. 1–15, and in Josephus, *Antiq.* xii. 327–334. At this time Antiochus iv died (164/163 B.C.). As we have seen (p. 12), the son and successor of Antiochus iv was but a child; his father had appointed Philip, one of his generals, as guardian of this boy-king, Antiochus v, Eupator, and as administrator of the realm. But Lysias managed to get hold of the child, and assumed the office of regent. It was not long before Lysias, taking with him the boy-king, came again to Palestine at the head of a formidable force. Judas met the Syrian army in battle by Bethzachariah; [1] valiantly as the Jews fought, they were unable to withstand the superior forces of Lysias, and suffered a severe defeat. Things looked very serious for Judas and his followers, when suddenly Lysias was called back to his own country owing to the fact that Philip, mentioned above, " was returned from Persia and Media, and with him the forces that went with the king, and that he was seeking to take unto him the govern-ment " (*i Macc.* vi. 56). This was a serious matter for Lysias; he realized moreover, as the sequel shows, that though he had defeated the Jews in the battle just fought, they were far from being permanently subjugated. He therefore recognized the wisdom of making peace with Judas, so as to be free to devote all his energies to settling the home troubles. The terms of peace offered to Judas were of extreme significance; here we must quote the words of Lysias as recorded in *i Macc.* vi. 58, 59 : " Now, therefore, let us offer the right hand to these men, and make peace with them, and with all their nation;

---

[1] Situated between Jerusalem and Bethsura, to the south.

and let us make a covenant with them that they (be permitted
to) walk after their own laws, as aforetime; for because of
their laws which we abolished, were they angered, and did
all these things." Now, the sole cause of the last five years'
fighting under the leadership of Judas had been the attempt
to abolish the religion of the Jews. The withdrawal of the
desire to bring this about at once resulted in peace between
the Syrians and the Jews. So far as championship on behalf
of the national religion was concerned, Judas had achieved a
great triumph. The Syrian rulers never repeated the foolish
attempt of Antiochus Epiphanes to stamp out Judaism.

At the same time, the Maccabæan war was far from being
ended; but the strife which was now soon to begin again
was not between the Jews and their suzerain; it was an
internal struggle between the hellenistic Jews and their
orthodox brethren. Religion thus played a considerable
part; but the primary cause was political, i.e. the striving
for rulership in the land. The suzerain power, it is true,
often interfered in this internal struggle; this was not, however, on its own initiative, but because its support was sought,
now by one, now by the other, of the contending parties.

The first step here was taken by the Jewish-hellenistic party.
Lysias, as we have seen, returned to his own country to deal
with Philip; " he removed in haste, and returned to Antioch,
and found Philip master of the city; and he fought against
him and took the city by force " (*i Macc.* vi. 63). The triumph
of Lysias was, however, short-lived. We have referred to this
above, and have seen how Demetrius i, Soter, came to the
throne (p. 12). This was in 162 B.C. Scarcely had he
assumed power when he was appealed to by the leader of the
Jewish-hellenistic party for help; " and there came to him ",
we read in *i Macc.* vii. 5, 6, " all the lawless and ungodly
men of Israel; and Alcimus was their leader, desiring to be
High-priest.[1] And they accused the people to the king, saying, Judas and his brethren have destroyed all thy friends,
and have driven us from our own land." In response to this
the king sent Bacchides, " a great man in the land ", to the

---

[1] According to Josephus, *Antiq.* xii. 385, xx. 235, Alcimus had already
been made High-priest through the influence of Lysias; cp. *ii Macc.*
xiv. 3.

help of Alcimus and his following. In spite of the " great host " that Bacchides had brought with him, it was thought advisable to proceed against the law-abiding Jews by craft; so " he sent messengers to Judas and his brethren with words of peace, deceitfully ". Judas wisely mistrusted them; but others were taken in by these apparently friendly overtures. Among the most ardent upholders of traditional orthodoxy were the *Chasidim,* mentioned above (Hasidæans in *i Macc.* vii. 13); as we have remarked, they are mentioned as though well known, and their formation as a party no doubt goes back to much earlier times. In a trustful spirit these peace-loving men came to Bacchides; but no sooner had he got them in his power than " he laid hands on threescore men of them, and slew them in one day ". Then, having, as he thought, " made sure the country to Alcimus ", and leaving a force with him, Bacchides returned to Antioch. But Alcimus soon found that Judas was too strong for him, and applied for help again to Demetrius. This time Nicanor, one of the " honourable princes ", was sent with another great host. We need not go into the details of all that followed; suffice it to say that Judas won a great victory at the battle of Adasa (north-east of Beth-horon) over Nicanor, who was himself slain. As this victory was won against Syrian forces, it was not to be expected that it could be ignored as of no account by Demetrius. He, therefore, once more sent Bacchides to Palestine to retrieve the loss of *prestige* suffered by Syria. This time Judas was opposed by such an obviously superior force that many of his followers were daunted, and " slipped away out of the army "; Judas was left with no more than eight hundred men to face an army of " twenty thousand footmen and two thousand horse ". To his honour be it said that Judas did not quail; he refused to flee: " If our time is come ", he is reported as saying, " let us die manfully for our brethren's sake, and not leave a cause of reproach against our glory." Foolhardy though it may have been, one cannot but admire the splendid spirit of self-sacrifice, of death if need be, for that which is highest and best of all that is worth living for. Battle ensued (the battle of Elasa), and Judas fell (160 B.C.). " Thereupon Jonathan and Simon took Judas their brother, and buried him in the sepulchre of his fathers at Modein. And they bewailed him, and all Israel made great lamentation for him, and mourned many days, and said, How is the mighty one fallen, the saviour of Israel ! " (*i Macc.* ix. 1–21).

With the loss of their leader the nationalist Jews were scattered; Bacchides instituted a cruel search for them, and many suffered, so that " there was great tribulation in Israel ". But even so, the Jews did not give way to despair. They now elected Jonathan, the brother of Judas, to be their leader. They could, however, only carry on a guerilla warfare in the hilly country, for Bacchides took measures to ensure his supremacy; he divided the land into districts over which he placed reliable officers (*i Macc.* ix. 25), and fortified a number of cities (*i Macc.* ix. 50–52). Having thereby placed Alcimus in a position of security, he returned to Antioch. Two years after this, however, Alcimus died. This necessitated the presence of Bacchides again in Palestine. But he found that in the meantime Jonathan had greatly strengthened his position, and that the task of subduing the patriots was beyond his power. He, therefore, made peace with Jonathan, and returned to Syria. " And the sword ceased in Israel," we read, " and Jonathan dwelt at Michmash. And Jonathan began to judge the people; and he destroyed the ungodly out of Israel " (*i Macc.* ix. 73). The Maccabæans were thus the actual rulers in the land in spite of the fact that the hellenistic pro-Syrian party in Jerusalem continued to be the nominal rulers.

Of what happened during the next five years our sources give us no information. But it is evident that Demetrius, the Syrian ruler, refrained from further interference; indeed, events in other parts of his kingdom would, in any case, have prevented this. Further, from the sequel it can be seen that the hellenistic party had lost its influence over the bulk of the people, who were now ranged on the side of the Maccabæans. Owing to the confused affairs in the Syrian kingdom (see above, p. 13), the Syrian kings could no more support the hellenistic party; they were, therefore, compelled, when external events induced them to seek Jewish support, to apply to the Maccabæan rulers. This occurred when, in 153 B.C., Alexander Balas appeared as a claimant to the Syrian throne.

Demetrius, whose position was by no means secure, vied with Alexander Balas in making promises to Jonathan for his support. In this Alexander got the better, for he offered the High-priesthood to Jonathan, who at once accepted it (*i Macc.* x. 18–21). The further offers of Demetrius to Jonathan (*i Macc.* x. 22 ff.) were not taken seriously (verse 46). The struggle for the Syrian throne continued for the next two years; and in the final battle, which took place in 150 B.C., Alexander was the victor, and Demetrius fell.

For some years, now, Jonathan ruled in peace and quietude. The hellenistic party, being now without their Syrian supporters, gave no trouble; and Jonathan remained on good terms with Alexander Balas. In Syria, however, new complications arose, and in these Jonathan soon became involved. The rightful heir to the Syrian throne, namely the son of Demetrius i, also named Demetrius, came forward to claim his own. His main supporter was Apollonius, the governor of Cœle-Syria; this was in 147 B.C. As Jonathan naturally sided with Alexander Balas, with whom he had always been on friendly terms, he was regarded by Apollonius as an enemy. He took measures accordingly, and attacked Jonathan. In the struggle which followed, Jonathan thoroughly defeated his opponent. In recognition of this signal proof of Jonathan's loyalty to him, Alexander Balas " gave him Ekron, and all the district thereof for a possession " (*i Macc.* x. 89). Elsewhere, however, the enemies of Alexander Balas proved too strong for him; he struggled on for some time; ultimately he was murdered (145 B.C.), and Demetrius ii was undisputed ruler (see below). As Jonathan had been the supporter of Alexander Balas, the new king naturally regarded him as an enemy, and undertook a campaign against him (*i Macc.* xi. 21, 22). But, presumably, Demetrius had in the meantime received information of renewed troubles in Syria, and thought it best to conciliate Jonathan; for we read (*i Macc.* xi. 28, 29) that " Jonathan requested of the king, that he would make Judæa free from tribute, and the toparchies (i.e. Ephraim, Lydda, and Ramathaim), and the country of Samaria; and promised him three hundred talents. And the king consented . . ." The renewed troubles in Syria, just referred to, which occasioned this means of conciliating Jonathan, had arisen owing to the

action of one named Trypho, who had been one of the generals
of Alexander Balas. He put forward a son of this latter,
Antiochus, as a claimant to the Syrian throne. Trypho's
efforts were attended with considerable success; so much so
that Demetrius again had to look to Jonathan for help. This
Jonathan consented to give on condition that the Syrian
garrison which had long occupied the *Akra*, in Jerusalem,
should be withdrawn,[1] and that certain other strongholds
should be handed over to him. Demetrius agreed, and
Jonathan sent three thousand men to his help, whereby he
was, for the present, able to hold his own (*i Macc.* xi. 41-51):
" And king Demetrius sat on the throne of his kingdom, and
the land was quiet before him " (*i Macc.* xi. 52). It is then
recorded, both in *i Macc.* xi. 53 and in *Antiq.* xiii. 143, that
he broke his word to Jonathan, " he lied in all that he
spake, and estranged himself from Jonathan ". It is not to
be wondered at that, in these circumstances, Jonathan transferred his allegiance from Demetrius to Trypho. The latter,
in consequence, rewarded Jonathan by confirming him in the
High-priesthood, and appointing him over " the four govern-
ments ", i.e. of Judæa, Ephraim, Lydda, and Ramathaim,
and making him one of " the king's Friends " (*i Macc.* xi. 57).
This meant that Jonathan was the recognized ruler over the
whole of Cœle-Syria, with the exception of Phœnicia. In
addition to this, moreover, Jonathan's brother, Simon, was
made captain (*stratēgos*) " from the Ladder of Tyre unto the
borders of Egypt " (*i Macc.* xi. 59). In consequence of all this
Demetrius resolved to take vengeance on Jonathan. His
efforts, however, met with no ultimate success; Jonathan
proved himself strong enough to defeat all the onslaughts of
the Syrian king.

The strength of the Maccabæans which had been so signally
demonstrated aroused in Trypho the fear that Jonathan might
frustrate his designs; what these were is recorded in *i Macc.*
xii. 39, 40: " And Trypho sought to reign over Asia, and to
put on himself the diadem, and to stretch forth his hand
against Antiochus the king. And he was afraid lest haply
Jonathan should not suffer him, and lest he should fight

---

[1] This part of the bargain does not, however, seem to have been carried
out, see below, p. 35.

against him; and he sought a way how to take him that he might destroy him." The sequel to this, so far as Jonathan was concerned, is told in *i Macc.* xii. 41–xiii. 24. The end was that Trypho, having secured the person of Jonathan by craft, put him to death (142 B.C.).

While Judas had gained religious freedom for his people, their greatest longing, Jonathan had achieved much in other directions: he had considerably extended the boundaries of the land over which he ruled; he had reduced the hellenistic party to impotence, and he had secured the office of the High-priesthood for his family. The leadership of the Maccabæans was now taken up by Jonathan's brother, Simon.

As already mentioned (p. 13), Trypho succeeded in his designs; he murdered the young king, Antiochus vi, and assumed the kingship as a rival to Demetrius ii. It was the latter who was recognized by Simon, naturally enough after Trypho's recent behaviour. But, with commendable foresight, Simon further strengthened his position in the event of any movement against him on Trypho's part: "And Simon built the strongholds of Judæa, and fenced them about with high towers, and great walls, and bars; and laid up victuals in the strongholds" (*i Macc.* xiii. 33). Trypho was, however, too much occupied in seeking to consolidate his position in Syria, where he "brought a great calamity upon the land". Simon was not again troubled by him. On the other hand, the position of Demetrius ii was by no means assured, owing to Trypho's efforts to gain the throne. It was, therefore, important for Demetrius to have Simon's support. Simon was willing to give this, but on conditions. He stipulated that his land should be free from tribute, which meant that Judæa should no longer be under Syrian suzerainty. Demetrius agreed to this, so that it could now be said that "in the hundred and seventieth year (i.e. 143/2 B.C.) the yoke of the heathen was taken away from Israel. And the people began to write in their documents and contracts, In the first year of Simon, the great High-priest and captain and leader of the Jews" (*i Macc.* xiii. 41, 42). Simon's achievement in gaining the independence of his country was an epoch-making event which he signalized by further proofs of his power and authority; he captured Gazara, Bethsura, Joppa, in all of

which " the enemies dwelt aforetime "; and, above all, he
drove out the Syrian garrison which had for long been in
possession of the Akra, in Jerusalem (i Macc. xiii. 43–53,
xiv. 33, 34). Judæa now enjoyed some years of peace and
prosperity. Simon's relations with Rome and Sparta, of
which we now read (i Macc. xiv. 16–24), greatly strengthened
his position. He wisely sought to renew the friendly relations
which had been established under Judas and Jonathan; this
was cordially responded to by both Rome and the Spartans.
Friendship with Rome was, of course, the more important for
Simon; we can, therefore, appreciate his action, recorded in
verse 24: " After this Simon sent Numenius to Rome with a
great shield of gold of a thousand pound weight, in order to
confirm the confederacy with them."

But quietude for the land was not destined to continue
indefinitely; and once more Simon became involved in the
ever-restless disputes for the Syrian throne. We have seen
(p. 13) that Demetrius ii was captured by the Parthians,
and that his brother, Antiochus Sidetes, came to dispute the
throne with Trypho. And now once more Simon's favour
was sought; Antiochus confirmed all that had been granted
by former kings, and promised, further, that when once he
had defeated Trypho and was established in his kingdom,
" we will glorify thee and thy nation and the Temple with
great glory, so that your glory shall be made manifest in all
the earth " (i Macc. xv. 9). Antiochus then moved against
Trypho, and soon got the better of him, though Trypho
himself remained at large. Thereupon he broke his word
with Simon and " set at nought all the covenants which he
had previously made with him, and was estranged from him "
(i Macc. xv. 27). Moreover, he sent one of his " Friends ",
Athenobius, to Simon demanding from him the surrender of
the cities he had taken, or else a heavy payment for the
same. In case of refusal Antiochus threatened reprisals.
Simon offered him but a small sum, whereupon Antiochus
determined to enforce his will. But as he had still to settle
matters with Trypho, he sent one of his generals, Cendebæus,
against Simon. Inasmuch, however, as Simon was now
getting on in years, he deputed his sons Judas and John to
deal with Cendebæus. Battle was soon joined, and the army

of Cendebæus was routed (137 B.C.). As long as Simon was alive no further attempt to invade Judæa was made; and the land had peace for about three years. Then, in 135 B.C., Simon was treacherously murdered by Ptolemy, the son of Abubus, his son-in-law. Ptolemy, of priestly family, was a captain of the Jewish army stationed in Jericho. The reason of the dastardly outrage was that Ptolemy's " heart was lifted up, and he was minded to make himself master of the country " (i Macc. xvi. 13). Simon's son and successor in the High-priesthood, John, named Hyrcanus, attacked Ptolemy and overcame him; but Ptolemy managed to escape without suffering his deserved punishment.

And now, once more, Antiochus Sidetes caused trouble, and this time with grievous success. We need not go into all the details; but Antiochus invaded Palestine, and ravaged the country; in the fighting he was wholly successful, and Judæa became again a vassal state of Syria. Having thus re-established Syrian suzerainty over Judæa, Antiochus, compelling John Hyrcanus to accompany him, undertook a campaign against the Parthians. Demetrius, who, as mentioned above, had been taken prisoner by the Parthians, was now released in order that he might attack Antiochus. At first Antiochus was successful, but ultimately he fell in battle, in 129 B.C., and Demetrius was undisputed king of Syria. What happened to John Hyrcanus we are not told, but he must certainly have returned to Palestine as soon as the opportunity offered. A new complication now arose in Syria in that Alexander Zabinas, the reputed son of Alexander Balas, came forward as a claimant to the throne; he was supported by the Egyptian king Ptolemy vii, Physcon. Alexander attacked, and defeated, Demetrius ii, near Damascus; the latter fled to Tyre, where he was assassinated (126/5 B.C.). Alexander Zabinas thought well to make a treaty with John Hyrcanus (Antiq. xiii. 269), foreseeing perhaps what was about to happen, for soon the rightful heir to the throne, Demetrius' son, Antiochus viii, Grypus, appeared upon the scene to claim his own. For some time indecisive fighting seems to have gone on; ultimately, Antiochus overcame his rival, and caused him to be put to death (122 B.C.). For the subsequent events in that kingdom see above, pp. 13 f.

The intermittent fighting for the throne in Syria since the death of Antiochus vii, Sidetes, in 129 B.C., prevented interference of any serious character with Hyrcanus, who was thus free to pursue his own designs of further extending the boundaries of his country. He captured Samaria, though not until after a siege lasting a year, and other territories; details of this are given by Josephus, *Antiq.* xiii. 272 ff., *War,* i. 64–66. He died in 104 B.C., " having administered the government in the best manner for thirty-one years. . . . He was esteemed worthy by God of the three greatest privileges, the government of his nation, the dignity of the High-priesthood, and prophecy; for God was with him. . . ." (*Antiq.* 299 f.). Little need be said of the very short reign of Hyrcanus' son, Aristobulus i; he reigned but for a year. The outstanding event of his reign was a further extension of the territory, to which was added " a part of the nation of the Ituræans "; this included the northern part of Palestine with Galilee to the south; it is probable that by " a part " Galilee is meant.

Of greater importance was the reign of Alexander Jannæus (102–76/5 B.C.), the brother of Aristobulus, on account of the further extension of territory acquired by him. But from our present point of view the importance of his reign centres elsewhere. There had been already in the reign of John Hyrcanus signs of differences between the more orthodox element among the people, led by the Pharisees, and the Hasmonæan high-priestly adherents. But in the time of Alexander Jannæus the entirely justified distaste at the *rôle* of the High-priest being held by one who was primarily a warrior was strongly felt. This was strikingly illustrated when once, during the feast of Tabernacles, Alexander Jannæus was pelted with citrons while officiating as High-priest at the altar (*Antiq.* xiii. 372). The power of the Pharisees tended constantly to increase, and occasioned bitter animosity on the part of the ruling powers. Their influence is graphically described by Josephus, who says that they have " so great a power over the multitude, that when they say anything against the king, or against the High-priest, they are presently believed " (*Antiq.* xiii. 288). Indeed, so great was their influence that Alexander Jannæus himself, shortly before his death, adjured his wife Alexandra, who was to succeed him as ruler, to " put some of her authority into the hands of the Pharisees, that they might commend her for the honour she had done them, and reconcile the nation to her; for he told her that they had authority among the Jews, both to do hurt to such as they hated, and to bring advantages to those to whom they were friendly disposed. . . . Promise them also that thou wilt do nothing without them in the affairs of the kingdom " (*Antiq.* xiii. 401 ff.). This advice was acted on by Alexandra after the death of her husband, when, according to his appointment, she ruled in his stead (75/4–67/6 B.C.). As she could not, of course, occupy the high-priestly office, she designated her eldest son, Hyrcanus, as High-priest, because he " permitted the Pharisees to do everything ". This was resented by her second, and more ambitious, son, Aristobulus, who sought both the throne and the High-priesthood. Immediately on her death he set about trying to accomplish his designs, and civil war broke out between the two brothers. This, however, was not destined to last very long, for with the appearance of Pompey, the Roman general, in 64 B.C., the whole aspect of affairs underwent a far-reaching change.

V

THE JEWS UNDER ROMAN SOVEREIGNTY

The strife between the two brothers, Aristobulus and Hyrcanus, was ended by Pompey. Aristobulus attempted to withstand the Roman power, and was transported to Rome. Hyrcanus, strongly supported by his minister, Antipater,[1] sided with Pompey, and was appointed both High-priest and Ethnarch of Judæa, which had now become part of the Roman province of Syria. Of this province Scaurus was appointed governor by Pompey (63 B.C.). So far as the Jews were concerned there followed now a few years of peace. But it is evident that beneath the surface machinations against Hyrcanus were proceeding. For when in the year 57 B.C. Aulus Gabinius became pro-consul of Syria, he was called upon to protect Hyrcanus against Alexander, the son of Aristobulus,

---

[1] He was the father of king Herod.

who aspired to the High-priesthood (Josephus, *Antiq*. xiv. 82, cp. *War*, i. 160, 161). Alexander seems to have had a considerable following, and he was foolish enough to challenge Gabinius. A fight ensued in which Alexander was beaten. But Gabinius evidently regarded Alexander's rising as serious, and took measures accordingly. Josephus records that while he "reinstated Hyrcanus in Jerusalem and committed to him the care of the temple", he ordained, on the other hand, that "the civil administration should be on the lines of an aristocracy. He divided the whole nation into five conventions (or councils), assigning one to Jerusalem, another to Gadara (Gezer), another to Amathus (east of Jordan), as the centre of government, a fourth to Jericho, and the fifth to Sepphoris, a city of Galilee. So the people were glad to be thus freed from monarchical government, and were governed for the future by an aristocracy" (*War*, i. 170; cp. *Antiq*. xiv. 91). This did not, however, prevent Alexander from challenging the Roman power. During the absence of Gabinius in Egypt (55 B.C.), Alexander attempted to seize the government of Judæa; but he was again defeated (*Antiq*. xiv. 100, *War*, i. 176, 177). The significant thing about these attempts on the part of Alexander is that they witness to the hatred of Roman domination among a large section of the Jewish people. This is further illustrated by the revolt, headed by Pitholaus, which took place in 53 B.C. The revolt was suppressed, and Pitholaus was put to death. For the next few years there is nothing of Jewish history to record.

With the advent of Cæsar a new order of things obtained in Judæa (47 B.C.). Hyrcanus had always shown himself the friend of Rome. In recognition of this he was confirmed in the High-priesthood, and received again the title of Ethnarch, of which Gabinius had deprived him. Various benefits were also conferred on the land of Judæa, which was definitely placed under the protection of Rome. But the assassination of Cæsar in 44 B.C. soon brought in its train evil days for Judæa. Misrule in Syria on the part of the proconsuls left the country in a grave state of anarchy, and increased the hatred for Rome. Antipater died in 43 B.C., poisoned by a rival, in Jerusalem. He was avenged by his son Herod. Hyrcanus was supported by Herod, and their friendship was

D

confirmed by Herod's betrothal to Mariamne, the grand-daughter of Hyrcanus. The years which followed were full of complications; into these details we shall not go, as this would be unnecessary for our present purposes. Hyrcanus was defeated by Antigonus, the son of Aristobulus,[1] who became High-priest; Hyrcanus was carried off to Babylon, and detained there in honourable captivity. Antigonus was supported by the Parthians who had invaded Syria; he was, therefore, the enemy of Rome.

The position of Herod was dangerous; his one hope lay in help from Rome. This, in due course, was forthcoming; and Herod was supported by the Roman pro-consul of Syria, Sosius. In 37 B.C. Jerusalem was besieged, and within three months fell. Antigonus was taken prisoner to Antioch and there put to death. Herod was made ruler of Judæa, receiving the title of king.[2] To Judæa was added the district of Samaria.

So far as the Jews were concerned the outstanding facts of Herod's reign may be, very briefly, described as follows. In spite of his ardent desire to live on good terms with his subjects, Herod found it to be impossible; the main reasons for this were that he was not a Jew, but an Idumæan, and also that he was a friend of Rome, and relied on Roman support. The further fact that Herod had displaced the Hasmonæan dynasty was a cause of hatred on the part of many Jews. In this popular feeling against Herod the Pharisees led the way; between them and Herod there was lasting animosity, evinced by the striking act of boldness in that they refused to take the oath of allegiance to him. On the other hand, Herod's friendship with Rome had great advantages for the Jews; for since Roman rule was exercised through the medium of a Jewish king, the people were not subject to the domination of Roman officials. Herod was directly responsible to Augustus without the intermediary of subordinates. This did not, however, assuage the bitterness felt against Rome by the mass of the people. Lastly, there was the renovation and enlargement of the Temple buildings, which he beautified in many ways. In addition to this, Herod adorned various

[1] His brother Alexander had been beheaded by command of Pompey (*War* i. 185).
[2] For fuller details reference may be made to Willrich, *Das Haus des Herodes* . . ., pp. 33 ff. (1929), and Jones, *The Herods of Judæa* (1938).

cities with buildings of one kind and another, and strengthened the fortifications of others.

These are, then, the matters of main importance to be noted during the reign of Herod. With his death in 4 B.C. our short historical survey comes to an end.

PART II: THE SOURCES

CHAPTER III

THE SCRIPTURES

I

THE HEBREW CANON

ANCIENT as so many of the Old Testament books are, and carefully as copies of them were preserved from age to age, it cannot be said that they were authoritative, as we now understand the word, prior to the exilic period. It was during the early post-exilic period, and as a result of scribal activity in its intensive study of the national records brought by the first exiles, that "Scripture", centring at first exclusively in "the law of Moses", began to assume a position of authority. The outstanding representative of the exilic teachers was Ezra; that he came to Palestine with the express purpose of inculcating the paramount authority of the law as envisaged in Babylonian Jewry, is clear enough from what is said in *Ezra* vii. 10: "For Ezra had set his heart to seek the law of Yahweh, and to do it, and to teach Israel statutes and judgements." It was owing to Ezra's zeal that, as is evident from what we read in *Neh.* viii–x; "the book of the law of Moses", called also "the book of the law of Yahweh", became the guide of life, religious, moral, and social. The law was recognized as directly commanded by God in all its details. The "book of the law", which Ezra brought from Babylon,[1] was not, however, the Pentateuch as it now appears in the Hebrew Bible, but that part of it which we call the Priestly Code, though that it received some further additions in subsequent

---

[1] See *Ezra* vii. 14; it must, however, be mentioned that some authorities regard the whole of *Ezra* vii. 12–26 as spurious; and that *Neh.* viii ff. refers to the book of the law already brought to Jerusalem, which had been ignored by the people; hence Ezra's activity, according to this view.

times is highly probable. The incorporation of the far older Yahwistic and Elohistic documents, together with the book of *Deuteronomy*, took place during the Greek Period. It was, therefore, during this period, doubtless during its early part, that the Pentateuch as a whole became recognized as the divinely given Law.

The Bible of the Jews thus consisted, in the first instance, of what was called the " Five books of Moses ". To these were added, in course of time, other writings which had been carefully preserved. First, the prophetical books and those containing the early, pre-exilic history of the nation. These, too, came to be regarded as Holy Scripture, i.e. as records of the revelation of the divine will concerning the people of Israel. Later still a further collection of writings was included ; many portions of these went back in their origin to much earlier days, and had received additions as time went on.

The Scriptures thus consisted of three bodies of writings : the Law, the Prophets, and the Writings, as these last were called (*Torah, Nebi'im,* and *Kethubim*). It is impossible to say precisely at what date the Bible of the Jews assumed this completed form. The earliest reference to this occurs in the Preface to *Ecclesiasticus,* or the *Wisdom of Ben-Sira,* to give the book its proper title; this Preface was written in 132 B.C. by Ben-Sira's grandson, who translated his grandsire's Hebrew work into Greek. He makes specific mention of " the Law, and the prophets, and the other books of our fathers ". This witnesses, therefore, to the existence of the Scriptures containing all three bodies of writings by, at any rate, 200 B.C., or thereabouts. But it must be emphasized that there is uncertainty as to which books were included among " the other books " mentioned by Ben-Sira's grandson. That some of those now regarded as canonical were not included among these is probable, for there was much controversy in later times among Jewish authorities as to whether *Proverbs, Song of Songs (Canticles), Ecclesiastes,* and *Esther,* were to be regarded as Scripture. It is, moreover, not without significance that in his " Praise of the Fathers of Old " (*Ecclus.* xliv. 1–l. 24) Ben Sira omits all mention of *Esther* and *Ezra*; *Daniel* is, of course, later. We have, further, another piece of evidence about the Scriptures in *ii Macc.* ii. 13–15, belonging to about

100 B.C., or a little later; the passage is a curious one, and
is regarded with some suspicion by scholars, but possibly it
echoes some earlier tradition; in reference to past Israelite
history, the writer says: " All these things are related in the
writings, namely, in the records of Nehemiah; and how he,
founding a library, gathered together the books about the
kings and prophets, and those of David, and letters of kings
about sacred gifts (i.e. offered by them for the temple).   And
in like manner, Judas also gathered together for us all the
writings which had been scattered owing to the war; and
they are still with us.   If, therefore, ye have need of them,
send some messengers to fetch them unto you."   Whatever
else is to be gathered from this passage, it will be seen that
so far as the " Writings " are concerned, only the *Psalms*
(" those of David ") are mentioned.   It is also worth noting
that in *i Macc*. i. 56 we are told that " the books of the Law "
were rent in pieces during the persecution under Antiochus
Epiphanes, but there is no mention of any other books of
Scripture.   Nevertheless, though the evidence is not as
decisive as might be wished, it may be regarded as certain
that the Scriptures consisted of the three bodies of writings
mentioned, variable as the last of these was, by the end of
the third century B.C.

We come now to draw attention to another matter regarding the Scriptures.   Authoritative as the books of the Law,
and of the Prophets, and the other Writings, had become
during the Greek Period, there was, as yet, no question of
what we understand by the technical expression " Canonical
Scriptures ", i.e. a collection of sacred writings distinct from
all other books, standing on an altogether higher plane because
directly inspired by God; a collection to which, on account
of its sacrosanct character, no addition might be made, and
from which nothing might be omitted.   The earliest evidence
we have of the definite formation of the Canon of Scripture is
that of Josephus, towards the end of the first century A.D.,
though what he says shows that the Canon was already fixed
by this time: " We have not ten thousands of books, dis-
agreeing with and contradicting one another, but only twenty-
two books, containing the record of the past time, rightly to
be believed.   And of these, five belong to Moses, which con-

tain his laws and the traditions of the origins of mankind till his death, for a period of nearly three thousand years. From the death of Moses till the reign of Artaxerxes, king of Persia, who reigned after Xerxes, the prophets who were after Moses wrote down what was done in their times in thirteen books. The remaining four books contain hymns to God, and precepts for the conduct of human life . . . and how firmly we have given credit to these books of our own nation, is evident by what we do; for during so many ages as have already passed, no one has been so bold as either to add anything to them, to take anything from them, or to make any change in them; but it is become natural to all Jews, immediately and from their very birth, to esteem these books as containing divine doctrines, and to stand by them, and, if occasion be, willingly to die for them " (*Contra Ap.* i. 38–42). The definite formation of the Hebrew Canon of Scripture here witnessed to was in all probability due to the decision of the leaders of the Pharisaic party who established a new Sanhedrin in Jabne (Jamnia) about twenty years or so after the destruction of the temple in A.D. 70. Under the presidency of Jochanan ben Zakkai this new Sanhedrin, consisting of seventy-two " elders ", became the central authority for the Jews not only of Palestine, but also of the Dispersion. It must be fairly obvious that any discussions as to the canonicity of books among the Jewish religious leaders must have taken place in Jabne, where the Sanhedrin gathered, and where the recognized Jewish scholars would be assembled. That such discussions were held is definitely stated in various passages in the Mishnah. So that, although it cannot be actually proved that the final and authoritative formation of the Hebrew Canon of Scripture took place at " the council of Jabne ", it is reasonably certain from the available evidence that the discussions concerning the canonicity of books held by the Sanhedrin assembled at Jabne resulted in what came to be regarded as the formal and authoritative fixing of the Canon.[1]

[1] Details of the evidence are given by Schürer, *op. cit.*, ii. pp. 432 ff.; see further Hölscher, *Kanonisch und Apokryph*, pp. 32 ff. (1905). Subsequent disputes as to the canonicity of *Esther*, *Ecclesiastes* and *Canticles* and others, among certain Rabbis, did not affect the decision arrived at.

II

THE GREEK CANON

Something must be said next about the Greek Canon of
Scripture. Although Jews were settled in various parts of the
world before the Greek Period, it was during this period that
they far more increasingly spread into all parts of the Greek-
speaking world; it followed that they used the Greek language
more and more, and in course of time lost all knowledge of
Hebrew.[1] This necessitated a Greek translation of the Scriptures. There can be no doubt that the want of such a version
of the Scriptures was felt primarily by the Jews who had
settled in Egypt, and especially by the large Jewish colony in
Alexandria, the city of Alexander's founding, in which those
Jews who so desired found, in settling there, a congenial
home, for they were admitted to full citizenship. The story
of how it came about that the Greek Version of the Scriptures
was made in Alexandria is told in the so-called *Letter of
Aristeas*. In this it is related that Ptolemy ii, Philadelphus,
285–246 B.C., caused a letter to be written to the High-priest
Eleazar at Jerusalem, requesting him to choose " six elders
from each tribe, men of high repute, well versed in the Law,
and able to translate ", since it is the royal will that " your
Law be translated from the Hebrew tongue in use among you
into Greek, that so these writings also may find a place in
our library with the other royal volumes ". On the arrival
of the seventy-two translators they were royally entertained
for a week. They were then conducted to the island of Pharos
along the mole, the *Heptastadion*, which connected the island
with the mainland, and provided with a dwelling-place and
all things needful for their task. The work was then begun.
" And so it came about that the translation was completed
in seventy-two days, as though this coincidence had been
intended." The translators were then presented with gifts by
the king, both for themselves and the High-priest, and dis-
missed with honour.

[1] This is true of the masses of the Palestinian Jews too, who spoke
Aramaic; the reading of the Hebrew Scriptures in the Synagogue was
always followed by an explanation in Aramaic, the origin of the later
Targums (" Translations ").

In discussing this *Letter of Aristeas*, Thackeray says: " We have, then, to deal with a work which in some respects is obviously fictitious, and in others appears deserving of respect. Behind the romantic and apologetic framework there lies, no doubt, an element of truth. The story appears to be based, in part at least, on ancient popular tradition. Philo tells us that in his day the translation was celebrated by an annual festival, attended by Jews and others, and held on the beach of the island of Pharos." [1] He regards the date of the Letter as most probably 120–80 B.C.; other scholars would place it slightly earlier.

Here it must be pointed out that the Septuagint was a potent means of bringing the knowledge of the Jewish religion to the Gentile world, with important results. " From the time when the Pentateuch, and later the other writings of the Old Testament, were translated into Greek, the fundamental documents of the Jewish faith were accessible to all whose curiosity, or whose zeal for truth, led them to explore the religious field. In the Jewish *Diaspora* there were many prepared to interpret and commend the teaching of these documents, meeting half-way the general tendencies of the thought of the time. One result of this was the gaining of proselytes, or semi-proselytes, to Judaism; and it is generally recognized that this was an important factor in preparing the way for Christian propaganda." [2]

In comparing the Greek Canon (the Septuagint) with the Hebrew Canon the first point to note is that the arrangement of books differs greatly between the two. In the former there is no division into Law, Prophets, and Writings; the Pentateuch and the historical books come first, then the poetical and wisdom books, and in the last place the prophetical books. This order varies, however, in the uncial manuscripts. But a much greater difference lies in the considerably larger number of books contained in the Greek Canon. All those included in what is erroneously termed " The Apocrypha " are, with two exceptions, part and parcel of the Septuagint. The exceptions are *ii* (*iv*) *Esdras*, which is not extant in Greek,

[1] *The Letter of Aristeas*, in the S.P.C.K. " Translations of Early Documents ", Series II, p. xiv (1917).
[2] Dodd, *The Bible and the Greeks*, pp. 243 f. (1935). See further, Causse, *op. cit.*, pp. 103 ff.

and the *Prayer of Manasses*, though this does appear in some
Septuagint manuscripts, while in some others it is found in
the "Canticles," or hymns, which are appended to the
Psalms.   On the other hand, in the Septuagint there are four
books of *Maccabees*; the "Apocrypha" has only two.

By the year 100 B.C., approximately, we have, thus, two
forms of the Jewish Scriptures: the Palestinian and the
Alexandrian.   The Jewish authorities of Palestine, as we have
seen, drew up a list of what they held to be inspired books,
but before this time, i.e. soon after A.D. 70, most of the books
excluded from the Hebrew Canon had been long in existence;
it is, therefore, pertinent to ask why the Palestinian Jewish
authorities did not include in their Canon those books of the
Greek Bible which are comprised in what we call the "Apocrypha"?   In answer to this, we must refer to the quotation
from Josephus given above (p. 45).   It is there said that
"from the time of Moses till the reign of Artaxerxes, king of
Persia, who reigned after Xerxes, the prophets who came after
Moses wrote down the things that were done during their
time in thirteen books . . ."   As Josephus is here indicating
what books were recognized as Scripture, it is clear that,
according to him, for a book to be regarded as canonical it
was necessary for it to have been written within a clearly
defined period, i.e. from the time of Moses to the death of
Artaxerxes,[1] regarded as the "prophetical period".   The
artificiality of this test of canonicity is shown by the fact
that, as Ryle says, "the mention of this particular limit seems
to be made expressly with reference to the book of Esther, in
which alone the Artaxerxes of Josephus (the Ahasuerus of the
Hebrew book of Esther) figures ".[2]   Moreover, Josephus con-
tradicts himself, for in the Preface to his *Jewish War* (18),
after referring to the "histories of our ancestors ", he goes on
to say that "where the writers of these things and our prophets
leave off, from there will I make the beginning of my history ",
and he begins with the time of Antiochus Epiphanes, who
came to the Syrian throne in 175 B.C.   In pointing, however,
to the "prophetical period" as that during which a book
had to be written in order to be canonical, Josephus was not

---

[1] Artaxerxes i is meant; he died in 424 B.C.
[2] *The Canon of the Old Testament*, p. 164 (1892).

expressing a theory of his own, for a similar view was held by the Rabbis, who, without doubt, received it from others before them.[1] But this view was one which was not only artificial in character, but also contrary to fact, for according to it, to quote Ryle again, " there never was or could be any discussion as to the number and limits of the canonical collection, which had from first to last an official character. Each new book was written by a man of acknowledged authority, and was added to the collection precisely as a new page would be added to the royal annals of an eastern kingdom. It is plain that this view is not in accordance with facts . . . Josephus's account of the Canon is a theory, and a theory inconsistent with the fact that we find no complete formal catalogue of Scriptures in earlier writers like the son of Sirach, who, in enumerating the literary worthies of his nation, had every motive to give a complete list, had he been in a position to do so; inconsistent also with the fact that questions as to the canonicity of certain books were still undecided within the lifetime of Josephus himself." [2]

Artificial, then, as this theory was, and contrary to facts, it nevertheless held sway in the Jewish Church. As a result, those books of the Greek Bible not represented in the Hebrew Bible, as fixed by the authorities of Jabne (Jamnia), were excluded from the Canon.

The books of the Greek Canon not included in the Hebrew Canon may be briefly enumerated as follows; as to their dates, they fall into five divisions, viz. (1) pre-Maccabæan; (2) those belonging to the second half of the second century B.C.; (3) those belonging to the earlier, (4) and to the later parts of the last century B.C., approximately; and (5) those which are post-Christian. Some differences of opinion exist in regard to a few of the books, but not of great extent.

The Wisdom of Ben-Sira (*Ecclesiasticus*). Written about 200 B.C., or a few years later; this book is in many respects the most important of the collection. It belongs, properly, to the Wisdom Literature, containing as it does a great number of precepts and wise counsels for guidance of life. The insight it gives into the social and religious conditions of

---

[1] For details see Hölscher, *op. cit.*, pp. 36 ff.
[2] *Op. cit.*, pp. 165 f.

the time marks it as a book of extreme value. It was written originally in Hebrew, of which about two-thirds have been discovered in recent years.

The Book of Tobit. This historical novel is of about the same date as the foregoing, and thus also pre-Maccabæan. From our present point of view its importance lies in the orthodox religious standpoint of the writer, and in its angelology.

These are the only two pre-Maccabæan books in the collection.

The Book of Judith. Here we have another historical novel; it was written possibly during the Maccabæan struggle; but we are of opinion that it belongs to a somewhat later time in the second century B.C., owing to the specifically Pharisaic doctrinal teaching which is one of its main characteristics; it is this which makes the book important regarding the Judaism of the Greek Period.

The Additions to the Book of Daniel. Of these five additions, all, with the exception of *The Story of Susanna* (see below), belong to the latter part of the second century B.C. The first, *The Prayer of Azariah*, is partly liturgical, and this applies also to the second, *The Song of the Three Holy Children* (= the " Benedicite, omnia Opera ", in the Prayer Book); the two stories of *Bel*, and *The Dragon*, have as their object the ridiculing of idolatry.

i Maccabees. From the historical point of view this book, written originally in Hebrew about 100 B.C., or a little later, is of the highest importance, since it gives a detailed account of the Maccabæan struggle. An outline of this era is given above (pp. 26 ff.); we need, therefore, only remark here that there are incidental references to religious belief and practice which are valuable for our special purposes. The standpoint is Sadducæan.

i (iii) Esdras. This book is also known as " The Greek Ezra ". It is a compilation made up of extracts from the canonical books of *ii Chronicles*, *Ezra*, and *Nehemiah*. It dates largely, therefore, from about 300 B.C., but in its present form it was written about 100 B.C. It contains, in iii. 1–v. 6, a section which is peculiar to it, namely the story of the young men of Darius' bodyguard; the object of which is to magnify Truth.

The Story of Susanna. Belonging to approximately the same date as the final form of the foregoing, this story was added to the book of *Daniel* on account of the name of the hero, " Daniel ", given to him because of his " spirit of discernment ". The story was composed with the object of urging the reform of the Law with regard to perjurers.

ii Maccabees. This is not a continuation of *i Maccabees*, as, e.g., *ii Kings* is of *i Kings*; the period covered is, in the main, different. As the writers of this book tells us, it is an epitome of a larger work the author of which was a certain Jason of Cyrene; of this historian and his work nothing is otherwise known. While purporting to give a history of the Maccabæan wars, the writer of our book, a Pharisee, deals almost wholly with the leadership of Judas Maccabæus. Though containing some details which may be regarded as historically valuable, the miraculous stories of heavenly messengers sent to aid the Jews, as well as historical errors of an obvious character, mark the book as much inferior to *i Maccabees* so far as reliable history is concerned. On the other hand, there are matters of religious teaching, of the Pharisaic type, which contribute to our knowledge of Judaism during the Greek Period. The date is approximately the middle of the last century B.C.

The Epistle of Jeremy. This writing purports to be a letter sent by the prophet. to " those who were about to be led captives by the king of the Babylonians ". It is, however, a not very skilfully composed polemic against idolatry, based largely on *Jer.* x. 1–16 and *Isa.* xlix. 9–19. It is probably of about the same date as *ii Maccabees*; but some authorities put it as early as 300 B.C., or thereabouts.

The Additions to the Book of Esther. These six additions are elaborations of episodes recounted in the canonical book. Their purpose is a religious one, but historically they cannot be said to be of value. Their date is about the same as the preceding.

The Prayer of Manasses. The date of this beautiful prayer is quite uncertain; some authorities assign it to the Maccabæan period, others to the first half of the third century A.D. Quite tentatively we suggest the latter part of the second, or the early part of the first, century B.C. At any rate, we believe it to be pre-Christian. It purports to be the prayer of Manasses referred to in *ii Chron.* xxxiii. 12, 13, 18, 19. The outstanding

themes of the Prayer are the greatness of divine mercy, and the efficacy of true repentance. The whole spirit is that of the writer of the fifty-first psalm. It has been incorporated in the *Didascalia* and the *Apostolical Constitutions*.

The Wisdom of Solomon. The unity of authorship and date of this important book—Solomonic authorship is, of course, out of the question—are subjects on which there are differences of opinion among scholars; to discuss all these would be out of place here. Upon the whole, the evidence, we venture to believe, favours dual authorship. Of the component parts, namely chaps. i–xi. 1, and xi. 2–xix. 22, the former we assign to the latter part of the last century B.C., the latter to the earlier part of the first century A.D. Both parts reflect, however, much earlier thought; the book is, therefore, of high value for the purposes of our present work. The first part is the more important on account of its teaching on retribution, the future life, and the nature of Wisdom. The second part extols the God of Israel, and shows, in contrast, the folly of idolatry. St. Paul's knowledge and use of the book is a matter of much interest; the author of the epistle of St. James also shows familiarity with it.

The Book of Baruch (*i Baruch*). Three short independent pieces have been combined in this book: i–iii. 8, iii. 9–iv. 4, and iv. 5–v. 9. The second of these belongs to the Wisdom Literature. There is much edifying religious teaching in each of them. They belong to the second half of the first century A.D., but before the fall of Jerusalem.

ii (*iv*) *Esdras* (the " Ezra Apocalypse "). This compilation belongs, in the main, to the Apocalyptic Literature. It is one of the most important books in the Apocrypha collection. Though late in date, the central portion belongs to the end of the first century A.D., the first two and last two chapters are much later—it echoes the teaching of earlier times, and is, therefore, important for our purposes. The book consists of three independent compositions: chaps. i, ii; iii–xiv; xv, xvi; of these the central one is by far the most important. It embodies a number of Visions, purported to have been seen by Salathiel, " who am also Ezra ".[1] Of particular importance

[1] On this see Box's admirable book *The Ezra-Apocalypse*, pp. 1 f. (1912). Mention must also be made of the recent work by Gry, *Les Dires prophétiques d'Esdras.* 2 vols. (1939).

among these Visions is that of " The Man rising from the
sea " (chap. xiii), on account of the conception of the transcendental Messiah. In his eschatological teaching the Seer
of the visions departs in some important particulars from the
older doctrines; " he does not look forward to a restoration
of the Jewish State, or a rebuilding of Jerusalem, nor to a
renewed and purified earth under the conditions of the present
world-order. His hopes are fixed on the advent of the new
and better world which will follow the collapse of the present
world. Consequently he anticipates merely the catastrophic
end of the present world-order; his theology does not allow
of any intermediate Messianic Age. The new Jerusalem
which is to come will be the Heavenly City . . . which
belongs to the future Age." [1]

For the Greek Text, we have Swete, *The Old Testament in
Greek* (3 vols., 1895, 1896, 1899), Rahlfs, *Septuaginta* (2 vols.,
1935). The text of the four extant Hebrew MSS. of *Ecclesiasticus* are given by Smend, *Die Weisheit des Jesus Sirach*
(Hebräisch und Deutsch, 1906); that of the subsequently
discovered fifth MS., containing xxxii. 16–xxxiv. 1, by Joseph
Marcus (1931). For the Latin Version of *ii (iv) Esdras*, see
Bensly, *The Fourth Book of Ezra* (1895); it is also published by
Violet, together with German translations of all the other
extant Versions, in *Die griechischen Christlichen Schriftsteller der
ersten drei Jahrhunderte, Ezra-Apokalypse, iv Esra* (1910).

III

THE USE OF THE SCRIPTURES IN THE NEW TESTAMENT

Thus, before the beginning of the Christian era the Jewish
Scriptures existed in two forms, Hebrew and Greek; the
former used by the Jewish teachers in Palestine and explained
in the vernacular, the latter being the Bible of the Jews of
the Dispersion. But there was no authoritative Canon of
Scripture.

With but few exceptions, the books of the New Testament
have a very large number of references to and quotations from
the Old Testament, and almost invariably these are from the
Septuagint. As a rule, the Old Testament is referred to as

[1] Box, *op. cit.*, p. xlvi.

" the law and the prophets ": *Matth.* v. 17, vii. 12, xi. 13 (" the prophets and the law "), xxii. 40, *Lk.* xvi. 16 (in *vv.* 29, 31 " Moses and the prophets "), in xxiv. 27, " And beginning from Moses and from all the prophets, he interpreted to them in all the scriptures . . ." seems to imply more than the law and the prophets; and in xxiv. 44 it is said, ". . . in the law of Moses, and the prophets, and the psalms." See further *Acts* xiii. 15, xxiv. 14, xxvi. 22 (" the prophets and Moses "), xxviii. 23, *Rom.* iii. 21. Phrases such as " that which is written ", or " the Scripture saith," occur of course often in reference to the Old Testament. But, as we should expect, there is nothing in the New Testament which in any way suggests the idea of a Canon. While there are not direct quotations from the books which we call the Apocrypha— and the same is true of *Esther, Song of Songs,* and *Ecclesiastes*— there are a number of instances in which familiarity with some of the books of the Apocrypha appears. As Swete says: " The careful student of the Gospels and of St. Paul is met at every turn by words and phrases which cannot be fully understood without reference to their earlier use in the Greek Old Testament. Books which are not quoted in the New Testament, e.g. the non-canonical books of *Wisdom, Ecclesiasticus,* and *Maccabees,* find echoes there; and not a few of the great theological words which meet us in the Apostolic writings seem to have been prepared for their Christian connotation by employment in the Alexandrian appendix to the Canon. Not the Old Testament only, but the Alexandrian version of the Old Testament, has left its mark on every part of the New Testament, even in chapters and books where it is not directly cited." [1] The Bible of the first Christians, as of the early Church, was the Septuagint, and it is highly probable that this had something to do with the repudiation by the elders at Jabne (Jamnia) of those books which do not appear in the Hebrew Canon. That these books were accepted as Scripture by the New Testament writers is shown not only by references to some of them, at least, but also by the fact that they are quoted by the early Church Fathers as such; this would not have been done unless the books in question

---

[1] *An Introduction to the Old Testament in Greek,* p. 404 (1900). See also Dittmar's very valuable *Vetus Testamentum in Novo* (1903).

had been recognized as Scripture from the beginning of Christianity. "Take the Septuagint in your hand", says Deissmann, "and you have before you the book that was the Bible of the Jews of the Dispersion and of the proselytes from the heathen; the Bible of Philo the Philosopher, Paul the Apostle, and the earliest Christian missions; and the Bible of the whole Greek-speaking Christian world; the mother of influential daughter-versions; the mother of the Greek New Testament." [1]

[1] *The Philology of the Greek Bible : its present and future*, p. 8 (1908).

CHAPTER IV

THE LAW AND THE ORAL TRADITION

I

THE LAW, OR TORAH

INCIDENTAL reference has already been made to the subject of the Law, but the dominating part which it played, in increasing measure, during the period with which we are specially concerned, demands some further consideration regarding its nature and scope. We are accustomed to use the term " Law " as equivalent to the Hebrew *Torah*; the word means " teaching ", or " instruction ", which has been given by God, and must, therefore, be obeyed.

It need hardly be pointed out that all law in ancient pre-Mosaic Israel, as among all the Semites, was originally based on tribal custom; the fact is here merely mentioned because a great deal of what was contained in the Hebrew Law during all periods of Israelite history had its source in the earliest ages. Moreover, as is well known, tribal custom was inseparable from religious custom because the tribe was under the special protection of its god, who was looked upon as directing the life of his worshippers in every sphere. This applied with special force to the Israelites because Yahweh was, from the time of Moses, always recognized as the God of Law and justice. It is, therefore, fully comprehensible that the Israelite Law was conceived of as having been created and commanded by Yahweh; so that the obeying of His Law was an act of worship. These points must be borne in mind, for, together with the belief that the Law of Yahweh was revealed to Moses, they conditioned the whole conception and observance of the Law throughout Israelite history. We are, however, not here concerned with the various stages of development through which the Law passed. Our starting-point is the form which the Law came to assume after the Exile. What is of para-

mount importance here to note is that the priestly ideals and
directions became more and more pronounced. This is seen
in the books of *Haggai* and *Malachi*, to a less extent in *Zechariah*;
but it is in some parts of *Isa.* lvi–lxvi that it becomes most
evident. Here we have, in lvi. 1, the two technical terms:
" Keep judgement ",[1] i.e. observe the Law, and " Do righteousness ", i.e. the righteousness of the Law. The two terms
are more or less parallel, and witness to the emphasis laid on
the observance of legal precepts. This is illustrated, for
example, by the inculcation of the proper keeping of the
Sabbath, which, as we see in later times, assumed an exaggerated importance. In lvi. 2 it is said: " Blessed is the man
that doeth this, and the son of man that holdeth fast by it,"
that is in reference to the Law in general; then it continues:
" that keepeth the Sabbath from profaning it." This is more
fully illustrated in *Neh.* xiii. 15–22, where it is told of the
drastic measures which Nehemiah took for preserving the
Sabbath from desecration. But it is in the Priestly Code
which belongs to the exilic and early post-exilic period that
the rigour with which Sabbath observance was insisted upon
is most clearly seen. It is said, for example, that the Sabbath
is to be kept as a " solemn rest ", and that " everyone that
profaneth it shall be put to death " (*Exod.* xxxi. 14). Other
laws belonging to this Code deal with the festivals, to which a
new importance is attached, and especially the New Moon
festivals. Further, the laws regarding sacrifices are much
developed; tithes, and other dues, likewise receive new
emphasis. In addition, laws affecting the affairs of ordinary
life become prominent, such as those which are concerned
with personal rights and obligations, and the law of contract.
Of far-reaching importance were the innovations in the
minutiæ of the ritual law, especially those which provided for
the priesthood. To give details of these various laws would
be wearisome; nor are they called for here. The main
point to emphasize is that the *developed form* of the ancient
Mosaic Law was that which held sway during the Greek
Period and after; though, as we shall see, unanimity on this
among the Jews did not obtain. But before we come to
consider in some detail the attitude to the Law and its require-

---

[1] The Hebrew word *mishpat* has here its secondary meaning of " justice ".

ments as presented in the post-Biblical literature of the last
three pre-Christian centuries, it is necessary that a brief word
should be said about the Oral Law.

II

THE ORAL TRADITION

The need for and the way in which the Oral Law came
into existence and developed were natural enough. Doubtless
from early times unwritten directions were put forth by way
of interpreting it and therefore supplementing the original
written Law. This would have been demanded in the nature
of things, for laws often need to be explained, and as time goes
on and conditions change, new laws are called for. But by
the " Oral Law " orthodox Judaism understood something
very different from this. The Hebrew equivalent for the term
is *Torah she-be-'al peh*, and means literally " Torah which is by
mouth ", i.e. given by word of mouth, as distinct from the
written form. The expression was derived, in the first instance,
from what is said in *Exod.* xxxiv. 27: " And Yahweh said
unto Moses, Write for thee these words, and according to the
tenor of (lit. ' the mouth of ', *'al-pi*) these words have I made
a covenant with thee and with Israel "; the second " these
words " was taken to mean spoken words, in addition to those
to be written. The passage was, therefore, interpreted in the
sense that the Almighty commanded Moses both to write
down " words ", and also to receive from him other words
not written. This extremely forced and unnatural interpretation of the passage became dominant; and the fiction arose
that God had given to Moses the Oral as well as the Written
Law. When exactly this took place it is impossible to say;
but the expression *Torah she-be-'al peh* was familiar by the
beginning of the Christian era, for it was employed by Gamaliel;[1] it must, therefore, have been in use before his time.
The idea was probably formulated somewhat earlier, in the
Greek period.

The Oral Law was, however, not universally accepted
among the Jews; it was repudiated by the Sadducees as well

[1] Zunz, *Die gottesdienstlichen Vorträge der Juden*, p. 47 (1892). Gamaliel
is mentioned in Acts v. 34.

as by the wealthier classes; thus, Josephus tells us that " the Pharisees have delivered to the people a great many observances by succession from their fathers, which are not written in the laws of Moses; and for that reason it is that the Sadducees reject them, and say, that we are to esteeem those observances as obligatory which are in the written word, but are not to observe what are derived from the tradition of our forefathers. And concerning these things it is that great disputes and differences have arisen among them while the Sadducees are able to persuade none but the rich, and have not the populace obsequious to them, but the Pharisees have the multitude on their side " (*Antiq.* xiii. 297, 298).

At first the supplementary material interpretative of the Written Law was of small dimensions; but this gradually grew, being developed and modified from time to time to meet the exigencies of changing circumstances. Then, after being subjected for some few centuries to these various influences, it assumed a fixed and official form in the Mishnah, promulgated by the patriarch Judah, about A.D. 190–200. But that this final form of the Mishnah had been preceded by earlier attempts at codification which prepared the way for Judah's work does not admit of doubt.

III

THE LAW IN POST-BIBLICAL JEWISH LITERATURE

In dealing now with the teaching concerning the Law, and the general attitude of the Jews towards it, during the Greek Period, there are one or two preliminary remarks which we feel impelled to make. It would be easy enough to give many quotations from the books comprised in the post-biblical literature which eulogize the Law in various ways; but this would not present the whole truth regarding the attitude towards the Law held by all circles of the Jews during the Greek Period. One must recognize the fact that in some of these books the subject of the Law receives but the scantiest attention, and even that in a merely conventional manner, while in others it is practically ignored. That is not to say that the writers of these books did not acknowledge the Law, but it means that the Law was not for them the central con-

sideration that it was for the more thoroughgoing, orthodox
Jew; its claims were not recognized as being binding to the
same extent as orthodox circles of the stricter type contended.
Quite apart from downright disloyal Jews, there were those
whose wider mental outlook taught them to see that in the
divine economy there were, for the godly, hopes and aspira-
tions that filled their minds with things which transcended
those earthly affairs, with which, as they contended, the
Law was mainly concerned. We are, of course, thinking here
of the Apocalyptists and their writings (see next chapter).
There are, however, other books, not belonging to the Apocalyptic Literature, in which the religious element is outstanding, but in which the Law receives but little mention; such,
for example, are *The Story of Achikar*, *The Life of Adam and
Eve*, *The Ascension of Isaiah*, and others. It cannot be argued
that it is not to be expected that in books like these the Law
should receive much notice because they deal with other
matters; for in such books, for example, as *Tobit, Judith,
i Maccabees*, the subjects are assuredly not of such a nature as
would lead one to expect references to the Law, yet the Law
is often referred to and deliberately brought in. In these
non-Apocalyptic books of which we are for the moment thinking, many admirable precepts are inculcated, dealing with
uprightness of living, the common dictates of humanity, and
the like; but these are taught because they are essentially
right in themselves, not because they happen to be included
in the Law. Acts of religious practice, or of kindliness, and
the like, can be prompted by a naturally benevolent disposi-
tion without being necessarily dictated by a legal precept.
The spirit of godliness calls forth many admirable injunctions
quite apart from anything commanded in the Law.

We contend, therefore, that, because in some of the post-
biblical writings precepts in conformity with the Law appear,
it does not follow that this is done with the purpose of exalting
the Law. We are led to make these observations owing to
the tendency, at times to be discerned in some modern books
on the subject, of piling up quotations from the writings in
question in order to illustrate what is held to be the universal
veneration for the Law; some of such quotations are not to
the point for the reasons given above.

It is not for a moment denied that the reign of the Law was dominant during the latter part of the Greek Period and after; we only plead for the recognition of the fact that there were God-fearing Jews who did not take the same view with regard to the Law as that held by the more strictly orthodox.

We shall now give a few illustrations from post-Biblical writings which describe the attitude of the orthodox Jews towards the Law. In *Ecclesiasticus* a point of particular interest is the identification of the Law with Wisdom, implying its existence before the Creation.[1] In the eloquent passage on the Praise of Wisdom (xxiv. 1–34) Ben-Sira says: "All these things (i.e. what he has been saying about Wisdom) are the book of the covenant of the Most High, the Law which Moses commanded; an heritage for the assemblies of Jacob" (v. 23). Again, the Law and Wisdom are used synonymously in xxxiv. 8: "Without deceit shall the Law be fulfilled; and Wisdom in the mouth of one who is faithful is perfection." But the essence of Wisdom is that it is " the fear of the Lord "; thus in xxi. 11 Ben-Sira says: " The fear of the Lord is the consummation (i.e. the Zenith) of Wisdom "; and again in xix. 20: " All wisdom is the fear of the Lord "; and similarly elsewhere. Now there is a point here which demands a slight digression. Ben-Sira, and in this he is in the following of other Wisdom-writers, both directly and by implication, makes the observance of legal precepts purely a matter of " the fear of the Lord ", i.e. of the relationship between the individual and his God. That, it will be said, goes without saying; we agree, but contrast this with the later teaching on the efficacy of the works of the Law, the attainment of justification in the sight of God by means of the piling-up of good works by man, and it will be realized that Ben-Sira's conception of spiritual religion is on a higher plane than that which represented man as the master of his own salvation. In this respect, therefore, Ben-Sira's conception of the Law differed markedly from that of the Pharisees.

In other directions, however, Ben-Sira's teaching on the Law shows a tendency approximating to the standpoint of the later Rabbinism. Thus, he says, for example, in xxxv. 1, 2:

---

[1] See *Prov.* viii. 22 ff. In the Midrash, *Bereshith Rabba*, on *Gen.* i. 1, it is said that the Torah was created before the creation of the world.

" He that keepeth the Law multiplieth offerings, and he that
giveth heed to the commandments sacrificeth a peace-offer-
ing." Again, in xxi. 11: "He that observeth the Law
becometh master of his natural tendency " (*yetzer*). And once
more: "He that observeth the Law guardeth his soul", but
here it is added: "and he that trusteth in Yahweh shall not
be ashamed " (xxxii. 24, this is from the Hebrew). A few
other passages of similar import occur, but not many.

One other point must be mentioned here; Ben-Sira's identification of the Law with Wisdom involves the belief in its
pre-existence before the beginning of the world. This, so far
as is known, is the earliest reference, if only implied, to what
became a cardinal doctrine of later Judaism.

In the book of *Tobit* we meet with a distinct tendency
towards the Pharisaic standpoint. Particular stress is laid on
the law of tithes (i. 6, 7); but the most significant passage is
in xii. 8–10: "Good is prayer with fasting and alms and
righteousness. A little with righteousness is better than much
with unrighteousness. It is better to give alms than to lay up
gold; alms doth deliver from death, and it shall purge away
all sin. They that do alms and righteousness shall be filled
with life; but they that sin are enemies to their own life."
The last passage is particularly Pharisaic, for alms and righteousness are made parallel; and life, referring to life in this
world, is made dependent on refraining from sin. Other
references to " the law of Moses " occur in vi. 12, vii. 13; but
general exhortations to right living, without any reference to
the Law being pre-supposed, are given in iv. 5, xii. 6, 7. It is
in the book of *Judith* that we find the most pronounced advo-
cacy of legal observances, more so, in fact, than in any other
book in the Apocrypha collection. It is said, for example, of
Judith on the death of her husband that " she made her a
tent upon the roof of her house, and put on sackcloth upon
her loins; and the garments of her widowhood were upon
her. And she fasted all the days of her widowhood, save the
eves of the Sabbaths, and the eves of the new moons, and the
new moons, and the feasts and the joyful days of the house of
Israel." Here we have legal observances followed in accordance with traditional practice; the wearing of the special
widow's garments, seclusion, and fasting (cp. *Gen.* xxxviii. 14,

19, *Deut.* xxiv. 17, *ii Sam.* xx. 3, *Job* xxxi. 16); these belonged to the duties of a widow in mourning. In xi. 12, 13, again, there is a reference to the laws regarding forbidden food, " which God charged them by his laws that they should not eat " (cp., e.g., *Lev.* xi, 13 ff., 29 ff., *Deut.* xiv. 12, 13). Elsewhere other laws are either mentioned or referred to. In some other books, viz. *i* (*iii*) *Esdras,* the two books of the *Maccabees, Baruch,* and *ii* (*iv*) *Esdras,* there is a similar tendency; but in the book of *Wisdom* the subject is rarely touched upon, and then only incidentally (ii. 12, vi. 4).

Turning now to the large number of other post-Biblical books, we do not propose to go into much detail, as this would take up a great deal of space. It will suffice to say that in the following books the teaching on the Law appears prominently: the book of *Jubilees,* the *Testaments of the XII Patriarchs, iv Maccabees,* the *Assumption of Moses,* the *Syriac Apocalypse of Baruch,* and the *Zadokite Fragments.* In all the rest (about a dozen, see the list on pp. 77 ff.) there is but the scantiest reference to the Law, in some it is never even mentioned.

In considering the whole of these two bodies of literature two facts stand out; the first is that the strictly orthodox attitude towards the Law was not adopted universally; there were those who, with due respect for the Law, did not accept what we understand by the Pharisaic standpoint. And the second fact is that the bulk of the apocalyptic writers had very little to say about the Law and its requirements. That they recognized it is not denied; but they were far too much occupied with more important things to think about it; beyond an occasional incidental mention. Their other-worldly outlook was not the only thing that occasioned a separation between them and the Pharisees; but it is important to lay stress upon this attitude of the Apocalyptists in view of much that we read in the New Testament.

Something must now be said about the specifically Pharisaic handling of the Law, and the minute regulations put forth regarding legal observances. For the details of this we have to go to the Mishnah; but, as has been pointed out, though not compiled until the end of the second century A.D., we have in it an immense deal of traditional matter. Numberless discussions appear here as to what the Law permits and prohibits; but the very differences of opinion illustrate the peculiar attitude of Jewish teachers towards what they conceived to be the demands of the Law. There is much of the most edifying character that was taught by the Pharisees, and those who followed them, on this subject. This must be strongly insisted upon, lest it should be thought, in view of some illustrations of a different nature to be given presently, that Pharisaic teaching was always of a puerile, hair-splitting character. We have, for example, sayings of the celebrated Hillel (the time of his main activity was 30 B.C.–A.D. 10 such as these: " Be a disciple of Aaron, a lover and maker of peace, love men and attract them to the Law " (*Aboth* i. 12). In a Talmudic passage we are told that on being asked by a pagan who wished to become a Jew, to express the essence of Judaism in a sentence, he replied: " What is hateful to thee, do not unto thy fellow-man; this is the whole Law; all else is but commentary " (*Shabbath* 31 a). Again, Simeon, the son of Shammai, the great opponent of Hillel in discussions on the Law, said with practical common sense: " Not the study of the Law, but the carrying out of it is the essential thing " (*Aboth* i. 17). In much the same spirit another early Rabbi taught: " Excellent is Law-study together with some worldly occupation, for the labour in both of them causes sin to be forgotten; and all Law-study without worldly labour ends in failure; and brings sin (in its train) " (*Aboth* ii. 2). Sentiments of this kind—and they could be multiplied—show that level-headed ideas about the Law were amply expressed by the most ardently orthodox. For one other illustration of this finer side of the picture we cannot do better than quote the following story of Rabbi Jochanan (end of the first century A.D.). Once, on walking with his disciple, Rabbi Chija ben Abba, in the country, they came to a field, to which Rabbi Jochanan pointed, saying: " This field belonged to me, but I sold it in order that I might devote myself to the study of the Law." They came to an olive-grove; he said: " This olive-grove belonged to me, but I sold it in order that I might devote myself to the study of the Law." Thereupon Rabbi Chija ben Abba wept and said to him: " I weep because thou hast nought laid up for thine old age." But the other answered: " My son Chija, my son Chija, is it then but a small thing in thine eyes that I sold something which was created in six days, and acquired instead something that took forty days and forty nights in giving? For the whole world was created in six days (*Exod.* xxxi. 17); but the giving of the Law took forty days " (*Exod.* xxxiv. 18).[1] It is a quaint story; but it tells of how a good man was prepared to give up all so that he might possess the divine gift of the Law.

A few illustrations of the other side of the picture may now be offered, for it must be recognized that these witness to the more prevalent ideas of the Law and its demands, held by the more strictly orthodox. A number of directions are given, for example, about the booth in which, according to the Law (*Lev.* xxiii. 42), people must dwell during the feast of Tabernacles; it must be of a temporary nature, not too high, i.e. not more than twenty cubits (*Sukkah* i. 1), it may not have a creeper growing over it (i. 4). Again, " He who sleeps under a bed in a booth has not fulfilled his obligation " (ii. 1), the reason being that there must be only one roof over his head, so that if he sleeps under the bed he is making it a roof in addition to the roof of the booth! Or, to turn to another subject, many rules are given about reciting the *Shema'* (" Hear, O Israel "), and saying one's prayers; thus, " he who recites it (i.e. the *Shema'*) in an irregular order has not fulfilled his duty " (*Berakoth* ii. 3). Again, " a man may not stand on a bed, or on a seat, or on a bench, and pray, for there may be no high position before God, since it is said, ' Out of the depths have I cried unto thee ' " (v. 17). Elsewhere it is said: " Should one be riding on an ass (i.e. when it is time to say his prayers) let him dismount; if he cannot dismount let him turn his face (i.e. towards Jerusalem); and if he cannot turn his face let him direct his intention towards the most Holy Sanctuary " (iv. 5). With regard to the washing of hands before meals it is said in the same tractate, viii. 2: " The School of Shammai say, Men wash their hands, and afterwards mix the cup. And the School of Hillel say, Men mix the cup and afterwards wash their hands." Finally, one or two miscellaneous rules about the Sabbath may be given. The tractate *Shabbath* opens with a passage which records what constitutes the profaning of the Sabbath so far as the

[1] *Pesikta* 178 *b*.

carrying of things is concerned; the Law is broken only when a man carries a burden from one place and also puts it down in another place; but if one person takes it up, and another puts it down, then neither has profaned the Sabbath. Again, the Sabbath rest is very jealously guarded; all kinds of things are mentioned as a breaking of the Sabbath, e.g.: "He who removes his finger-nails, whether one with another, or with his teeth; he who pulls out his hair, or the hair of his upper lip, or of his beard; so, too, a woman who plaits her hair, or who paints her eyebrows, or who colours her cheeks red"; in all these cases the guilty person has to bring a sin-offering (x. 6). In another tractate ('*Eduyoth* iv. 1) it is recorded that the School of Hillel pronounced it as a profanation of the Sabbath to eat an egg which a hen had laid on this day; the School of Shammai were more lenient, and permitted this!

These few illustrations will give some idea of the less edifying side of Pharisaic teaching on the Law; and it must be confessed that there is every reason to believe that this played the dominating part during the last century or so of our period and after.

IV

THE NEW TESTAMENT AND THE LAW

To deal in any way exhaustively with what is said in the New Testament about the Law would demand a great deal of space; we shall therefore restrict ourselves to the mention of some of the points of outstanding importance. That Christ accepted the Law in principle is clear from such words as: "Think not that I came to destroy the law or the prophets; I came not to destroy, but to fulfil" (*Matth.* v. 17), i.e. by teaching its true meaning and spirit; for "destroy" the Syriac Version has the word *shera*, lit. to "remit", i.e. to set aside its obligations. At the same time, when it goes on to say that "till heaven and earth pass away, one jot or one title shall in no wise pass away from the law till all things be accomplished", there is a distinct repudiation of the belief in the eternal duration of the Law as taught by orthodox Judaism (see above, p. 61); and the context (*v.* 20) goes on to show that in the Kingdom of Heaven the Law will be something very different from that taught by the Pharisees (cp. *Lk*. xvi. 16, 17). That our Lord was not hostile to the Law *per se* is shown by the episode recorded in *Mk*. i. 40 ff., in the words: " Go thy way, show thyself to the priest, and offer for thy cleansing the things which Moses commanded " (v. 44, cp. *Lev*. xiv. 2 ff.); the addition of the words " for a testimony unto them ", i.e. the priests, further emphasizes our Lord's recognition of the legitimate demands of the Law. The sacrificial system as a whole was certainly accepted by Christ, though there is great significance in what is said to the scribe who proclaimed his belief in the two great commandments of the Law being " much more than all whole burnt-offerings and sacrifices "; to him it is said: " Thou art not far from the Kingdom of God " (*Mk*. xii. 28–34). The implication is that the sacrificial system was of a secondary character (cp. *Mk*. xiii. 2; *Jn*. iv. 19, 20).

The specifically Pharisaic point of view is, as we all know, repudiated by our Lord; e.g. in the matter of fasting (*Matth*. ix. 14 ff., *Mk*. ii. 18 ff., *Lk*. v. 33 ff.), and of eating with " unwashen hands " (*Mk*. vii. 1 ff., *Matth*. xv. 1 f.), and regarding Sabbath observance. As to this latter an interesting point comes out in *Lk*. xiv. 1–6, in the account of the healing of a man with the dropsy on the Sabbath; the lawyers and Pharisees seek occasion to accuse our Lord of desecrating the Sabbath; but instead of replying to the two questions He puts to them, " they held their peace ", and " they could not answer again unto these things ". The reason for this was that, in finding fault with our Lord's action, they were going against their own teachers; for there can be no doubt that traditional teaching is recorded in the Mishnah (*Yoma* viii. 6) when it is said that in the case of danger to life Sabbath laws may be disregarded. In other respects the Oral Law is directly condemned, e.g. in *Mk*. vii. 8: " Ye leave the commandment of God, and hold fast the tradition of men "; so, too, in the verses which follow, on a man's duty to his parents (9–13); see further *Matth*. vii. 29, and elsewhere. But the strongest condemnation occurs in such a passage as *Matth*. xxiii. 4: " Yea, they bind heavy burdens, and grievous to be borne, and lay them on men's shoulders; but they themselves will not move them with their finger " (cp. *Lk*. xi. 46);

here we have the thought of " the yoke of the Law ", the expression occurs in the Mishnah, *Aboth* iii. 6, or " the yoke of the commandments " (*Berakoth* ii. 2) ; as against this Christ says : " Come unto me, all ye that labour and are heavy laden, and I will give you rest. Take my yoke upon you, and learn of me. . . . For my yoke is easy, and my burden is light " (*Matth.* xi. 28–30).

St. Paul, in *Romans* and *Galatians*, has a great deal to say about the Law; into the details of this we cannot go, but the central point of his teaching here is his repudiation of the doctrine of justification by works : " By the works of the law shall no flesh be justified in his sight " (*Rom.* iii. 20, cp. *vv.* 27, 28, x. 4 ff., *Gal.* ii. 16, iii. 11). It is only fair to point out that such a teacher as Jochanan ben Zakkai said : " If thou hast practised much Torah claim not merit for thyself, since for this purpose wast thou created " (*Aboth* ii. 9) ; but this is exceptional; and excellent as this precept is, it omits to add the supreme element which must take the place of merit, namely justification by faith (*Rom.* iii. 23, 24).

The conclusion, therefore, is that while Jewish teaching on the Law had much to commend it, and had a necessary place in the background of Christianity, it lacked the possibility of conferring the glorious gift described by St. Paul in the words : " For freedom did Christ set us free;—stand fast, therefore, and be not entangled again in a yoke of bondage " (*Gal.* v. 1). Pharisaism had created the oral tradition to be a fence for the protection of the pious against sin, and the nobler side of Pharisaism so regarded it. To the less noble side of Pharisaism the fence had become of all-absorbing interest, transcending that which it guarded, so that St. Paul could regard it as the fence of imprisonment rather than the fence of protection.

CHAPTER V

THE APOCALYPTISTS AND THEIR LITERATURE

WE shall deal here with the Apocalyptic Literature in the more restricted sense, that is to say with books not included in the canonical Scriptures. Brief reference may, however, be made to those parts of some of the Old Testament books which contain apocalyptic elements. Thus, in *Isa.* xxiv–xxvii we read of the coming world-catastrophe, after which the judgement of the angels, and also of the kings of the earth, takes place. Thereupon Yahweh Himself comes to Zion in glory. Following upon this the ingathering of the Jews from the lands of the Dispersion occurs, and they, together with their brethren in the home-land, " shall worship Yahweh in the holy mountain at Jerusalem ". Fuller apocalyptic descriptions occur in the book of *Daniel*, chaps. viii–xii; but as references to these will come before us as we proceed we need not dwell upon them here. The book of *Joel* is also largely apocalyptic. First there is a lurid description of the Day of Yahweh: " Alas for the day! For the day of Yahweh is at hand, and as destruction from Shaddai shall it come " (i. 15). It is a day of darkness and gloom; a mighty people will overrun the land, and lay it waste; the earth will quake; the heavens will tremble, the sun and the moon, and the stars, will become dark (ii. 1–11). When these terrors have passed Yahweh will pour His spirit on all flesh. The dispersed of Israel will return, and the nations will be punished. Then there will be prosperity for the people of Yahweh, for He will come and dwell in Zion (iii, in the Hebrew text iv). In *Zech.* xii, xiii, and especially iv, there are also apocalyptic elements, but less pronounced; the central thought is the coming of Yahweh, Who will reign over all the earth.

These are the main portions which, in the canonical books, are of an apocalyptic nature. They belong to the Greek Period.

Our purpose here, however, is to say something about the non-canonical apocalyptic writings, together with a few preliminary remarks about the writers.

I

THE APOCALYPTISTS

From the point of view of our present investigation, namely, Jewish teaching as a preparation for Christianity, the Apocalyptists and their Literature are of profound importance.

" The Jewish Apocalypses ", says Burkitt, " themselves, and the state of mind that produced them, had a great and formative influence on the minds of the earliest Christians; I venture to think we can go so far as to say that without some knowledge of the Jewish Apocalypses, and a fairly clear realization of the state of mind in which they were composed, it is impossible to understand the earliest Christianity, impossible to enter at all into the hopes and fears of the ' multitude ', of the crowd, that forms the background of the Gospels." [1]

The conviction that it was through divine inspiration that the Apocalyptists were enabled to reveal things to come is expressed at the beginning of i Enoch,[2] in the words: " Enoch, a righteous man, whose eyes were opened by God, saw the vision of the Holy One in the heavens " (i. 2), after which follows the Seer's prophecy of the future advent of the " Holy Great One ". This is from the latest portion of the book; pre-Christian, however, and echoes the claim of the Apocalyptists of every generation. Thus, like the prophets of old, they believed themselves to be instruments chosen of God, recipients of divine truths which they were to proclaim among men. That the purport of their messages centred largely on the occurrences which were to take place at the end of the present world-order was in great measure due to the circumstances of the times. During the last two pre-Christian centuries and the first century A.D. there was, with the exception of the period of the later Hasmonæan rulers, almost incessant

---

[1] In *Judaism and the Beginnings of Christianity*, Lecture II, pp. 51 ff. (1923).
[2] For the reasons why the names of ancient Israelite worthies were adopted by the Apocalyptists, see p. 74.

unrest. The Maccabæan wars, approximately 170 B.C.–
120 B.C., and the Roman dominion from 63 B.C. onwards,
plunged the country into prolonged and grievous turmoil.
It was largely during these periods that the Apocalyptists
flourished; and owing to the conditions of the times they
resuscitated the hopes of the advent of a deliverer who would
overcome the enemies and rule in a renovated world. Such
hopes had been expressed in earlier times, but the pressure
of the evils now suffered caused these hopes to be renewed
with unprecedented force. This is not the place to describe
in detail the ever-increasing bitterness that arose between the
Jews and their Roman oppressors during the later part of
this period; [1] the important thing to note, from the present
point of view, is that the unrest of the times gave constant
cause to the Apocalyptists to propagate their teaching. One
result was that masses of the people, fired by their words and
inspired by their prophecies, grew ever more turbulent; that,
again, exasperated the Romans, and more vigorous measures
were taken against the Jews; it was a kind of vicious circle
the reactions of which thundered along in disastrous career
until the final crash.

The fact is worth emphasizing that the Apocalyptists were
not concerned solely with literary activity; there is evidence
to show that, again in the following of the prophets, they
were oral teachers as well as writers. Direct contact between
them and the masses is graphically described, for example, in
ii (iv) Esdras xii. 40 ff. The Seer tells of how he had withdrawn for seven days so that in solitude he might receive a
vision; then he goes on to say: " And it came to pass, when
all the people saw that the seven days were past, and I came
not again into the city, they gathered them all together, from
the least unto the greatest, and came unto me, and spake
unto me, saying, ' Wherein have we offended thee, and what
evil have we done against thee, that thou hast utterly forsaken us, and sittest in this place? For of all the prophets
thou only art left to us, as a cluster of the vintage, and as a
lamp in a dark place, and as a haven for a ship saved from
the tempest . . .' And they wept with a loud voice." Elsewhere in the same book (xiv. 27–36) we have another picture

---

[1] See Oesterley and Robinson, A History of Israel, ii. pp. 332 ff. (1934).

F

of the Seer among the people: "Then went I forth . . . and gathered all the people together, and said . . ." This book is among the latest of the Apocalyptic Literature, but there can be no doubt that it reflects the usage of these teachers in earlier times too.

The religious fervour of the Apocalyptists is evident on every page of their writings; they were profoundly convinced, as we have said, that the revelations accorded in visions were divinely inspired, and that they were the instruments of God, chosen to proclaim His will. They were in a real sense true prophets among the people, and were intensely concerned with the spiritual condition of individuals. Their exhortations to men to lead righteous lives were in the spirit of the prophets. One or two illustrations of this will be instructive. In *i Enoch* xci. 3 ff., for example, it is said: "Love uprightness, and walk therein; and draw not nigh to uprightness with a double heart, and associate not with those of a double heart, but walk in righteousness, my sons, and it shall guide you on good paths, and righteousness shall be your companion." It is in the *Testaments of the XII Patriarchs* that exhortations of this kind occur most frequently; a few examples may be given: "Keep yourselves, therefore, my children, from every evil work; and cast away wrath and all lying, and love truth and longsuffering" (*Dan* vi. 8). In *Gad* vi. 1, again, it is said: "And now, my children, I exhort you, love ye each his brother, and put away hatred from your hearts; love one another in deed, and in word, and in the inclination of the soul." This beautiful urging to show forth love is nowhere more exquisitely set forth than in the words: "Love ye one another from the heart; and if a man sin against thee, speak peaceably to him, and in thy soul hold not guile; and if he repent and confess, forgive him" (*Gad* vi. 3).

Exhortations of this kind are again and again supplemented by words of hope; and here we are coming to what lies at the base of all that the Apocalyptists teach. In *i Enoch*. i. 8 the Seer says: "But with the righteous He (i.e. Yahweh) will make peace; and He will protect the elect, and mercy shall be upon them. And they shall all belong to God, and they shall be prospered, and they shall all be blessed; and He will help them, and light shall appear unto them, and

He will make peace with them." The Seer is here referring to the time when the present world-order will have passed and the age to come will have been established. The final reward of the righteous is thus described : " I know a mystery, and I have read the heavenly tablets, and have seen the holy books; and I have found written therein and inscribed regarding them (i.e. the righteous) : That all goodness and joy and glory are prepared for them, and are written down for the spirits of those who have died in righteousness; and that manifold good shall be given to you in recompense for your labours, and that your lot is abundantly beyond the lot of the living. And the spirits of you that have died in righteousness shall live and rejoice; and your spirits shall not perish, nor your memorial from before the face of the Great One " (i Enoch ciii. 1–4). Not less direct are the words of condemnation uttered against the wicked; and here again we are constantly reminded of prophetical denunciations; for example, it is said in i Enoch v. 5 : " But ye,—ye have not been steadfast, nor have ye fulfilled the commandments of the Lord; but ye have turned away, and have spoken proud and hard words with your impure mouths against His greatness. Oh, ye hard-hearted, ye shall find no peace. Therefore shall ye execrate your days, and the years of your life shall perish . . . and ye shall find no mercy." There are many other passages to the same effect. The final punishment of the wicked is thus described : " Woe to you, ye obstinate of heart, who watch in order to devise wickedness; therefore shall fear come upon you, and there shall be none to help you. Woe to you, ye sinners, because of the words of your mouth, and because of the deeds of your hands which your godlessness hath wrought; in blazing flames burning worse than fire shall ye burn " (i Enoch c. 8, 9).

Passages like these, and similar ones occur in other apocalyptic writings, illustrate the way in which the Apocalyptists worked among the people. Prophetical influence is easily discernible, but the Apocalyptists were by no means always dependent on this.[1]

We come next to consider the literature of the Apocalyptists, so far as this has come down to us.

---

[1] See further, Lagrange, Le Judaïsme avant Jésus-Christ, pp. 70 ff. (1931).

II

THE APOCALYPTIC LITERATURE

The writings of the Apocalyptists which have come down
to us belong approximately to the period 200 B.C. to A.D. 100.
All of them have false names in their titles, for which reason
they are known as the *Pseudepigrapha*. The purpose of this,
to us, strange procedure has been differently explained.
Charles believes it to have been necessary owing to the
supremacy of the Law; inspiration was dead, and the Canon
was closed; how otherwise were the Apocalyptists to obtain
acceptance for their books? [1] There is much force in some
things that Charles says, but it is possible that ideas of a
different nature may have played a part here. It may, at
any rate to some extent, be accounted for by the desire to
gain the recognition of an authoritative character for the
writings in question; the writers believed that they were
expressing what the honoured heroes of the past would have
thought and said under the conditions which had now supervened. Or, once more, we may be permitted to give the
following quotation: " The apocalyptic writers almost certainly drew their material in some directions from popular
tradition. Many of the ideas which receive various embodiment in this literature were doubtless derived from the common stock of popular consciousness; their ascription to or
association with the great heroic figures of antiquity, like
Enoch, Abraham, Isaiah, or the twelve Patriarchs, may also
be a feature from the popular consciousness. The men who
reduced the various elements to writing, or utilized them for
enforcing religious views or lessons may, on this view, be
acquitted from any charge of fraud or dishonesty; they implicitly trusted the popular tradition so far as to believe that
the ideas to which they were giving expression really did go
back to the heroic figures of old. Their estimate, moreover,
of the function and importance of authorship probably differed
fundamentally from that of the moderns; it was far less self-

[1] See *Eschatology, Hebrew, Jewish, and Christian*, pp. 202 ff. (1913), where
the theory is fully worked out; but we are unable to follow Charles when
he says that " the Canon was closed ".

conscious, and was the natural outcome of a literary modesty which was *naïve*." [1]

But however this may be, there is a matter of far greater importance to which attention must be drawn next. It cannot be too strongly emphasized that the Apocalyptic Literature contains elements which go back to a far-distant past. The Apocalyptists utilized a great deal of non-Hebrew material; [2] but while retaining this in their writings, they often superimposed upon it their own ideas, prompted by a variety of motives. Hence the manifold incongruities occurring in their writings.

Again, while on the one hand the Apocalyptists laid prophetical eschatology under contribution, they made use of material quite alien to anything that the prophets taught on the subject.

Thus, in this literature the presence of three elements must be recognized: extraneous material, prophetical eschatology, and the Apocalyptists' own teaching.

It is now very necessary that we should begin here by considering whence the first of these came. This will have to be only in brief outline, for to deal with it adequately would require a volume for itself.

There were two periods in Jewish history during which great tides of extraneous influences poured over the Jewish world of thought. The first was during the Babylonian Exile; and the second was during the Greek Period, as a consequence of the conquests of Alexander the Great. In the former of these the influences were twofold. There was, in the first place, Babylonian mythology, inextricably mixed up with religious ideas; these exercised a profound influence on Jewish thought, as is amply illustrated in the book of *Genesis*, the final redaction of which took place during and after the Exile, as well as in other books of the Old Testament. Of these Babylonian elements there are many signs in the Apocalyptic Literature. But, in the second place, Babylonian religion had itself become permeated with the teachings of Zoroastrianism, i.e. the religion of ancient Persia, or

---

[1] Oesterley and Box, *The Religion and Worship of the Synagogue*, p. 36 (1911).

[2] Cp., e.g., Hölscher, *Geschichte der israelitischen und jüdischen Religion*, pp. 153 ff. (1922).

Iran.[1] So the extraneous religious influences which played upon the Jews during and after the Exile had this twofold strand, Babylonian and Iranian.   It must, however, be added, that Iranian influences on Jewish religious beliefs were not always mediated through Babylonian thought; the evidence shows that in various directions Iranian influences were direct; illustrations of this will come before us later.

So much, then, for the first wave of extraneous religious thought by which Jewish thinkers were influenced. The second, during the Greek Period, was more complicated in its action.   As already pointed out, owing to the conquests of Alexander the Great, Hellenism had an enormous effect on the world in general during the centuries which followed. The Greek language, Greek culture, Greek modes of thought, became world-wide.   Hellenism brought about, furthermore, a fusion of races; and, most important of all from our present point of view, this fusion of races was the means of an inter-mingling of religious beliefs, together with an appreciation of ancient mythological elements with which these were per-meated.   As Scott-Moncrieff points out, " in Asia Minor and Egypt, Hellenism was only a veneer covering lower strata which were essentially oriental, and had inherited civilizations and religions far more ancient than anything Greek.   In Asia Minor, especially in the great towns near the Mediter-ranean, Greek influence had permeated deeply the life of all classes and a large number of religious cults had become hellenized." [2]   The influence of Hellenism in all its varied forms extended not only over all the lands bordering on the Mediterranean (Egypt was a partial exception), but also into the farthest East, into Babylonia and Persia, and even into far-off India.   For since Alexander's world-empire embraced the eastern countries, including even India, the intermingling of races, and consequent influences on religion, meant that the religions of the nations of the east and far east affected the religious beliefs of the nations of the nearer east.   We have already said that in the earlier period, during which extraneous influences poured over the Jewish world, those of

---

[1] See, further, pp. 88 ff.

[2] *Paganism and Christianity in Egypt*, p. 1 (1913); see also *The Labyrinth* (ed. S. H. Hooke), Lecture iv, " The Cult of Sabazios ", pp. 113 ff. (1935).

Babylonia and Persia were strong; but this applies in an emphasized degree to this second period. For Hellenism itself was far from being unaffected by oriental influences; so that wherever the Greek spirit made itself felt, there appeared also in more or less degree that of the East. Thus, both directly and indirectly the religious beliefs of the western peoples were affected by oriental thought.

The presence of extraneous material, then, is the first of the three elements mentioned above which figure in the Apocalyptic Literature. Of the two others, prophetical eschatology and the teaching of the Apocalyptists set forth on their own part, it is unnecessary to say anything here as abundant illustrations of each will come before us in the succeeding chapters.

We must now give a list of the writings comprised within the Apocalyptic Literature, together with the briefest possible indication of their character and contents. Dates of composition cannot be given with exactitude, and even with regard to approximate dates there is not always unanimity of opinion among experts. For our purposes, however, it will be quite sufficient if we indicate the writings as respectively: Pre-Maccabæan, Maccabæan, Post-Maccabæan, and Post-Christian (not later than the first century A.D.). It must be emphasized that inasmuch as the writings belonging to this last period embody much ancient material, they can be quoted in support of beliefs held in pre-Christian times. The reason for making the Maccabæan period a dividing line, as it were, will be clear from what has been said above (pp. 26 ff.); it was an epoch-making period in the post-exilic history of the Jews.

Pre-Maccabæan

i Enoch xii–xxxvi, xci. 12–17, xciii; to these must be added the fragments of the " book of Noah " embodied in this book, namely vi–xi, liv. 7–lv. 2, lx, lxv–lxix. 25, cvi, cvii. *i Enoch* is known as the " Ethiopic " Enoch, to distinguish it from the " Slavonic " Enoch (*ii Enoch*, see below). Our book is the most important of the Apocalypses. It is, however, not a single book, but a collection of various writings, the oldest of which is comprised in the chapters here indicated. Of these

xii–xxxvi form a separate book, containing visions of Enoch,
and accounts of his journeys on the earth and down to Sheol.
Angelology plays a great part. The myth of the fallen angels
is referred to (cp. *Gen.* vi. 1, 2); they are said to have brought
sin on to the earth; their final doom is decreed in spite of
Enoch's intercession. Of special interest are the subjects of
the Judgement, the Garden of Righteousness, and the Tree
of Life. A pronouncedly ethical note runs through the whole.
Chapter xciii, to which xci. 12–17 belongs, seems to be an
independent piece; it is called " The Apocalypse of Weeks ",
i.e., the first seven weeks of the history of the world, referring
to the past, and the Judgement, which will take place during
the last three weeks, referring to the future. As Charles says,
" The Book of Enoch, like the Book of Daniel, was written
originally partly in Aramaic and partly in Hebrew. From
an Aramaic original is derived vi–xxxvi, and possibly lxxxiii–xc,
while the rest of the book comes from a Hebrew original."
Of the two extant Versions, the Ethiopic is the most complete; this has been translated by Charles, *The Book of Enoch*
(1912); our quotations have been taken from this edition,
consideration having been also taken of Beer's translation in
Kautzsch's *Die Apokryphen und Pseudepigraphen des Alten Testaments*, ii. 217 ff. (1900). Charles has also published a translation in the S.P.C.K. Series, " Translations of Early Documents " (1917). The text of the Greek Version, so far as this
is extant, is given by Charles in Appendix I of his book just
mentioned. A recently discovered manuscript of chaps.
xcvii. 6–civ, cvi, cvii, has been edited by Campbell Bonner,
The Last Chapters of Enoch in Greek (1937).

MACCABÆAN

i Enoch lxxxiii–xc. These chapters contain the " Dream-
Visions ". The most important subjects dealt with in them
are the Judgement, the New Jerusalem, the Resurrection, and
the Messiah.

THE BOOK OF JUBILEES [1]

Probably written originally in Hebrew, this book is called
also " The Little Genesis ", on account of its being based on

---

[1] Some authorities regard this book as post-Maccabæan.

the *Genesis* narratives of the Creation and subsequent events up to the time of Moses. The most complete extant Version is the Ethiopic. The standpoint of the writer is of particular interest, for in some respects, such as the upholding of the Law, he seems to represent Pharisaism; but in other directions he is strongly anti-Pharisaic. There is not a great deal of an apocalyptic nature in the book; but there are some interesting eschatological passages; the near advent of the Messiah is expected. The Ethiopic Version has been translated by Charles, *The Book of Jubilees* (1902), also in the S.P.C.K. Series (1917), from which our quotations are taken. A German translation is given by Littmann, in Kautzsch, *op cit.* ii. 39 ff.

Post-Maccabæan

The books under this heading are given in chronological order; more or less, for it is recognized that in some cases the views of experts differ on the question of date.

The Sibylline Oracles, Book III. The value of this book, written in Greek, from our present point of view, lies in the large amount of eschatological material which it contains. The belief finds expression that the Messiah's appearing is imminent. Of much interest also are the indications given of the existence of opposed parties among the Jews. The Greek text is published by Geffcken, *Die Oracula Sibyllina* (1902). An English translation is published by H. N. Bate, in the S.P.C.K. Series, *The Sibylline Oracles Books III–V* (1918).

The Testaments of the XII Patriarchs. This book was originally written in Hebrew, but only a few fragments of this have been preserved. The most important Version is the Greek, but there are also Armenian and Slavonic Versions extant. The writer of the book was a Pharisee, but later portions were added of an anti-Pharisaic character. So far as the eschatology of the book is concerned, the Patriarchs are represented as prophesying about the last times, in which a falling-away of their descendants is foretold. The special characteristic of the book centres in its ethical teaching, which is of a high order. The Greek Version was published by Sinker, *Testamenta XII Patriarcharum* (1869); Charles published an English translation in 1908, *The Testaments of the Twelve Patriarchs*; also in the S.P.C.K. Series (1917).

i Enoch xxxvii–lxxi. This section of the book contains "The Parables", or "The Similitudes". It is a very important part of the book, on account of its Messianic teaching, of the doctrine of Sin held, and of what is said about angels and demons. The names which are applied to the Almighty form a special feature.

i Enoch xci–civ. There are some points of similarity between this and the section just mentioned; but they are of independent authorship. These chapters were written by a Pharisee of the extreme type. The eschatological teaching is an important element.

The Psalms of Solomon. These are eighteen psalms, written originally in Hebrew. That the writer, or writers, were Pharisees does not admit of doubt. The Messianic outlook is nationalistic. An important point in these psalms is the witness they bear to the existence of party strife during the middle of the last century B.C. Greek and Syriac Versions are extant; the latter is a translation of the Greek, the text of which is given in the Septuagint editions of Swete and Rahlfs. English translations are published by Ryle and James, *Psalms of the Pharisees* (1891) and by Gray in vol. ii of Charles *The Apocrypha and Pseudepigrapha* . . .

iii Maccabees. How this title came to be applied to the book is not clear; it has not the remotest connexion with the Maccabæans. It is included in our list because it represents the rigidly orthodox and nationalistic type of Judaism during the last century B.C. Antagonism against the hellenistic Jews is strongly expressed. The Greek text of both this and the following book are given in the Septuagint editions of Swete and Rahlfs. English translations of each by Emmet will be found in the S.P.C.K. Series (1918).

iv Maccabees. This book is of slightly later date than the preceding. In this case the title is appropriate, since its main subject is the martyrdoms of the aged priest Eleazar, and of the mother with her seven sons, recorded in *ii Macc.* vi, vii. Like the preceding, it was written in Greek. The writer regards Greek philosophy as fully embodied in the Mosaic Law. Our main interest in the book centres, however, in its teaching on the Resurrection and the Future Life.

i Enoch i–v. These chapters seem to be an independent

section; "they look like an introduction to the entire book written by the final editor ", according to Charles. The section contains an apocalyptic poem of much interest, describing the happy lot of the righteous, and the fate of the ungodly hereafter.

The Zadokite Fragments. These are Hebrew remnants of a body of writings originating probably towards the end of the last century B.C. The point of view, as one would expect, is anti-Pharisaic; but the " Zadokites " from whom the writings emanated were not Sadducees as ordinarily understood. They called themselves " the sons of Zadok ", thus retaining an ancient name to which they had a right in so far that they were priests and Levites (v. 7); they, therefore, probably originated among the Sadducees, but broke away from them. The eschatological material contained in these Fragments is important; the near advent of the Messiah is looked for; but the Messiah is not of the house of David; he is described as " from Aaron and Israel ". The strife of parties among the Jews which is witnessed to is also of interest. The Hebrew text is edited by Schechter *Fragments of a Zadokite Work edited from Hebrew manuscripts* . . . (1912); see also Rost, *Die Damaskusscrift*, in Lietzmann's *Kleine Texte* (1933). Our quotations are from Charles' translation in vol. ii of *The Apocr. and Pseudepigrapha*. . . .

Post-Christian

The Assumption of Moses. This book, of a composite character, was written, originally in Hebrew, by a Pharisee; that is seen by his devotion to the Law. Nevertheless, he is in some ways quite anti-Pharisaic; thus, he holds a doctrine of divine grace and human good works which approximates to Christian teaching. He is also against the political tendencies of the Pharisees in his day, i.e. the very beginning of the Christian era. In chap. x. 1–10 there is a poem of much interest on the advent of the Kingdom of God; it contains some familiar apocalyptic *traits*. The place of the Messiah, however, seems to be taken by the archangel Michael. The extant Latin Version, translated from the Greek, which in its turn was translated from the original Hebrew, is published by Clemen, *Die Himmelfahrt des Moses* (1904), in the *Kleine*

Texte . . . Series, ed. Lietzmann. An English translation is published by W. J. Ferrar in the S.P.C.K. Series (1917).

The Sibylline Oracles, Book V. The eschatology of this book is what specially concerns us. The Messianic King comes from the heavens to destroy the enemies of God, and to set up a new temple. His rule is terrestrial, and prior to his advent the woes of the last days will harass mankind.

ii Enoch. This book is known also as " The Secrets of Enoch ". It was written originally in Greek, but only the Slavonic Version is extant. Some sections, according to Charles, were originally written in Hebrew. So far as authorship is concerned this book is in no way connected with *i Enoch*; and it is of far less importance in the matter of apocalyptic teaching. But it deals with some subjects which are of much interest, viz. the doctrine of Sin, the Millennium and the Seven Heavens. With regard to this last, the book describes the belief in greater detail than is found elsewhere. An English translation is published by Charles, *The Book of the Secrets of Enoch* (1896), from which our quotations are taken.

The Life of Adam and Eve. The original writing was in all probability in Hebrew, but nothing of this has survived. There are extant Versions in Greek, Latin, Armenian, and Slavonic. The erroneous title of " The Apocalypse of Moses " is also given to this book. It contains teaching on the Judgement, the Intermediate State of the soul in Paradise, and on the Resurrection. Belief in guardian-angels is also taught, and emphasis is laid on the efficacy of their prayers on behalf of the departed. It is urged, further, that the prayers of righteous men should be offered for the departed. English and German translations, by Wells and Fuchs respectively, are given in the collections of Charles and Kautzsch; to these we are indebted for our quotations.

The Apocalypse of Abraham. This apocalypse was written originally in Hebrew or Aramaic; only a Slavonic Version is extant. It illustrates the divergence of view regarding some elements in the eschatological drama which existed among the Jews. It knows nothing of the Resurrection, and there is no belief in an Intermediate State; the righteous dead go at once to the heavenly Paradise, the Garden of Eden; and the

wicked go immediately down to the underworld. The figure
of the Messiah, the " Elect One ", appears at the sound of
the trumpet-blast (cp. *Matth.* xxiv. 31, *i Cor.* xv. 52, *i Thess.*
iv. 16, *Rev.* ix. 14). The Judgement then takes place, and
the wicked are annihilated, while the dispersed of Israel are
gathered together to enjoy the blessings of the " Age of
righteousness." The part played by the Messiah is, however,
very limited. An English translation of the Slavonic is
published by Box and Landsman in the S.P.C.K. Series, *The
Apocalypse of Abraham* (1918); our quotations are from this
translation.

ii Baruch. " The Syriac Apocalypse of Baruch." Comparatively late in date as this book is, it contains a great deal
of material handed down from earlier times. It is one of the
most interesting among our sources, and is of importance for
its teaching on the Law, including a reference to the " Unwritten Law ", i.e. the Oral Tradition, for its doctrine of Sin,
and for what it says of the nature of the risen body. A translation from the Greek and Syriac is published by Charles in
the S.P.C.K. Series (1917), from which our quotations are
taken.

The Testament of Abraham. This book, written probably
originally in Greek, has come down to us in two Greek recen-
sions, both of which have clearly been considerably abridged;
they disagree with one another on some points. It was
probably written during the first century A.D., but James
assigns it to the second century. A curious feature of the
eschatological teaching is that there are three Judgements,
the final one alone being presided over by the Almighty; the
two others by Abel, and the twelve tribes of Israel, respectively
(cp. *i Cor.* vi. 3). The Messiah plays a very subordinate part.
One recension emphasizes the need of intercessory prayer for
the departed, but the other one does not mention this. Three
classes of people who pass into the other world at death are
recognized: the righteous who enter Paradise, the wicked
who go to Gehenna, and those who are neither very good nor
very bad; these, too, go to Gehenna, where they are purged
by fire, then they are released. It is worth adding that
mention is made of the righteous in Paradise who rest in
" Abraham's bosom " (cp. *Luke* xvi. 22). The Greek text

was published by James, *The Testament of Abraham* . . . (1892). An English translation by Box is given in the S.P.C.K. Series (1927).

The Ascension of Isaiah.   This is a composite work comprising three originally distinct writings: "The Martyrdom of Isaiah", "The Testament of Hezekiah", and "The Ascension of Isaiah". The first of these is probably pre-Christian. The "Testament" is a Christian writing, so, too, are the final chapters of the "Ascension", which describe the vision of Isaiah. The compilation contains much that is of importance for the study of beliefs held in the early days of Christianity. Possibly the original was in Hebrew or Aramaic; the principal extant Version is the Ethiopic. There is an English translation by Charles in the S.P.C.K. Series (1917), from which our quotations are taken.

iii Baruch.   "The Greek Apocalypse of Baruch". This is a Jewish writing worked over by a Christian. It is quite independent of the other two books of Baruch. The two subjects of main importance are the doctrine of mediation of angels, and what is said about the Fall. The belief in the Seven Heavens is also prominent. The Greek text has been published by James in "Texts and Studies", vol. v., No. 1 (1897). An English translation is given by Hughes, in Charles' *The Apocrypha and Pseudepigrapha* . . ., vol. ii.

Belonging to this literature is ii (iv) Esdras, "The Ezra Apocalypse"; but this has already been referred to above, pp. 52 f.

It is hoped that this brief outline of the more outstanding subjects dealt with in this literature may suffice for the present; many illustrations from the writings mentioned will come before us in the following chapters.

CHAPTER VI

THE INFLUENCE OF PERSIAN THOUGHT AND TEACHING

IT is necessary that we should include in this introductory part of our study some observations regarding the religion of ancient Persia. This is because there is every reason for believing that in certain directions the Judaism of our period reflects the influence of Persian religion. Though primarily in the domain of Eschatology, this influence is to be discerned in other spheres too. We shall, however, be concerned here only with Eschatology.[1]

I

THE STAGES PRECEDING AND FOLLOWING ZOROASTRIANISM

During the middle of the second millennium B.C. the Persians [2] (Iranians) from the West occupied Bactria together with the neighbouring country in north-western India, the land of the Asurs. These people took their name from their supreme god, *Asura Mazda*, " the Lord of High Knowledge ". The Persians settled down among them, and thus the Indo-Iranian branch of the Aryans was formed. Later, this branch divided, the Aryan-Indians migrated into the Punjab, while the Persians proper were in possession of Bactria to the frontiers of India. But before this division took place there had been an intermingling of the ancient religion of the Persians with that of the Asurs. This is demonstrated by comparing much that occurs in the *Rigveda* with the sacred writings of the Persians. *Rig* means " praise ", and the ancient sacred literature of India is contained in the four *Vedas*; the word comes from the Sanscrit root *vid*, " to know "; the fourth of these, and the most important, is the *Rigveda*, which contains a collection of praises to the gods; hence its name.

[1] See further for this influence the chaps. on Angelology and Demonology.
[2] The name is derived from the ancient *Parsa*, the *Persis* of the Greeks.

Thus it is important to realize that some of the vital elements of Persian belief were derived from the religion of the Asurs. As just pointed out, among the Indians *Asura* means Lord, or Deity; the corresponding name among the Persians was *Ahura*, whose outstanding quality was his wisdom, hence the name *Ahura Mazda*, the " Wise Lord " (Ormazd), among the latter in later times. In course of time the conceptions held with regard to this deity and his lesser fellow-deities degenerated, and in other respects the religion of the Persians had become debased. Thus, reform was called for; and a reformer was forthcoming in the person of Zarathustra, or Zoroaster, the more familiar form of his name. He appeared about 1000 B.C., according to most authorities.[1] Zoroaster was not the founder of a new religion, for his teaching was based on what had gone before; his reform was concerned with the purification and spiritualization of the beliefs of his time; and he brought an ethical spirit into the traditional religion which it had never before possessed. Zoroastrianism was thus a second stage in the development of the religion of ancient Persia. After Zoroaster's death degeneration again supervened, and once more there was great need for another reformation. It is necessary to mention this, because in the sacred writings which have come down to us there is much that belongs to the reformed religion after the age of Zoroaster. At the same time, late in date as these writings are, they reflect in many instances teaching ultimately derived from Zoroaster himself.

II

THE ANCIENT PERSIAN SCRIPTURES

The sacred literature of the Persians, representing not more than fragmentary portions of what must have existed at one time, is contained in the *Avesta*, or " Law "; from the old Persian word *Abasta*. Attached to it is its commentary, or explanation, called *Zend*; hence the oft-used title of the scriptures, *Zend-Avesta*; but, as Darmesteter says, this is " a very improper designation; as *Zend* was applied only to explanatory texts, to the translations of the *Avesta* ".[2]

[1] Other authorities hold that he lived in the sixth century B.C.
[2] *The Sacred Books of the East*, vol. iv, p. xxx (1880).

The *Avesta*, then, as now existing, contains the following *Nasks*, or " Books " :—

The *Yasna* (" Ritual ") ; this is a collection of litanies, but it includes also the *Gathas* (" Hymns "), seventeen in number, which are the most ancient part of the Persian Scriptures. It contains also *Yashts* (the word means the act of " Worship "), which are also hymns, though of a different kind from the *Gathas*. There is also a separate book of *Yashts* consisting of twenty-one hymns of praise. Next, there is the *Visperad*, meaning " To all the gods " ; it contains invocations to many deities, and also litanies for the sacrifices. Further, there is the *Vendîdâd*, the " Law against demons " ; but it contains other laws as well, many of which are ancient ; and also mythical tales. This book belongs to the second century B.C., but in spite of its lateness it is important on account of much traditional material which is embodied ; among other things it contains the Yima legend, the equivalent to the " Golden Age " myth. So far the *Avesta*. A much later work is the *Bundahish*, the " Original Creation " ; according to West,[1] " the actual name of the treatise was *Zand-akas*, ' knowing the tradition ' ". This, too, is an important book because it purports to give details concerning Zoroastrian beliefs, and doubtless in many respects echoes original material. With the *Kordah Avesta*, or " Little Avesta ", we are not concerned, as this is very much later.

. . . .

Selected Literature :—

Darmsteter, in *Sacred Books of the East*, vols. iv, xxiii (1880, 1883) ; West, in the same Series, vols. v, xviii, xxiv (1880, 1882, 1885) ; Böklen, *Die Verwandtschaft der jüdisch-christlichen mit der parsischen Eschatologie* (1902) ; A. V. Williams Jackson, *Zoroaster, the Prophet of Ancient Iran* (1889) ; Geldner, in Bertholet's *Religionsgeschichtliches Lesebuch*, pp. 323–359 (1908) ; Moulton, *Early Zoroastrianism* (1913), and *The Treasure of the Magi* (1917) ; Scheftelowitz, *Die altpersische Religion und das Judentum* (1920) ; Gressmann, *Die orientalischen Religionen im hellenistisch–römischen Zeitalter*, pp. 124–138 (1930) ; Waterhouse, *Zoroastrianism* (1934).

---

[1] *The Sacred Books of the East*, vol. v, p. xxiii (1880).

G

III

AN OUTLINE OF PERSIAN ESCHATOLOGICAL BELIEFS

It may be said that at the base of Persian eschatology there lies the fundamental *dualistic conception* of the Persian religion; namely, the irreconcilable antagonism between the highest god, Ahura-Mazda, who is all-good, and Angra-Mainyu, the great spirit of evil. They are in unceasing conflict for the possession of the world. The entire history of the world and of mankind presents the outcome of this perpetual struggle with its varying successes for one or the other. And the end of the world, with the final judgement, coincides with the triumph of the all-good god over the powers of evil. But the struggle between the forces of good and evil for the possession of the world is conceived of as passing through different phases, or world-epochs. Thus, the world is to exist for a period of twelve thousand years. The first six thousand consisted of two eras; during the first era of three thousand years all and everything was invisible. During the second era Ahura-Mazda created the material, good world, and the first man. Then comes the second period of six thousand years, likewise divided into two eras. It is during both of these eras that the conflict between Ahura-Mazda and Angra-Mainyu takes place. The first three thousand years of this second great division of the world's history is the time of the complete ascendancy of Angra-Mainyu, the evil spirit. But at the end of these first three thousand years there appears the figure of Zoroaster; with his advent there arises the hope of better things, though the conflict between the powers of good and evil continues. Then, at a certain time, there occurs the miraculous birth of Saoshyant, of the seed of Zoroaster and the virgin Hvov. Saoshyant is to be the saviour of the world, and his work is to be the gradual improving of the world until it reaches perfection. Then the end will come.

The sequence of the great eschatological events is not clearly stated, and the fantastic details with which the whole drama of the " last things " is overloaded makes it difficult to find one's way through the maze of subject-matter. But this confused presentation is only to be expected seeing that our sources are of different authorship, and belong to widely separated periods. It is generally recognized, nevertheless, that, as already remarked, even in the latest writings echoes of earlier thought and teaching have been preserved.

The *signs of the end* are dealt with in great detail in *Bahman Yasht* ii. 24 ff.; a few quotations may be given. Of the catastrophic happenings in the natural world it is said, for example, that " the sun will be more unseen and more spotted; the year, month, and day shorter . . . the crop will not yield the seed . . . vegetation, trees, and shrubs will diminish . . ." (ii. 31). Again, in ii. 42 : " And a dark cloud makes the whole sky night, and the hot wind and the cold wind arrive. . . . and it does not rain, and that which rains also rains more noxious creatures than water; and the water of rivers and springs will diminish, and there will be no increase . . ." There is much more to the same effect. Another of the signs of the end will be the melting of metal on the hills and mountains; this " will remain on the earth like a river " (*Bundahish* xxx. 19). But apparently in connexion with this the *Judgement* takes place, for it is said that " all men will enter into the molten metal, and will become pure. To him that is righteous it will appear as though he were passing through warm milk; but to him that is godless it will be as though he were constantly passing through molten metal " (xxx. 20). Sometimes an intermediate state after death and before the Judgement seems to be referred to (e.g. *Vend.* xix. 27). The " Great Judgement " is spoken of in the *Gatha* xxx. 2, where every individual is urged to secure the favour of Ahura-Mazda by right living before it takes place; and in *Yasna* li. 9 reference is made to the testing by " red fire ", whereby Ahura-Mazda will discern between guilt and merit; by means of molten metal the mark will be impressed upon all, to the detriment of unbelievers, but for the gain of true believers. As a result of the Judgement the power of the Drujes, the evil spirits in the service of Angra-Mainyu, will be brought to an end; but those who are faithful to Ahura-Mazda will enjoy happiness in the " blissful fields " (cp. the *Elysii Campi* of Greek mythology); this is described in the *Gatha* xx. 10.

While belief in immortality is thus expressed in the *Gathas*, and often elsewhere, it is remarkable that in the former the subject of the *Resurrection* is never mentioned. For this we have to turn to the later writings. Thus, in *Yasht* xix. 88–90 mention is made of the world to come, where the dead will have risen; then there will be no old-age, no death any more, no decaying, and no corruption; all evil will come to an end. But it is in the *Bundahish* xxx. 3–16 that the fullest details are given. It is the coming of Shaoshyant, the saviour, which will bring about the resurrection: " After Shaoshyant comes they prepare the raising of the dead " (4). First the bones are raised up; " whoever is righteous, and whoever is wicked, every human creature, they raise up from the spot where its life departs. Afterwards, when all material living beings assume again their bodies and forms, then they assign to them a single class ", i.e. there are no distinctions of rank. Mutual recognition of relations and friends will then take place (7–9). The first act of men after they are risen will be to praise Ahura-Mazda and the Archangels "with loud voices " (23). According to the *Gathas* (*Yasna* xxxiv. 11), they will then receive the food of immortality.

This, then, is a brief outline of the more outstanding elements of Persian eschatological beliefs. Many details of minor importance have not been touched upon; but what has been said represents the fundamental points.

IV

THE PERIOD OF PERSIAN INFLUENCE ON JEWISH ESCHATOLOGY

A question of some difficulty arises when we seek to determine the time or times during which Jewish teachers came under the influence of Persian eschatology. The fact of this influence is generally recognized by scholars, and we shall see in the chapters to follow that they are justified in this.

Now this influence was brought to bear owing to the close contact of the Jews with Babylonian–Persian beliefs during the Exile,[1] and after, and doubtless also during the earlier part

---

[1] This is well brought out, among others, by Waterhouse, *Zoroastrianism*, pp. 115 ff. (1934).

of the Greek Period. The question, therefore, naturally arises as to why no signs of Persian influence appear in the post-exilic Biblical books, nor in the books of the Apocrypha,[1] nor (with the exception of the earliest sections of the book of *i Enoch*, *circa* 200 B.C.) in the Apocalyptic Literature until post-Maccabæan times, when these signs became prominent. Such eschatological *traits* as appear in post-exilic prophetical books and in some of the later psalms are due to the influence of earlier prophetical writings, not necessarily to that of Persian religion. That there should have been a period of several centuries from the time that Persian influence was exercised before its marks became prominent in Jewish literature, must strike one as strange. How this is to be accounted for certainly raises a difficulty. We must, however, seek to offer some explanation. On the return from the Exile the Jewish religious leaders were intent upon the study of the Law, and in seeking to instil its precepts among their people. This naturally involved concentration on what concerned the present world to the exclusion of speculations regarding the " Last Things " and the future Messianic Age. Practical religion was not concerned with what may well have been regarded as outside the sphere of present religious needs. Moreover, that future age had been indissolubly connected with a ruler of the house of David, subordinate as that rule was to the Kingship of Yahweh. But the monarchy had come to an end; a fact which had dispersed the expectations connected with the Messianic Age. This may well explain why thoughts of an eschatological nature, which occupied so large a part in Persian religion, did not occupy the minds of the official Jewish religious teachers. Nevertheless, the sequel forces us to believe that, in spite of official discouragement, there were circles of religious-minded men who, from the Exile onwards, fostered the belief in what had been taught by the prophets, a belief which was strengthened through contact with Persian religion. These men handed on their teaching; and this, though discountenanced by the official religious leaders, continued in spite of them to gain adherents. The time then came when these apocalyptic teachers, as we

[1] *ii* (*iv*) *Esdras* belongs to the Apocalyptic Literature.

must call them, attained sufficient influence to be able to assert themselves and their teaching in their writings, so many of which have come down to us. It is in these writings that the marks of Persian influence appear. To this references will be made in later chapters.

PART III: THE THEOLOGY OF EARLY JUDAISM

CHAPTER VII

MONOTHEISTIC BELIEF

In considering this fundamental tenet of Jewish belief, we must glance, though it be but cursorily, at the teaching of the Old Testament belonging to the earlier phases of Israelite history. Why this is necessary will become clear as we proceed. There are various theories held regarding the tendencies and causes which led to monotheistic belief in general; and there is much that can be urged in support of these theories; indeed, they are substantiated by what is known about monotheistic tendencies among ancient peoples. Nevertheless, we cannot get away from the conviction that the underlying impulse which led men step by step to the truth that there is, and can be, only one God, was due to the gradual self-revelation of God Himself to man, according to man's capacity for apprehension. We fully recognize that the tendencies which ultimately led to a monotheistic belief were preceded by many ages of gradual religious development. It took untold centuries of groping on the part of man before he reached even a polytheistic stage, a stage which was the precursor of that in which first a tribal, and later a national, god was deemed to be more worthy of worship than gods of other tribes or nations. These were the preceding steps, and they are indicated in the Old Testament. We shall here, however, be concerned only with the step that immediately preceded monotheistic belief, before coming to that belief itself.

I

MONOLATROUS WORSHIP

Here our thoughts turn naturally to the work of Moses, whose teaching centred in the belief in One God, vastly superior to all other gods; but the reality of the existence of these lesser gods was not denied; Moses, therefore, was the founder of monolatrous worship among the Hebrews, but not of purely monotheistic belief. The great merit to be ascribed to Moses is that he responded to the divine approach made in infinite condescension to him. Human free-will, granted by God, lays on man the responsibility and duty of responding to the divine call. As much as in him lay, Moses responded; but, as the subsequent religion of Israel shows, it was long before the people followed in his steps. The Old Testament Scriptures make it only too plain that contact with the Canaanites engendered a syncretistic form of worship in which the God of Israel had not, in the eyes of the bulk of the people, that uniqueness on which Moses had laid such immense stress. The God of Israel was worshipped, but other gods, the Baals, were also worshipped. And when we come to the time of the grand pre-exilic prophets, there is no getting away from the fact that even they, with all their exalted conceptions of the God of Israel, His uniqueness, His majesty, His sublimely ethical nature, His creatorship, His mercy and loving-kindness, His righteousness and justice, His Lordship over Nature, His directing will in world-history,—in spite of all this, the pre-exilic prophets did recognize the possibility of the existence of other gods, infinitely inferior to Yahweh from every point of view, yet existent. Their belief in God was not, therefore, a true uncompromising monotheistic faith. Incidentally it may be pointed out that the most honoured title applied to Yahweh, viz. 'Elyon, " Most High ", is an implicit recognition of the existence of other gods less high (e.g. *Num.* xxiv. 16, *ii Sam.* xxii. 14, *Isa.* xiv. 14, and often in the Psalms). Attention must also be drawn to *Deut.* vi. 4: " Hear, O Israel: Yahweh our God, Yahweh is One "; this formed the basis for the future dogma of Monotheism; but in itself the passage does not express monotheistic belief. Yahweh is " our God ", i.e. the God of Israel, for whom He is the one and only God; but this does not exclude the belief that other nations had their gods, for in *vv.* 14, 15 it goes on to say: " Ye shall not go after other gods, of the gods of the peoples which are round about you; for Yahweh thy God in the midst of thee is a jealous God . . ." It was not until the time of the great unnamed exilic prophet whom we call Deutero-Isaiah that we find the utterance of the dogma expressed in the words: " Thus saith Yahweh, the King of Israel, and Redeemer, Yahweh of hosts, I am the first, and I am the last; and beside me there is no god " (*Isa.* xliv. 6). Words of similar import occur often in his teaching. Even with this great prophet in their midst the ingrained belief of many of his people still asserted itself and called forth his rebuke: " They shall be greatly ashamed that trust in graven images, that say to the molten images, Ye are our gods " (*Isa.* xlii. 17). One sees, indeed, what a stupendous task it must have been for the great prophet and his small following to try to wean their people from an age-long belief that there were many gods besides Yahweh.

Now, bearing in mind this deep-seated belief in the existence of a multiplicity of deities, and especially that each nation was believed to have its own special tutelary deity—Chemosh the god of the Moabites, Ashtoreth the goddess of the Zidonians, Milkom the god of the Ammonites, and so on (cp. *ii Kgs.* xxiii. 13)—we shall do well to consider for a moment the condition of the Jews who returned to Palestine from the Babylonian exile. The Old Testament gives us ample information on this subject. To begin with, the returned exiles found that the homeland embraced now but a very circumscribed area. Jerusalem was a more or less ruined city. The Temple likewise was a ruin, though there is reason to believe that an altar still existed there (cp. *Jer.* xli. 5). The population was very scanty. Outside enemies were not wanting. There was a drought over the land, as the prophet Haggai records (*Hag.* i. 11); and there was evidently a great food scarcity. And, perhaps most fatal of all, the people were not free; they were a subject-race; Palestine was part of a Persian province. Such being the state of things, what was likely to have been the attitude of the bulk of the people towards their national God? What was He doing to help them? How much stronger had the gods of the Medes and Persians proved themselves to be! Was it worth while rebuilding the Temple for a God who did nothing for His people? So the Temple remained in its ruined condition full twenty years. We have drawn attention to this simply to show how difficult it must have been for the first generation of those who returned from the Exile to cling to the monotheistic belief taught by Deutero-Isaiah. That faith was upheld by a comparatively few faithful ones in the land, from generation to generation; and, but for them, it is difficult to see how pure Monotheism could have survived; for there is no disguising the fact that even among many who were ardent worshippers of Yahweh the belief in the existence of other gods, however immeasurably inferior to Him, still persisted. Many passages in a number of Psalms belonging to the post-exilic period continue to bear witness to this. But what is especially noteworthy is that in some of these later psalms there are distinct indications of the existence within the Jewish community of those who had altogether withdrawn from the worship of Yahweh; it is clear, for example, from many verses in *Ps.* cxix that the Jews were divided into distinct and opposed parties, namely, those who feared Yahweh (e.g. *vv.* 63, 74, 79), and those who scorned the divine commandments (e.g. *v.* 21), and the law of God (e.g. *vv.* 126, 136, 150, 155). The psalmist's enemies were godless men, who spurned the precepts of Yahweh; and they were Jews, not Gentiles. The many references in this psalm to this rift within Jewry are of particular interest and importance in the present connexion, because the psalm belongs to the early Greek period. The conception of the Law is too developed for the psalm to belong to the time of Ezra, to whom were due the beginnings of its exaltation; on the other hand, its presentation and the utterances in regard to it are quite different from the " yoke " that it became later. It may, therefore, be claimed that *Ps.* cxix (and the same is to be said of some other psalms) gives us some insight into the religious conditions of the Jews in Palestine during the third century B.C.

It must thus be recognized that during the two or three generations immediately preceding the beginning of the Greek

Period (roughly B.C. 300) a monotheistic belief was by no means yet accepted by the Jews as a whole. We have to face the fact, in approaching the Greek Period, which is our main concern, that while, on the one hand, Monotheism was vigorously championed by those who followed the teaching of Deutero-Isaiah, and later by Ezra, there was, on the other hand, a section of the people who opposed this teaching. Of the Jews of the Dispersion during these generations we have but the scantiest knowledge, but judging from the clear evidence offered during the Greek Period, the conditions obtaining among them were similar to those among their brethren in Palestine; for it may be assumed that this evidence reflects, and continues to set forth, the characteristic of Jewish belief during the immediately preceding times.

II

THE GREEK PERIOD

We come now to consider in some detail the Greek Period. And here it will not be out of place if we draw attention, first, to the interesting fact that a tendency to a monotheistic belief is to be observed during this period in certain Gentile circles. Dodd, in his very instructive work, *The Bible and the Greeks*, pp. 6, 7 (1935), says: ". . . The philosophers and poets, influenced by them, had much to do with turning this vague sense of a divine Somewhat within or beyond the gods of popular worship, into a real belief in one supreme divine Being. When Plato [1] identified ὁ θεός with the ἰδέα τοῦ ἀγαθοῦ, he took a step which was directed towards a monotheism not altogether unlike that of Judaism. In the Hermetic writings, largely influenced by Platonism, θεός is frequently used in a genuinely monotheistic sense . . ." This may well have helped in furthering Jewish propaganda in the Dispersion, in spite of the fact that "the tendency towards Monotheism was accompanied by a view of the divine as immanent and impersonal", which was not in agreement with the Jewish conception of God. To this we now turn.

So far as the canonical books of the Old Testament belonging to this period are concerned, such as *Isa.* xxiv–xxvii,

[1] He was born in 428 B.C.

Jonah, Joel, Zech. ix–xiv, *Daniel* and some of the *Psalms,* since monotheistic belief is taken for granted by the writers, we do not expect to find expressions of this belief in so many words; nevertheless, here and there they occur, though mostly by implication. Once the belief finds definite expression, where the prophet speaks in reference to the Gentiles: " And Yahweh shall be king over all the earth; in that day shall Yahweh be one, and his name one " (*Zech.* xiv. 9); and the truth is implied in *Zech.* xii. 1. Again, in *Joel* ii. 27 it is said: " And ye shall know that I am in the midst of Israel, and that I am Yahweh your God, and there is none else." On the other hand, there are some passages which suggest that, as in previous ages, there were those who did not accept a monotheistic belief. Thus, in *Zech.* xiii. 2 we read, in reference to " the house of David " and " the inhabitants of Jerusalem ", these words: " And it shall come to pass in that day, saith Yahweh of hosts, that I will cut off the names of the idols out of the land, and they shall no more be remembered." A refusal to acknowledge Yahweh is mentioned also in *Isa.* xxvi. 10: " Let favour be shewed to the wicked, yet will he not learn righteousness; in the land of uprightness will he deal wrongfully, and will not behold the majesty of Yahweh "; the context shows that " the land of Judah " is referred to (cp. also *Isa.* xxvii. 9, 11). The same is found in some of the *Psalms* belonging to the Greek Period.

We must consider next the writings belonging to the *Apocrypha,* as well as some other writings which offer some points of interest. As it is not always possible to decide with certainty the home of these, though for the most part they are not Palestinian, we shall not, in each case, be able to indicate whether they belong to Palestine or the Dispersion; not that this much matters, for national unity comes more and more to be recognized, whatever the locality in which Jewish communities were settled. Indeed, it must be pointed out that among the Jews of the Dispersion, living as they were in Gentile surroundings, with every inducement to conform to alien types of worship, monotheistic belief must have been very firmly established, since its champions often not only withstood the assaults made upon it, but courageously sought to gain non-Jews to accept belief in One God. This must mean that in the Dispersion monotheistic belief had long been held by generations of loyal Jews. Nevertheless that there were renegade Jews in the various centres of the Dispersion, as there were in Palestine itself, the evidence will show.

In illustration of what has been said, we shall now give some quotations from writings belonging to the Greek Period; some of these are Jewish, others Gentile; some are Palestinian, others were written in centres of the Dispersion, some by Jewish, others by Gentile authors. As to their dates, there are often differences of opinion among experts; but a chronological order of the quotations is not of great moment, as the writings from which they are taken all come within the period, approximately, between B.C. 300 and the eve of Christianity.

If we begin by quoting from a book belonging to the later part of our period, *i Maccabees* (its date is generally acknowledged to be soon after 100 B.C., but it records the history of the preceding century), it is because of the need of emphasizing the truth that the champions of a monotheistic faith were, until after the Maccabæan wars, incessantly opposed by those of their own race. It is not always realized with what an age-long struggle the loyal Jews were faced in upholding their monotheistic faith. When in the final stages of this struggle, as late as about the middle of the second century B.C., Antiochus Epiphanes made his mad attempt to stamp out Judaism, it is perfectly clear that he was supported by a strong party among the Jews themselves; and such a party had obviously existed previously. Thus, in *i Macc.* i. 11–15 we read: " In those days came there forth out of Israel transgressors of the law, and persuaded many, saying, Let us go and make a covenant with the Gentiles that are round about us; for since we were parted from them many evils have befallen us. And the saying was good in their eyes. And certain of the people were forward herein . . ."; the passage is quoted in full above (p. 23). In verse 43 it is said, further: " And many of Israel consented to his (i.e. Antiochus Epiphanes) worship, and sacrificed to the idols, and profaned the sabbath." How widespread the evil was is shown by the action of Judas Maccabæus, who " went about among the cities of Judah, and destroyed the ungodly out of the land " (iii. 8, see also

verse 15 and *ii Macc*. iv. 13). On the other hand, it need
hardly be said, a true monotheistic faith was proclaimed again
and again. To revert now to somewhat earlier times; the
book of *Tobit*, approximately 200 B.C. or possibly a little
earlier, is in the nature of a novel, written, however, with
specific religious purposes. The scene is laid in Nineveh,
whither, soon after the fall of Samaria, in 721 B.C., Tobit,
with many others of his race, is purported to have been
carried captive. Reflecting, no doubt, the conditions of his
own time, the writer makes Tobit tell of how many of his
own race fell away into idolatrous practices, though he himself
remained faithful in his worship of the God of Israel; and he
looks forward to the time when " all nations shall turn to
fear the Lord God truly, and shall bury their idols ". The
writer of this book was one of those who, living in the midst
of Gentile surroundings, probably in Egypt, was loyal to the
God of his fathers. His book witnesses to a true monotheistic
belief; but he deplores the falling away of many of his race.
The prevalence of idolatry during this period must have been
widespread among renegade Jews, otherwise it would be
impossible to account for the existence of Jewish writings,
written for Jews, which contain vehement denunciations
against the worship of idols. This is seen, for example, in
the two curious little stories contained in the writings called
Bel and *The Dragon*, where idolatry is ridiculed in the most
drastic fashion, and the chicanery of the priests who served
in idol-sanctuaries is mercilessly exposed. The stories illustrate the effort made by a Jew, strong in his monotheistic
faith, to warn his people against idolatry. In this connexion
mention must be made of the remarkable polemic against
idols contained in the book of *Wisdom* xiii–xv; this, written in
Egypt, is directed against Jews of the Dispersion, who, living
in the midst of Gentile surroundings, were, again, exposed to
the dangers of idolatry which they saw practised around them;
and this book was written, probably, as late as the beginning
of the Christian era, though some authorities date it a little
earlier.

A few illustrations must now be given from some of the
books of the Apocrypha in which Monotheism is proclaimed
in definite form. Thus in *Ecclus*. xxxvi. 1–5 (the Hebrew

text), Ben-Sira prays: "Save us, O God of all, and cast thy fear upon all the nations. Shake thine hand against the strange people, that they may see thy power. As thou hast sanctified thyself in us before their eyes, so sanctify thyself in them before our eyes; that they may know, even as we know, that there is none other God but thee." Similarly in xlii. 21: "The mighty works of his wisdom hath he ordered; One is he from everlasting." And again, in the *Song of the Three Holy Children*, Azarias prays that the enemies of his people may know "that thou art the Lord, the only God, and glorious over the whole world". And, once more, in *Wisd.* xii. 13 it is said: "For neither is there any God but thee, who carest for all." Many other illustrations could be given showing the firmly established monotheistic belief among the better type of Jew. So that we learn from this body of literature that, though opposition was encountered from men of their own race, Monotheism was too strongly implanted in the hearts of orthodox Jews to suffer harm.

We must examine next what is said on this subject in the Apocalyptic Literature, belonging approximately to 200 B.C.–A.D. 100; [1] but even in the latest of these writings a great deal of much earlier material is embodied. This literature is of particular interest because it represents a type of Judaism which in some important respects differs from orthodox teaching; but it is, as will be seen, a standing witness to monotheistic belief during the last two pre-Christian centuries.

It would be wearisome to give too many quotations from these writings, but a few representative ones are called for in order to set forth from every side the Jewish attitude towards Monotheism during the Greek Period.

In all the component parts of *i Enoch* the Unity of God is obviously taken for granted; in what is the earliest of these, the "Dream-Visions" 165–161 B.C., we have the following beautiful confession of faith:

"Blessed be thou, O Lord, King,
  Great and mighty in thy greatness,
  Lord of the whole creation of the heaven,
  King of kings, and God of the whole world.

[1] Apocalyptic-eschatological material occurs also in writings not belonging to the Apocalyptical Literature proper.

And thy power and kingship and greatness abide for ever
   and ever,   ♦
And throughout all generations thy dominion;
And all the heavens are thy throne for ever,
And the whole earth thy footstool for evermore."

Without actually defining monotheistic belief, these words
constitute a convincing witness to it. Again, in an apocalyptic
portion of the *Sibylline Oracles*, belonging to the middle of the
second century B.C., we have a passage which, in its condemnation of idols, implies monotheistic belief; in extolling
the righteous, the writer says: " For to them alone hath the
Mighty God given wise counsel, and faith, and excellent
wisdom in their hearts; in that they give not themselves to
vain deceits, nor honour the work of men's hands that fashion
images of gold and brass, of silver and ivory, wood and stone,
idols of clay smeared with vermilion, pictured likenesses of
beasts, such things as men with minds void of understanding
honour; but instead they lift up to heaven holy hands . . ."
(iii. 584–591). A passage of somewhat similar import occurs
in the book of *Jubilees* xii. 2–6, which is, however, too long to
quote. Its date is approximately the same as the preceding.
We refrain from giving further quotations from the apocalyptic
writings because monotheistic belief is assumed in all of them.

Finally, we must draw attention to some other writings of a
miscellaneous character belonging to this period; their special
interest lies in the evidence they afford both of the existence
of monotheistic belief among the Jews of the Dispersion, and
also of the efforts made to propagate this belief among non-
Jews. Fragments of a writing under the assumed name of
Hecatæus of Abdera, belonging to the end of the third century
B.C., are preserved by Josephus in his *Contra Apionem*. The
writer was a Jew, living in Egypt. While not directly men-
tioning the monotheistic belief of the Jews, he imples its existence among them; he says that when, because of their belief,
" they have torments inflicted upon them, and are brought to
the most terrible kinds of death, they meet them after an
extraordinary manner, beyond all other people, and will not
renounce the religion of their forefathers " (*Contra Ap.* 191).
He says, further: " When those who came to them in their

country built themselves temples and altars, the Jews demolished them all " (*ibid.* 193). Again, Josephus refers to the rhetorician, Apollonius Molon (first century B.C.), saying that he wrote against Jews accusing them of the crime of associating with those who held opinions about God differing from theirs (*ibid.* ii. 258); the reference must certainly be to their monotheistic belief. Further, in the *Letter of Aristeas* (second century B.C.), the writer, speaking of Moses, says: " In the very first place of all he taught that God is One, and that his power is made manifest through all things, every place being filled with his sovereignty, and that none of the things done in secret by men on earth are hidden from him, but all that a man does and all things that are yet to be are manifest in his sight " (132). He then goes on to show the uniqueness of Jewish monotheistic faith in saying that " all other men except our nation consider that there are many gods, although they are themselves far more powerful than those whom they vainly reverence " (134), i.e. the worshippers are more powerful than the things worshipped. These must suffice, though various other illustrations could be given.

III

DIVINE TRANSCENDENCE

Monotheistic belief necessarily and rightly engendered an increasingly exalted conception of God. Based, in the first instance, on much that the prophets had taught, the greatness and majesty and power of God became more and more realized. So that, prompted by feelings of reverential awe and adoration, there arose a conception of divine transcendence which brought momentous results in its train. These results cannot be chronologically set forth, for they became intermingled irrespective of periods; but what ultimately underlies them all is the feeling that God, the Everlasting Who dwells in the heavens above, is too great and sublime to be concerned *directly* with mere man and the things of the earth; His will must be accomplished by means of intermediary agencies. This may go back in origin to the references to " the angel of Yahweh " of early times, though in essence the later belief differed entirely from that. But it is more likely

H

that the more developed belief in the ministry of angels which arose in post-exilic times was laid under tribute in formulating the doctrine of intermediate beings between God and man. The subject of angelology will occupy us later (Chap. XXII). It is mentioned here because, if we may so express it, the putting afar of God from man demanded the belief in intermediate agencies to carry out the divine will on earth.

We must now examine in some detail another way whereby, as it was conceived, the Almighty fulfilled His purposes among men without detriment to His majesty by direct contact with humanity. This was by means of the hypostatization of divine attributes, i.e. the personification of abstract qualities of the divine nature; things which belonged indissolubly to the Person of God, but which could be thought of, in some sense, as distinct from Him.

What was probably the earliest of these to be formulated, though originally conceived of as purely abstract, was the *Spirit of God*. Thus, for example, when we read in Gen. i. 2 that " the spirit of God brooded on the waters ", the thought is that of a divine life-giving power; and the use of the expression elsewhere shows that it connoted the divine influence granted to men, especially to the prophets. But the tendency to personification arose comparatively early, for Deutero-Isaiah uses expressions which are suggestive of something more than abstractions, though we must not discern here anything more than a tendency. He says, for example, in *Isa.* xl. 13: " Who can direct the spirit of Yahweh, or being his counsellor can teach him? " This differentiation between Yahweh and His spirit appears again in xlviii. 16: ". . . and now Yahweh God hath sent me, and his spirit "; what these words mean is difficult to say, but, at any rate, they make a distinction between Yahweh and His spirit, see also lxiii. 10. But it is when we come to the Greek Period that we find a clear hypostatization of the spirit of God. A few illustrations must be given. It is clearly in reference to the divine spirit when in the *Testaments of the XII Patriarchs, Judah* xx. 5 (third century B.C.), it is said: "And the spirit of truth testifieth all things, and accuseth all "; that suggests independent action on the part of the spirit; but words like this must, it is granted, be balanced by such passages as: " And the spirit of understanding and sanctification shall rest upon him " (*Levi* xviii. 7) ; and, " the spirit of holiness shall be on them " (*Levi* xviii. 11), where there is no question of personification. In taking passages like these together, one realizes a kind of mental struggle as to how far personality is to be imputed to the spirit of God. On the other hand, in the book of the *Wisdom of Solomon* personification is pronounced; thus in i. 5 it is said : " For the holy spirit of discipline fleeth from deceit, and starteth away from foolish thoughts, and is abashed at the approach of unrighteousness " ; and in verse 7 : " For the spirit of the Lord filleth the inhabited earth." In these passages, as in ix. 17, the spirit seems to be identified with Wisdom, in which case personification would be the more pronounced (see below) ; in xii. 1, however, there is no connexion with Wisdom in the context : " For thine incorruptible spirit is in all things." Once more, in *The Ascension of Isaiah* v. 14, where the legend of Isaiah's martyrdom is recorded, we read : " And when Isaiah was being sawn asunder (cp. *Hebr.* xi. 37), he neither cried aloud nor wept, but his lips spake with the holy spirit until he was sawn in twain."

Of great interest is, next, the hypostatization of the *word of God*. Here again the beginnings of this profoundly important speculation must be sought in the Old Testament. The step from the thought of the divine utterance as fulfilling the divine will to that of conceiving of the utterance, or word, as something individualistic, is not so difficult to envisage when one realizes that it is because of the word that something happens. At any rate, direct power was imputed to the word of God, and from this, personification of the word ensued. Thus, in *Isa.* lv. 11 we have the striking passage : " So shall my word be that goeth forth out of my mouth; it shall not return unto me void, but it shall accomplish that which I please, and it shall prosper in the thing whereunto I sent it." Again, in *Ps.* cvii. 19, 20 it is said : " They cried unto Yahweh in their trouble, and he saved them out of their distresses he sent his word to heal them, and to deliver them . . ." ; similarly in *Ps.* cxlvii. 15 : " He sendeth out his commandment on earth, his word runneth very swiftly." Passages like these present the word of God as His messenger to accomplish His will. In the later non-canonical books passages of similar import occur; e.g. in the Hebrew of *Ecclus.* xlii. 15, "By the word of God are his works"; this recalls *Ps.* xxxiii. 6; the same thought is found in the *Wisdom of Solomon* ix. 1 : "O God of our fathers, and Lord of mercy, who madest all things by thy word" (cp. xvi. 12). So, too, in *ii (iv) Esdras*, which, though belonging to the first century A.D., contains much earlier material; e.g. in vi. 38: "O Lord, of a truth thou spakest at the beginning of the creation, upon the first day, and saidst thus, Let heaven and earth be made; and thy word perfected the work." These are but a few illustrations of many that could be given.

Although not of the same importance as foreshadowing Christian truth, some reference must be made to the personification of *Wisdom*, for this is presented as the most definite of all the hypostases. Moreover, we find that Wisdom is sometimes identified with the Word; in the *Wisdom of Solomon*, ix. 1, 2, quoted in part above, it is said: "Who madest all things by thy Word and by thy Wisdom thou didst form man . . ." Again, just as Wisdom sits on the throne of God, "Give me Wisdom, her that sitteth by thee on thy throne" (ix. 4), so, too, the same is said of the Word: "Thine all-powerful Word leaped from heaven out of the royal throne" (xviii. 15). Familiar as the chapter is, a few verses from *Prov.* viii, the classical passage, must be quoted. While, on the one hand, it definitely personifies Wisdom, thus emphasizing the divine transcendence, the outcome of monotheistic belief, that belief is carefully guarded, and Wisdom is throughout presented as subordinate; she herself is created, she is God's "child", His instrument; the actual Creator is God alone. Wisdom is made to say: "Yahweh created (lit. formed) me at the beginning of his ways (so the Septuagint), as the first of his works, of old. I was set up from everlasting, from the beginning, or ever the earth was . . ." (*vv.* 22–30). Teaching quite similar to this is given by Ben-Sira, in *Ecclus.* xxiv. 3–9: "I came forth", Wisdom is made to say, "from the mouth of the Most High, and as a mist I covered the earth. In the high places did I fix my abode, and my throne was in the pillar of cloud. Alone I compassed the circuit of heaven, and in the depth of the abyss I walked. . . . He created me from the beginning, before the world; and I shall never fail."

Here we have again the distinct personification of Wisdom, while monotheistic belief is preserved by emphasizing that Wisdom was created by God. Even in the *Wisdom of Solomon*, with its mixture of Greek with Hebrew ideas, and where Wisdom is sometimes presented as of almost divine nature, the Unity of God is nevertheless safeguarded. In vii. 25, 26, e.g. Wisdom is thus described: " For she is an exhalation of the power of God, and a clear effluence of the glory of the Almighty . . . she is a reflection of everlasting light, and an unspotted mirror of the working of God, and the image of his goodness." Further, Wisdom is omnipresent (vii. 23, viii. 1), omnipotent (vii. 27), omniscient (ix. 11), and sits on the throne of God (ix. 4); but with all these divine attributes she is yet represented as subordinate to the Almighty (e.g. ix. 10).

One other matter demands brief mention as offering one more illustration of what the conception of divine transcendence entailed. This was the impulse to avoid the direct mention of the Name of God, and to express this by means of circumlocution. The inexpressible majesty of the One and Only God, unimaginably greater than man, forbade the utterance of His name, which, it must be remembered, was identified with the person of the bearer, and the same applies in the present connexion. In place, therefore, of pronouncing the name of God, expressions of deep reverence were used. We do not propose to give quotations from the large number of uncanonical, and other, books belonging to the Greek Period in which these expressions occur; it will suffice if we enumerate a few of them by way of illustration. Among them are these: *The Most High, The Holy Great One, The Great Glory, Heaven, The Eternal King, The Righteous One, The Lord of spirits, The Head of Days, The Immortal One,*—and others. And this brings us, of course, to the subject of the utterance of the name of Yahweh. This touches very closely on Monotheism; for a proper name, such as this, implies, whatever its origin may have been, that, just as other nations had their supreme gods, with their names, so Israel had their special God with His name; in other words, to speak of God as Yahweh was, in effect, a denial of Monotheism, for national gods were distinguished from each other by their names. Hence the gradual elimination of the name of Yahweh in utterance, while reverencing it as that which denoted the One and only God, the Creator, Who alone exists. In writing it was a little different, for it could be denoted by an abbreviation; but even this came to be avoided; and Adonai, " Lord ", was used instead, the vowels of which were attached to the consonants of the Hebrew form of Yahweh. In many of the later psalms, and in *Ecclesiastes*, the name of Yahweh never occurs,[1] and only two or three times in post-biblical books. Ultimately, the holy name was never uttered except in the Temple-worship when the priestly benediction (*Num*. vi. 24–26) was given (cp. *Ecclus*. l. 20).[2] In later days, in the Rabbinical literature there is the expression *Shem-ha-Mephōrash*, in reference to the *Tetragrammaton* (the four letters of the Hebrew form of Yahweh); it means the name that is *separate* and different from all other names.

We have sought to set forth Jewish monotheistic belief, and the struggle whereby this was attained. We have also drawn attention to the conception of divine transcendence which monotheistic belief engendered, together with the personification of divine attributes. All this must be regarded as tending towards the fuller revelation of truth as seen in the teaching of Jesus Christ; a sanctified groping after reality which could not be apprehended by man without further exhibition of divine love; and this was forthcoming.

IV

JEWISH TEACHING AND CHRISTIAN BELIEF

We must now briefly consider the bearing of what has been said on Christian teaching and belief. Inadequate as Judaism was in almost every particular, it can claim to have been, under divine guidance, a true preparation for Christianity: " Salvation is from the Jews " (*Jn*. iv. 22). That our Lord accepted Jewish monotheistic belief, so far as it went, is seen by His reference to the *Shema'*,[3] (" Hear "), which, if it can

---

[1] In the book of *Job*, apart from the prologue and epilogue, it occurs only four times.
[2] There are various theories as to the meaning of the divine Name; but the root from which it comes is quite uncertain.
[3] I.e., *Deut*. vi. 4–9; xi. 13–21; *Num*. xv. 37–41.

be so described, constituted the creed of Judaism: "Jesus answered, The first (commandment) is this, Hear O Israel; the Lord our God, the Lord is One " (*Mk*. xii. 29 and *Matth*. xxii. 37, *Lk*. x. 27). But there are other sayings of our Lord which point to the inadequacy of Jewish monotheistic belief; e.g. in passages in which He implies His divinity; [1] and although it occurs in the later, fourth Gospel, it is impossible not to believe that such a saying as " I and the Father are One " (*Jn*. x. 30, see also xiv. 9. 10, xvi. 28) was uttered by Him. The Unity of God as taught by Judaism did not, and could not, envisage the fullness of truth; though we recognize that it was a preparatory foreshadowing of this. Such a foreshadowing is also to be discerned in the Jewish teaching concerning the Spirit of God; here the fullness of truth is indicated by our Lord in His words ". . . until ye be clothed with power from on high " (*Lk*. xxiv. 49), which must be read in connexion with *Acts* i. 8, "But ye shall receive power, when the Holy Ghost is come upon you." This is not the place to deal with the doctrine of the Holy Trinity; but we may be permitted to quote Dr. Fulton's comment on *ii Cor*. xiii. 14 (" The grace of the Lord Jesus Christ, and the love of God, and the communion of the Holy Ghost . . ."); he says: " If the passage contains no formulated expression of the Trinity, it is yet of great significance as showing that, less than thirty years after the death of Christ, His name, and the name of the Holy Spirit could be employed in conjunction with the name of God Himself. Truly, if the doctrine of the Trinity appeared somewhat late in theology, it must have lived very early in devotion." [2] That our Lord taught belief in God the Father, in Himself as One with the Father, and in the Divine Spirit as the power of God,—in other words, that He taught the truths which we describe as the doctrine of the Holy Trinity, must be recognized. And we may well believe that He saw in the Jewish teaching of His day tendencies which He accepted as adumbrating truths which He set forth in their fullness.

In Jewish teaching, further, we have seen the importance attached to the Word of God. Our Lord, it is true, never

---

[1] We deal with the doctrine of the Messiah in chaps. X, XI.
[2] *Encycl. of Religion and Ethics*, xii. 458 *b* (1921).

directly applies the *Word* to Himself; but the significance of
Jn. i. 1–4 cannot be ignored; the conception is the fully
developed truth of what had been adumbrated in earlier Jewish
teaching.   As Hoskyns [1] says: " The texture of the prologue
(i.e. of the Fourth Gospel) is taken from the Old Testament
Scriptures (e.g. Gen. i, Prov. viii); but it is altogether
Christian."

[1] *The Fourth Gospel,* Vol. I, p. 130 (1939).

CHAPTER VIII

UNIVERSALISM AND PARTICULARISM

THESE two opposed principles, which in turn were such prominent elements in the outlook of Judaism, were each, though in different ways, connected with monotheistic belief. If, on the one hand, Yahweh was the One and only true God, He, and He only, should be worshipped by all men, to the exclusion of so-called gods. Here we have the universalistic outlook. On the other hand, Yahweh was the God of Israel, attached throughout the nation's history to the land of promise, which contained the Temple, the special place of His abode; therefore, Yahweh was the God of Israel, and of them only; Gentiles were outside the pale of His care and mercy. Each of these two conceptions must now be considered.

I

THE UNIVERSALISTIC OUTLOOK

How far back we may go in seeking for the beginnings of the universalistic outlook is a disputed question. Certain passages in pre-exilic books which sound the note of Universalism are held by some authorities to be later additions; they may be right. At any rate, for our present purposes, we need go no farther back than exilic times; for there we have, long before the Greek period, some of the noblest passages imaginable, expressing the universalistic outlook, together with the reason that prompts it. Here we look again to Deutero-Isaiah. Thus, in *Isa.* xlv. 22–24, the prophet, putting the words into the mouth of Yahweh, says: " Turn ye unto me and be saved, all the ends of the earth; for I am God, and there is none else. By myself have I sworn, gone out from my mouth is righteousness, my word shall not go back, that unto me every knee shall bow, every tongue shall swear. ' Only in Yahweh ' shall it be

said, ' is righteousness (or " victory ") and strength,' . . ."
Again, after an exhortation to His own people, Yahweh is made
to say: " Instruction shall go forth from me, and my justice
shall be for a light of the peoples.   My righteousness is near,
gone forth is my salvation, and mine arms shall judge the
peoples; the isles shall wait for me, and on mine arm shall they
trust " (li. 4, 5).   And, once more, for the glory of the people
of Yahweh it is said: " Behold, I have given him (i.e. David
and his house) for a witness to the people, a prince and commander of the peoples.   Behold, a nation that thou knowest not
shalt thou call, and a nation that knew not thee shall run unto
thee, because of Yahweh thy God, and because of the Holy One
of Israel; for he hath glorified thee " (lv. 4, 5).   Echoes of
this universalistic note resound again in slightly later times.
Opinions differ to some extent about the date of the chapters
Isa. lvi–lxvi (" Trito-Isaiah "), and they certainly do not all
belong to the same date; [1] but we may with some confidence
assign the following passage to about a century after the time of
Deutero-Isaiah: " And the strangers that join themselves to
Yahweh, to serve Him and to love the name of Yahweh, to be
his servants, every one that keepeth the Sabbath not to profane
it, and holdeth fast by my covenant; I will bring them to my
holy mountain, and make them joyful in my house of prayer;
their burnt-offerings and their sacrifices shall be accepted upon
mine altar; for mine house shall be called a house of prayer
for all peoples " (lvi. 6, 7).   Further, striking evidence of the
universalistic outlook is afforded by the books of *Ruth* and
Jonah; both were written before the beginning of the Greek
Period, but not long before.   In the former the indication of
this wider outlook, being merely incidental (e.g. iv. 10, 11), does
not detract from the tendency, rather the contrary, since it is
taken for granted.   In the book of *Jonah*, however, we have a
story composed specifically for the purpose of inculcating the
universalistic outlook, illustrating, as it does, the divine mercy
accorded to a non-Jewish people.

But if this universalistic outlook was thus clearly propagated
in the earlier part of the post-exilic period, still more was it
likely to have been in evidence during the Greek Period, when,

---

[1] For a discussion on the subject see Oesterley and Robinson, *An Introduction to the Books of the Old Testament*, pp. 282 ff. (1934).

as we have seen, the intermingling of the peoples took place as
a result of the conquests of Alexander the Great.   This naturally
fostered sympathetic intercourse between Jews and Gentiles,
together with the hope, on the part of the former, that the One
and only God would become recognized as the God of all.
Here again, the evidence is of much interest, so that some
further quotations must be permitted.   The writings from
which these are taken are of various dates which cannot in
every case be determined with certainty; but they all belong
to the last two pre-Christian centuries.   Some were written in
Palestine, others in the Dispersion.   We shall begin with the
former, giving them as far as may be in their chronological
order.   Ben-Sira was a devout Jew, though not of the strictly
orthodox type.   With striking broadmindedness, he embraces
all humanity in putting the question and answer thus: " An
honourable race is what?   The race of men.   What manner
of seed is honourable?   They that fear the Lord.   What manner
of seed is without honour?   The seed of man, (viz.): A
contemptible seed is that which transgresseth the commandment " (*Ecclus.* x. 19); this verse is not extant in Hebrew, but
v. 22, from the Hebrew, runs: " Sojourner and stranger,
foreigner and poor man, their glory is the fear of God."   There
is no distinction in these verses between Jew and Gentile.   The
same spirit is manifested in a passage which has been inserted
in the *Testaments of the XII Patriarchs, Judah* xxiv. 5, 6; as
Charles rightly points out, " the main body of the *Testaments*
could not have been written by any other than a Jew of the
Pharisaic school "; so that when a passage like that to be
quoted occurs, it cannot be doubted that it is a later insertion;
its interest from our present point of view lies in the fact that it
illustrates the opposition of one of universalistic outlook to
what had now become the dominant attitude (the passage
belongs to the first century B.C.).   In reference to the Messiah
of the tribe of Judah it is said: " And the sceptre of my kingdom shall shine forth: and from your root shall arise a stem;
and from it shall grow up a rod of righteousness unto the
Gentiles, to judge and to save all that call upon the Lord "
(cp. also *Levi* ii. 11).   The significance of the passage lies in the
fact that elsewhere in this book the Messiah is always represented as arising from the tribe of Levi, i.e. the Messiah will be

primarily a priest, which represents the particularist standpoint. In some passages, it is true, Levi and Judah are mentioned jointly as those from whom the salvation of Israel will proceed; but even in these Levi is always given precedence.

In writings originating in the Dispersion the universalistic outlook is, naturally enough, more prominent. Thus, in *Tob.* xiii. 11 (Cod. א) it is said in reference to the New Jerusalem: " A bright light shall shine unto all the ends of the earth; many nations shall come from afar, and the inhabitants of the utmost ends of the earth unto thy holy name; with their gifts also in their hands unto the King of heaven, generations of generations shall utter rejoicing in thee, and thy name that is elect unto the generations of eternity." This striking anticipation of the salvation of the Gentiles is repeated in xiv. 6, 7, where the Messianic Age is again referred to: " And all the nations which are in the whole earth, all shall turn and fear God truly, and all shall leave their idols, who err after their false error. And they shall bless the everlasting God in righteousness." In what follows the Jews are also included, showing again that there is no distinction between them and the Gentiles. Similarly in *i Enoch* x. 21: " And all nations shall offer adoration, and shall praise me, and all shall worship me." In a later portion of the book (" The Similitudes ", middle of the first century B.C.) it is said, in reference to the Son of Man: " He shall be a staff to the righteous whereon to stay themselves and not fall, and he shall be the light of the Gentiles. All who dwell on earth shall fall down and worship before him and shall praise and bless and celebrate with song the Lord of Spirits " (xlviii. 4, 5).

These illustrations will suffice. They show that from the exilic period onwards there were enlightened teachers among the Jews, living both in Palestine and in the Dispersion, whose conception of God demanded a wide and sympathetic outlook on humanity, realizing that their brethren were not restricted to those of their own race. There was One God, and none other, and therefore all men were His children; there could be no limit put to His mercy and grace.

II

JEWISH PARTICULARISM

In contrast to this edifying picture of God and man, we turn to consider the particularistic attitude which characterized much of the outlook of Judaism during the same periods. Not that this attitude is to be condemned; far from that. It was inevitable, and was prompted by well-intentioned motives.

We may begin by observing how matters stood, so far as the Jews were concerned, during the Exile. First, we have the undoubted fact, proved, above all, by the subsequent history, that Babylonian Jewry represented all that was best in the traditional religion, viz. the worship of Yahweh to the exclusion of all other cults, and an ardent observance of His Law. The enforced cessation of sacrifices only increased activity in the study and elaboration of the Scriptures, copies of which were brought by the priestly circles from the homeland. But the exiles—and this is our second fact—were living in the midst of Gentiles of higher culture, whose religion, with its visible deities and imposing ritual, was calculated to captivate many of those among the exiles for whom the religion of their fathers offered nothing of corresponding grandeur. They must not be judged too harshly; the Babylonians were a great people; their gods, according to the popular belief, had overcome the most cruel of all the enemies of Israel, the Assyrians; very powerful gods, therefore, were they. But the people of Yahweh were in captivity; how had His power been shown forth? That many among the exiles had very soon been faithless to their religion is evident from what the prophet Ezekiel says, when he was " among the captives by the river Chebar " (i. 1), about the "impudent and stiffhearted ", and "rebellious ", among his people (ii. 1–7, iii. 7).[1] Thus, the religious leaders in the land of exile were not only living amid idolatrous Gentile surroundings, but were also harassed by the presence of renegades among their own people. The natural and inevitable result was for the upholders of the worship of Yahweh to become " a close society, guarding themselves as far as might be from the influences around them, preserving their own

[1] Passages such as *Isa.* xliv. 9–20, xlvi. 5–8, xlviii. 4, 5, are held to be later insertions by various commentators.

religion, and resisting that practised by their neighbours. Particularism was the condition of survival for Yahwism in Babylonia, and it was here that Particularism began." [1]

Of the details, so far as they can be gathered, of the religious and social condition of the returned exiles, it need only be said that while enjoying full religious freedom, it is evident that there was a gradual deterioration of both the moral and religious standards. There appears, too, to have been much maltreatment of the poor on the part of the more wealthy; religious contention was also rife. On the other hand, from what is said in *Mal.* iii. 16, 17, it is to be gathered that there was a loyal section of those " that feared Yahweh ", and encouraged one another; it is said of them that " they shall be mine, saith Yahweh of hosts, in the day that I act, yea, mine own possession ". With the advent of Nehemiah and, later, Ezra, from the Jewish community in Babylonia more vigorous action was taken for the upholding of the ancestral religion. If they brought with them the particularistic attitude nurtured in Babylonian Jewry, [2] there can be no doubt that it was welcomed by the faithful adherents of Yahwism in Palestine. It may not be altogether fanciful to surmise that their polemic against intermarriage with aliens was first prompted by what had been seen to be its consequences among the exiles in Babylonia. We recall in this connexion Tobit's words to his son, bidding him take " a wife of the seed of thy fathers, and take not a strange wife, which is not of thy father's tribe " (*Tob.* iv. 12 ; see further below). The prohibition on the part of Nehemiah and Ezra was intended to have a twofold effect : purity of race and purity of religion, the latter largely conditioned by the former. Then followed Ezra's championship of the Law, which likewise originated in Babylonia, and represented a particularistic attitude. It is important to note that Particularism, wholly necessary as it was if the worship of Yahweh in its purity was to survive, had the further effect of creating a nationalistic spirit, which, in times to come, played an important *rôle* in Jewish history. But ultimately it was recognized that the interests and claims of nationalism were incompatible with the demands of true religion.

[1] Rowley, *Israel's Mission to the World*, p. 42 (1939).
[2] Differing herein from Deutero-Isaiah ; but the champions of either attitude respectively, appear throughout, from the exilic period onwards.

That the work of Ezra bore abundant fruit is sufficiently evident from the later history; unfortunately, however, we have but little information regarding its consolidation during the century (the fourth) immediately succeeding his time. It is seen, however, in the literature of the Greek Period that the particularistic attitude which he championed was a living force. A few illustrations may be offered. Nothing could more forcibly set forth the spirit of Jewish exclusiveness than the following passage from the *Testaments of the XII Patriarchs, Levi* xxii. 16: " Separate thyself from the nations and eat not with them; and do not according to their works, and become not their associate; for their works are unclean, and all their ways are a pollution and an abomination and uncleanness." The prohibition even to associate with Gentiles is evidence of a bitter spirit of exclusiveness. Again, special reasons, into which we cannot enter now, prompted the thought of the destruction of the Gentiles by the expected Messiah; in the *Psalms of Solomon* vii. 27–31 it is said: " He shall destroy the godless nations with the word of his mouth, and at his rebuke nations shall flee before him . . . and neither sojourner nor alien shall sojourn with them (i.e. the Jews) any more." The contempt in which the Gentiles were held is graphically expressed in the *Assumption of Moses* i. 12, where Moses is made to say to Joshua: " He hath created the world on behalf of His people." Similarly in *ii (iv) Esdras*, of late date, but echoing earlier thought, we read: " But as for the other nations, which are descended from Adam, thou hast said that they are nothing (cp. *Isa.* xl. 17), and that they are like spittle; and thou hast likened the abundance of them to a drop falling from a bucket (cp. *Isa.* xl. 15): . . . if the world hath indeed been created for our sakes why do we not enter into possession of our world ? " (vi. 56–59). The polemic against intermarriage, pointing to an exclusive nationalism, finds frequent expression; thus, in the *Test. XII Patr., Levi* ix. 10, it is commanded: " Take, therefore, to thyself a wife without blemish or pollution, while thou art yet young, and not of the race of strange nations "; and in much stronger language it is said in the book of *Jubilees* xxx. 7: " And if there is any man in Israel who wished to give his daughter or his sister to any man who is of the seed of the Gentiles, he shall surely die, and they shall stone him with stones; for he hath wrought shame in Israel; and thou shalt burn the woman with fire, because she hath dishonoured the name of the house of her father; and she shall be rooted out of Israel "; and again in verse 11 : " And do thou, Moses, command the children of Israel, and exhort them not to give their daughters to the Gentiles, and not to take for their sons any of the daughters of the Gentiles, for this is abominable before the Lord " (see also verses 13 ff.; xxii. 20). Further illustrations are unnecessary.

From what has been said, then, it will have been seen how strongly represented were these antagonistic attitudes adopted respectively by the champions of Universalism and Particularism. There is one other movement, characteristic of the Greek Period, which demands mention; for, from different points of view, it could be claimed as proper to each of these schools of thought, viz. Proselytism. By the teachers of Universalism, with their belief in Yahweh as the God of all men, it could be rightly insisted on that the Gentiles should be gathered into the fold of true believers; while the teachers of Particularism could likewise claim that, provided that Gentiles were prepared to accept the strict demands of Judaism, they would be received into the community of God's chosen people. Proselytism, therefore, comes within the purview of both Universalism and Particularism. Into the details of the activity shown in this respect by the champions of each of these schools of thought we shall not go, since they have already to some extent been illustrated.[1]

III

THE NEW TESTAMENT TEACHING

That the two attitudes of thought and their practical carrying-out had their part in the preparation for Christianity both in Palestine and in the Dispersion is undoubted. This may, however, be illustrated by a few references to the New Testament, and especially to the teaching of our Lord. Just as the words in *Jn.* iv. 22, " Salvation is from the Jews ", endorse the Particularistic attitude at its foundation, so those in *Mk.* xvi. 15,

[1] The subject is dealt with in great fullness by Schürer, *Geschichte des Jüdischen Volkes* . . ., iii, pp. 1–70 (1909).

" Go ye into all the world, and preach the Gospel to the whole Creation ", show Christ's acceptance of the Universalistic spirit. In spite of the opposition of the Pharisees, the exponents *par excellence* of Particularism, it is certain that our Lord accepted much for which they stood. Judaism *per se* contained nothing that was antagonistic to Christianity; it was its inadequateness, and the perversion of some of its original teaching by the Pharisees, together with their failure to recognize this that was one of the main causes of their opposition to our Lord. Another main cause, which will be dealt with more fully later, was our Lord's recognition of the truth of much that was taught by the Apocalyptists for whom the Pharisees had no love. As the upholders of a true monotheistic belief, so far as they were able to conceive of this, the Pharisees had His entire sympathy (see, e.g., *Mk.* xii. 29 and parallel passages). The same is true of their belief in the Resurrection, and of their reverence for the Scriptures; similarly in regard to the Law; but here their methods of its observance, and the exaggerated importance which they attached to the claim of reward for fulfilling its precepts, were not in accordance with what earlier teachers had inculcated. " Think not that I came to destroy the law and the prophets; I came not to destroy, but to fulfil . . ." (*Matth.* v. 17–20); but the Pharisaic standpoint and attitude precluded the possibility of that fulfilment.

Universalism was likewise a preparation for Christianity in ways which, so far as our Lord Himself was concerned, were of the deepest import; with this, however, we deal fully in Chaps. X, XI. But in another direction Universalism had played an indispensable part in the preparation for Christianity; for owing to it, Jewish communities had taken root in centres throughout the world of those days; these became centres for the teaching of Judaism among the Gentiles; in consequence of this there were numbers of cities in all lands in which the teaching of Christianity by the apostles found a fruitful soil, in so far as Judaism foreshadowed Christian truths.

Thus, both Particularism and Universalism had their part in the preparation for Christianity.

I

CHAPTER IX

THE KINGDOM OF HEAVEN

WE shall be dealing here with important subjects which, in some respects, are indissolubly connected with others which will come before us in later chapters. We shall, however, attempt to deal with them separately, so far as this is possible, because from another point of view they are, individually, self-contained. Thus, when we study the subject of the origin and development of the conception of the Kingdom of Heaven, points are reached at which the background of Messianic belief, and, later, that belief itself, become inseparably connected with the Kingdom; yet the seed-plant from which Messianic belief grew is, initially, an independent growth; and the study of the Person of the Messiah is again one which demands individual treatment. Then, once more, the whole of the great eschatological drama, including the Signs of the End, the Judgement, the Resurrection, and the After-life, are all inextricably bound up in one way or another with the coming of the Kingdom of Heaven, as finally conceived of. Nevertheless, these, too, as individual occurrences, require to be dealt with separately. In this chapter, however, we shall confine ourselves to conceptions concerning the Kingdom of Heaven, and the signs which herald its advent, and we shall attempt to trace out briefly the original ideas from which, with the progressive divine self-revelation to man in accordance with his capacity for apprehension, the fullness of truth was ultimately attained.

The other subjects belonging to the eschatological drama, namely the Judgement, the Resurrection, and the After-life, are dealt with in Chap. XIII.

I

THE TIME OF PRIMEVAL HAPPINESS, AND ITS LOOKED-FOR RETURN

The belief that a time of happiness existed in the primeval age, and that this time of happiness will once more be the lot of man on earth, was widespread in the ancient world. Myths of a Golden Age in the far-distant past, when gods and men lived together in blissful peace and contentment, formed the background of all ancient religions; and the return, sooner or later, of this Golden Age was confidently looked for. This is not the place to discuss theories as to what may have prompted the myth of the Golden Age; [1] the fact that it was widespread in the ancient world is common knowledge. Many illustrations could be given; it will suffice if we make a brief reference to the belief among the three peoples who exercised a profound influence upon the Hebrews in various directions. The Babylonians taught that after the beginning of all things there existed the age of perfection, corresponding to the Golden Age. "Just as pure knowledge, revealed by the Godhead, lies at the beginning, so that it is the task of science to discover the original truth by observation of the book of revelation written down in the stars, and to obtain freedom from the errors which have crept in through human guilt, so also the Age of pure happiness lies at the beginning"; this, as Jeremias says, was an axiom among the Babylonian thinkers.[2] But through human guilt, sin and unhappiness came into the world, and times of distress and violence supervened; but ultimately these evil times will be brought to an end by the destruction of the world. Then the happy time as at the beginning will come again. This, put very briefly, was the Babylonian belief (see also pp. 141 f.).

Similarly, the Egyptians held that there was a happy time long, long ago, when the gods ruled on earth; it was never thought of without its return being yearned for. When it was desired to express something which was delightful beyond imagination, they would say: "The like was never seen since the days of King Ra", in reference to the happy time

[1] See the present writer's *The Evolution of the Messianic Idea*, pp. 35 ff. (1908).
[2] In Hastings' *Encycl. of Religion and Ethics*, i. 187 *a* (1908).

at the beginning [1] (see, further, p. 141). Once more, in the Persian Scriptures similar beliefs find expression; thus, in the Yima legend it is told how Yima the good shepherd, and most glorious and radiant of mortals, ruled in the age of bliss long ago. In that time death existed not; there was neither hunger nor thirst, nor cold nor heat, and there was no such thing as old-age. This happy time will return, it is said, when a saviour, Shaoshyant, the renewer of humanity and of the world, will come; then will be the age of the victory of Ormazd (Ahura-Mazda), the supreme god, over the powers of evil, and happiness and material prosperity will again be the lot of men (*Yasht* ix. 8 ff., xv. 15, *Yasna* ix. 4, 5, *Vend.* ii). Further, in *Yasna* xliii. 10, 16, Zoroaster himself is brought into the closest connexion with Ahura-Mazda; and in li. 1 Zoroaster, in addressing this deity, claims to be preparing " for us " the coming " good kingdom, which will bring a happy destiny to mankind " (cp. also xxx. 6, xliv. 2, 16).[2]

We come now to consider the early Hebrew ideas concerning the primeval time of happiness, and its return.

The Hebrew conception and form of the Golden Age myth are preserved in the Paradise story (*Gen.* i. 26–ii. 25). Much to the point here are Dillmann's words : " When one examines the thought-connexion of the story (and its sequel) it is seen that the starting-point lies in the enigmatical fact that man, although standing in relationship to God, and capable of striving for that which is highest, and ever making progress in conquering and impressing his power upon all things outside of himself, is, in spite of all this, subject to unnumbered sufferings, evils, and hardships, and, more especially, that although filled with an ineradicable yearning for permanent happiness, he never reaches this goal, but, on the contrary, succumbs, like all other earthly beings, to death and corruption. The contradiction which is seen to exist here has from of old led men to the conviction that all things cannot originally have been so. It was, moreover, easy to see that these evils had tended to increase rather than to decrease with the march of history, and that men were happier in the earlier,

[1] Maspero, *Geschichte der morgenländischen Völker im Alterthum*, übersetzt von R. Pietschmann, pp. 36 ff. (1877).

[2] See, further, Gressmann, *Die Orientalischen Religionen* . . ., p. 131 (1930) ; Otto, *Reich Gottes und Menschensohn*, pp. 141 ff. (1934).

simpler conditions of life. Hence it has come about that among all races a belief in a happier time long ago has been formulated, differing in form according to the genius of each race."[1] This belief in a happy time long ago was thus shared by the Israelites; but no less firm was their belief in its return, which became known as " the Day of Yahweh ". The prophetical conception of the " Day ", with the prophets' teaching on the ethical righteousness of Yahweh, entirely revolutionized the traditional outlook. The popular expectations, which reflect the current and original beliefs, were very different. When in *Amos* v. 18 the prophet says: " Woe unto them that desire the Day of Yahweh ", used as a kind of technical term, all those being addressed by him know precisely what he is referring to (cp. viii. 9, 13); it is, therefore, clear that the term must have been long in use. How the prophet conceived of that " Day " is graphically set forth in chaps. v, viii, ix. 1–4 [2] in his book; and when, rebuking the people for desiring the advent of that " Day ", he says that " it is darkness and not light " (v. 18), he is obviously correcting what he knows to be the people's idea of it; and the purpose of his teaching on the subject was to show that it was the very reverse of what they expected. What the popular ideas were is abundantly described in many passages; they should all be consulted, but to quote them in full would demand a good deal of space (see, e.g., *Amos* ix. 13, 14, *Isa.* xi. 6, 7, xxx. 23, 24, xxxv. 1, 2, 7, 9, lxv. 25, *Hos.* i. 10, ii. 18, 19, and a number of others). Their general content may be briefly summarized as follows: it will be a time of happiness, contentment, and peace; there will be no ills or sorrows among men; righteousness will flourish; and there will be no more iniquity. That this time of happiness represented what was believed to have been the Golden Age of primeval days, the return of which was looked for, is instructively illustrated by the use of the technical term *Shûb Shebûth*: this Hebrew phrase cannot be literally translated, but it may be freely paraphrased: " Bring back the restoration ", i.e. the restoration of the primeval age of happiness (see, e.g., *Amos*

---

[1] *Die Genesis*, p. 43 (1886).
[2] Chap. ix. 5–15 is generally recognized as being a later addition to the passage.

ix. 14, *Jer.* xxxii. 44, xxxiii. 11, 14–16, 26, *Ezek.* xvi. 53, xxxix. 25, *Ps.* lxxxv. 2).[1] The phrase, as Dietrich shows, is of foreign origin; and, as originally used, was not thought of as being preceded by any cosmical catastrophe. When the prophet speaks of the " Day of Yahweh " as being one of " darkness and not light ", it illustrates the developed, prophetical, conception of the ethical righteousness of Yahweh. Again and again in his book Amos declares that it was because of the sins of the people that the " Day " would be one of terror. The question arises as to whether the " Day of Yahweh " is to be understood in the later eschatological sense, i.e. the end of the present world-order and the setting up of the Kingdom of Yahweh; this must be answered in the negative. The passage in which the prophet speaks of the " Day ", when punishment will overtake the people, culminates in the pronouncement, " therefore will I cause you to go into captivity beyond Damascus " (v. 27); the same applies to all the pre-exilic prophets as well as to much that some of the later prophets taught, e.g. Joel (fourth century). The popular conceptions were, of course, far from envisaging anything of the kind.

II

THE KINGDOM OF YAHWEH

Although this is in continuation of what has just been said, we must devote a special section to it. It hardly needs pointing out that the phrases, the " Kingdom of God ", or the " Kingdom of Heaven ", never occur in the Old Testament. If here again we have to mention some things which are matters of common knowledge, this must be pardoned; it cannot well be avoided in seeking to cover the whole ground.

We must begin by observing that the earliest conception of the Kingdom of Yahweh was that which pictured Him as ruling over Israel. Thus, in *i Sam.* viii. 7 we read: " And Yahweh said unto Samuel, Hearken unto the voice of the people in all that they say unto thee; for they have not

---

[1] The phrase is studied and illustrated with convincing detail by Dietrich, שׁוּב שְׁבוּת, *Die endzeitliche Wiederherstellung bei den Propheten* (1925).

rejected thee, but they have rejected me, that I should not be king over them." Again, in *i Sam.* xii. 12: "And when ye saw that Nahash, the king of the children of Ammon came against you, ye said unto me, Nay, but a king shall reign over us; when Yahweh your God was your king." Many other passages to the same effect could, of course, be quoted. At a time when the nation's God was thought of as the nation's king (cp. *i Kgs.* xi. 7) this was natural enough. But the conception of Yahweh as Israel's king appears also in *Isa.* vi. 5: "Then said I, Woe is me! for I am undone; because I am a man of unclean lips, and I dwell in the midst of a people of unclean lips; for mine eyes have seen the King, Yahweh of Hosts." Once only elsewhere in the pre-exilic prophetic books is this found, viz. in *Hos.* x. 3: "Surely now shall they say, We have no king; for we fear not Yahweh: and the king, what can he do for us?"[1] There can thus be no doubt that, however envisaged, Yahweh's Kingdom, in the first instance, was thought of as embracing the land of Israel only. It may be that even before the Exile the beginnings of a more exalted conception of Yahweh's kingship and the scope of His rule were held in some rare instances; but there is no proof of this.

When, however, we come to post-exilic times there is no more instructive passage proclaiming this truth than *Ps.* cxlv. 13: "His kingdom is an everlasting kingdom, and his rule unto every generation." The parallelism between "kingdom" and "rule" illustrates the truth that Yahweh's kingship is not conceived of as exercised over a restricted area, but that it is an illimitable dominion, which recognizes neither national nor geographical boundaries; and further, that it is independent of time, from everlasting to everlasting. For the former conception we have also *Ps.* ciii. 19: "His kingdom ruleth over all", where there is no thought of the "kingdom" being used in reference to any one country, such as we naturally associate with the idea of a kingdom (cp. *Ps.* xxii. 29). It must be emphasized that neither of these psalms is eschatological in the sense of envisaging the end of the present world-order.

We have here, then, two conceptions regarding the Kingdom

[1] *Isa.* xxxiii. 22 is a post-exilic passage.

of Yahweh which are wholly incompatible. On the one hand, the Kingdom is described as comprising the land of Israel; on the other, as world-embracing. This incongruity can be accounted for only on the assumption that alien influences [1] were brought to play upon the traditional circumscribed ideas of Israel's teachers.

It is unnecessary to deal at length with the teaching that the scene of Yahweh's Kingdom is, in the Old Testament, invariably presented as existing on this earth.

When we think of Yahweh's Kingdom and of His kingship, whether national or universal, the question naturally arises as to how we are to explain the existence of what appears as a concurrent rulership, viz. that of Yahweh and that of an earthly king. And further, there is the appearance of an idealized ruler far transcending in character and rulership any Davidic king; how are we to explain the exercise of this twofold kingship by the ideal ruler and by Yahweh at one and the same time? These questions are purposely postponed because they must be dealt with in connexion with Messianic Belief (Chap. X).

III

THE SIGNS OF THE END

Incidental reference has been made to the idea of world-annihilation as a prelude to the return of the Golden Age, interpreted by the prophets as the Kingdom of Yahweh. In the Hebrew writings this cosmical cataclysm takes the form of what we designate as apocalyptic pictures. While the great prophets of Israel taught that Yahweh would intervene to put an end to the existing world-order, it is, with the exception of the exilic prophet Ezekiel, only in post-exilic prophetic writings that we get the details of the results of Yahweh's intervention, i.e. apocalyptic *traits*. The reason of this is that it was during the Exile, and after, that Jewish teachers came under the influence of Persian eschatology, with its strong apocalyptic elements (see, further, Chap. VI). It can hardly be doubted that the earlier prophets were influenced by Persian beliefs, which had been absorbed by the Babylonians,

[1] See, further, p. 142.

and adapted them to the religion of Yahweh. In spite of this, however (be the reason what it may), the fact is that they did not embody apocalyptic elements in the developed sense in their writings. We shall take the writings which come into consideration in their chronological order, so far as may be, while recognizing that in some cases there are differences of opinion as to date. It will not be necessary, however, to quote all the relevant passages in full. First we have, in the book of *Ezekiel*, a number of references to the final cosmical catastrophe which is to come about at the advent of the " Day " : darkness and cloud (xxxiv. 12), storm and tempest (xiii. 11), fire (xx. 47, 48, in Hebr. xxi. 3, 4), blood and sword (v. 15–17). There is also much in chaps. xxxviii, xxxix, which are, however, held by many scholars to be of post-exilic date. A striking passage occurs in *Zeph*. i. 14–18, part of which is well worth quoting : " The great day of Yahweh is near. . . . That day is a day of wrath, a day of trouble and distress, a day of wasteness and desolation, a day of darkness and gloominess. . . . And I will bring distress upon men, and they shall walk like blind men, because they have sinned against Yahweh; and their blood shall be poured out as dust, and their flesh as dung . . . the whole earth shall be devoured by the fire of his jealousy; for he shall make an end, yea a terrible end, of all that dwell on the earth." The ethical note which is struck here will not be missed. In *Nah*. i. 2–10 there is what appears to be part of an acrostic psalm which has been inserted after the opening verse; it is, unfortunately, very corrupt as regards its text; a few of the verses must, however, be quoted : " Yahweh hath his way in the whirlwind and in the storm, and the clouds are the dust of his feet. He rebuketh the sea, and it becometh dry, and he drieth up all the rivers. . . . The mountains quake at him, and the hills melt; and the earth is upheaved at his presence, yea, the world, and all that dwell therein . . . his fury is poured out like fire, and the rocks are broken asunder by him." It should be added that some commentators assign a Maccabæan date to this psalm; but opinions differ on this. Belonging to the middle of the fourth century B.C. we have the book of *Joel*, which contains a number of apocalyptic *traits*; a short quotation may be given : " And I will show wonders in the heavens, and in the earth, blood and fire, and pillars of smoke. The sun shall be turned into darkness, and the moon into blood, before the great and terrible Day of Yahweh come " (ii. 30, 31, see also i. 15–20, ii. 10, 11). The chapters xxiv–xxvii of the book of *Isaiah* are apocalyptic, contemporary historical events being placed in an eschatological setting. That the whole section belongs to about 200 B.C. is generally recognized.[1] As an illustration of the particular point under review we have in xxiv. 21–23 the following: " And it shall come to pass in that day that Yahweh will punish the host of the height in the height, and the kings of the earth on the earth. . . . And the moon shall be confounded, and the sun ashamed; for Yahweh of hosts shall be king in mount Zion, and in Jerusalem, and before his ancients there shall be glory " (following the Septuagint; lit. " it shall be glorified ").

We have now briefly considered, so far as the Old Testament is concerned, the belief in the Golden Age and its return; the Kingdom of Yahweh, conceived of as restricted to the land of Israel, but also as embracing the whole world; and, finally, the belief in a cosmical catastrophe preceding the advent of the Kingdom. We turn now to take a glance at the Apocalyptic Literature in order to see how these subjects are treated there.

IV

THE TEACHING OF THE APOCALYPTISTS

What especially strikes the investigator here is the bewildering intermingling of traditional beliefs with extraneous elements, the latter often predominating. Added to this are the manifold and often highly imaginative speculations of the Apocalyptists themselves.

The important fact has also to be borne in mind that the " otherworldliness " of the Apocalyptists makes their outlook very different from that of all who preceded them. While concerned with " this world " as well as with " the world to come ", their thoughts are far more centred on the latter than on their present surroundings. We can do no more than give

---

[1] An exception to this is Lindblom in his *Die Jesaja-Apokalypse* (1938).

a few illustrative quotations from some of the writings, for the material is very large. In doing so we shall sometimes have to ignore the context, because older ideas are placed in new settings, and for the present we are concerned only with pointing out the fact that the subjects spoken of above were utilized and often elaborated by the Apocalyptists.

From the nature of the apocalyptic writings it is not to be expected that we should find many references to the Golden Age. Here and there, however, a passage occurs which seems to re-echo this old-world belief. Thus, in *Sib. Orac.* III. 744 ff., which gives an account of the happy time to come, it is difficult not to perceive the underlying conception of the primeval time of happiness; the materialism of the whole passage only bears this out: " For earth, the universal mother, shall give to mortals her best fruit in countless store of corn, wine, and oil. Yea, from heaven shall come a sweet draught of luscious honey; the trees shall yield their proper fruits; and (there will be) rich flocks, and kine, and lambs of sheep, and kids of goats. He will cause sweet fountains of milk to burst forth. And the cities shall be full of good things, and the fields rich. Neither shall there be any sword throughout the land, nor battle din; nor shall the earth be convulsed any more with deep-drawn groans. No war shall there be any more, nor drought throughout the land; no famine, no hail to work havoc on the crops. But there shall be a great peace throughout all the earth; and king shall be friendly with king till the end of the age, and a common law for men throughout all the earth shall the Eternal perfect in the starry heaven in place of all those things which have been wrought by miserable mortals." Doubtless the writer envisages here the Messianic Age, but this is, as we have seen, to be the return of the primeval days of bliss.

Passing mention may be made here of the idea of the millennium which represents the return of the Golden Age. In *ii Enoch* (the *Secrets of Enoch*) xxxii. 2–xxxiii. 2 we read: " And I blessed the seventh day, which is the Sabbath, for in it I rested from all my labours. Then also I established the eighth day. Let the eighth be the first after my work, and let the days be after the fashion of the seven thousand (each day of the Creation is reckoned as equivalent to a thousand years, cp. *Ps.* xc. 4, *ii Pet.* iii. 8). Let there be at the beginning of the eighth thousand a time when there is no computation, and no end; neither years, nor months, nor weeks, nor days, nor hours." This is the earliest occurrence of the Jewish conception of the millennium. Charles explains its origin thus: " The account in *Genesis* of the first week of creation came in pre-Christian times to be regarded not only as a history of the past, but as a forecast of the future history of the world so created. Thus, as the world was created in six days, so its history was to be accomplished in 6000 years; for 1000 years are with God as one day . . . and as God rested on the seventh day, so at the close of the 6000 years there would be a rest of 1000 years, i.e. the millennium." [1]

We turn next to the various conceptions held with regard to the Kingdom. First, we may mention, though it does not belong to the Apocalyptic Literature, what Ben-Sira says on this subject. In the prayer contained in *Ecclus.* xxxvi. 1–7 supplication is made that God would " hasten the end, and ordain the appointed time "; and it continues: " Gather all the tribes of Jacob, that they may receive their inheritance, as in days of old. Have mercy upon the people that is called by thy name, Israel, whom thou didst name Firstborn. Have mercy upon thy holy city, Jerusalem, the place of thy dwelling. Fill Zion with thy majesty, and thy Temple with thy glory. . . . Hear the prayer of thy servants, according to thy favour towards thy people. That all the ends of the earth may know that thou art the Eternal God." Here we have the national conception of the Kingdom, the Almighty being thought of as dwelling in Jerusalem. But more usual, as we should expect, is the universalistic view. In *i Enoch* lxxxiv. 2, for example, it is said: " Blessed be thou, O Lord, King, great and mighty in thy greatness. Lord of the whole creation of the heaven, King of kings, and God of the whole world. And thy power and kingship and greatness abide for ever and ever, and throughout all generations thy dominion; and all the heavens are thy throne for ever, and the whole earth thy footstool for ever and ever." So, too, in *Dan.* ii. 44:

---

[1] *The Book of the Secrets of Enoch,* pp. xxix f. (1896). That the millennium conception was due to Persian influence is highly probable, see p. 88.

"The God of heaven shall set up a kingdom, which shall never be destroyed. . . ." These two incongruous conceptions, the national and the universalistic, occur, as we have seen, in the Old Testament, but there is a further element in regard to them appearing prominently in the Apocalyptic Literature which is most significant, namely, the transference of the Kingdom from earth to the spheres above, or else as including both Heaven and earth, as, for example, in *i Enoch* xlv. 4, 5: "And I will transform the heaven and make it an eternal blessing and light, and I will transform the earth, and make it a blessing; and I will cause mine elect ones to dwell upon it. . . ." Again in *Sib. Orac.* III. 767 ff.: "And then indeed will he raise up his Kingdom for all ages over men, he who once gave a holy law to godly men, to all of whom he promised to open out the earth and the world, and the portals of the blessed, and all joys, and everlasting wisdom and eternal gladness." In the *Assumption of Moses* x. 9, 19, it is said in reference to Israel: "And God shall exalt thee, and bring thee to the heaven of the stars, the place of his habitation. . . ."

Lastly, there are the signs preceding the advent of the Kingdom. A long account of these is given in *Sib. Orac.* III. 669–697, from which a few verses may be quoted: "From heaven shall fall fiery swords down to the earth . . . and earth, the universal mother, shall shake in those days at the hand of the Eternal . . . and the towering mountain peaks and the hills of the giants shall he rend, and the murky abyss shall be visible to all . . . the rocks shall flow with blood, and each torrent shall flood the plain. . . . And God shall judge all with war and sword, and with fire and with cataclysms of rain; and there shall be brimstone from heaven, yea, stones and hail incessant and grievous. . . . Wailing and lamenting through the length and breadth of the land shall come with the perishing of men; and all the shameless shall be washed with blood. . . ." Passages like this occur frequently; we refrain from giving further quotations, some of the references are: *i Enoch* xcix. 4–10, c. 1–6; *ii (iv) Esdras* iv. 52–v. 13, vi. 13–28, ix. 1–6, xiii. 16 ff.; *Syr. Apoc. of Bar.* xxv–xxvii, xlviii. 30–38, lxx; *Assumpt. of Moses* x. 3–7.

The subjects dealt with do not, of course, exhaust all those connected with the Eschatological Drama; but, as we have pointed out, others will necessarily come before us in other connexions, therefore in order to avoid repetition we do not mention them here. This applies especially to Chaps. X, XI, where Messianic belief in connexion with the Kingdom is considered.

V

THE TEACHING OF THE NEW TESTAMENT

What has been said forms the background of much that we read in the New Testament. To this latter we must now direct our attention.

The idea of the Golden Age, it need hardly be said, does not come into consideration here. The first point to note is that the incongruity regarding the national and universalistic conceptions of the Kingdom which occurs in the earlier Jewish teaching disappears. That earlier teaching contained the foreshadowing of truth, but the separation of two aspects of the truth made each, taken by itself, inadequate; combined, they present the whole truth: " Art thou the king of the Jews? " asks Pilate; and Christ answered, " Thou sayest " (*Lk.* xxiii. 3). That is one side of the truth. The other is contained in the words: " And this gospel of the kingdom shall be preached in the whole world for a testimony unto all nations " (*Matth.* xxiv. 14). Similarly, St. Paul teaches: " There is no distinction between Jew and Greek; for the same Lord is Lord of all, and is rich unto all that call upon him " (*Rom.* x. 12).

Further, in the earlier development of the conception concerning the Kingdom the most outstanding element was its ethical character, as taught by the prophets. So far as this went, it was divinely-guided truth; but it is only in weighing the manifold purport of our Lord's parables of the Kingdom that we see the full development of this truth. To enter into the details of this here is not called for; it may be hoped that they are sufficiently familiar. But one element must be emphasized. Whereas in the earlier teaching the ethical character of the Kingdom finds *general* expression, our Lord's words touch the *individual* at every turn. Here again it is unnecessary to go into details; the most cursory reading of the parables in question brings home the truth in vivid consciousness.

Notice was directed above to the other-worldliness of the Apocalyptic Teachers in general regarding the Kingdom. This, contrasted with the ordinary Jewish conceptions of the Kingdom, is sufficiently striking. But, once more, it will be realized how great an element of truth there is in either conception. The Apocalyptists, with their heavenward gaze, concentrated their thoughts on what they believed to be the only true sphere of divine rule. On the other hand, materialistic as orthodox Jewish ideas of the Kingdom often were, in so far as the Kingdom was thought of as existing also on earth, they witnessed to the truth. Both these conceptions concerning the Kingdom find their place in the teaching of our Lord. This must be examined in some detail. Attention may be drawn first to those passages in which the Kingdom is spoken of as *present*. In *Matth.* xi. 12 (cp. *Lk.* xvi. 16) there is the difficult passage about taking the Kingdom of Heaven by force; according to some commentators the reference is to fanatical nationalists who held that the Messianic Age must be established by force of arms, i.e. the Zealots; [1] we venture to believe, however, that the reference is to the death of John the Baptist, and that the final words of the verse, " and men of violence take it by force "—rendered in the Syriac Version " and the violent take it away ", or " grasp it "— refer to the Jewish religious leaders; cp. *Lk.* xi. 45 ff., especially verse 52, ". . . for ye took away the key of knowledge; ye entered not in yourselves, and them that were entering in ye hindered "; for the " key " in reference to the Kingdom see *Matth.* xvi. 19, " I will give unto thee the keys of the kingdom of heaven ". But whatever may be the right interpretation of the passage, there is no doubt that the Kingdom of Heaven is represented as in present existence. The same applies to *Lk.* xi. 20 (cp. *Matth.* xii. 28), where we read: " But if I by the finger of God cast out demons, then is the kingdom of God come upon you." Again, in *Mk.* x. 14 (cp. *Matth.* xix. 14, *Lk.* xviii. 16) it is said: " For of such is the Kingdom of God ", in reference to the little children. Then we have our Lord's words of warning to the Scribes and Pharisees who shut up

[1] See Josephus, *Jewish War*, iv. 193 ff., 224 ff., 305 ff., v. i ff.

the Kingdom of Heaven against men: "For ye neither go in
yourselves, neither suffer ye them that are entering to go in"
(*Matth.* xxiii. 13, cp. *Lk.* xi. 52); and there is also His rebuke
to the chief priests and elders: "The publicans and harlots
go into the Kingdom of God before you" (*Matth.* xxi. 31).
Even more striking are the definite statements: "The time is
fulfilled, and the kingdom of God hath drawn nigh" (*Mk.* i. 15,
cp. *Matth.* iv. 17, x. 7, *Lk.* x. 9), and: "The Kingdom of
Heaven is within you", or, "in the midst of you", as the
Syriac version reads (*Lk.* xvii. 21). And, once more, the
same is taught in some of the parables of the Kingdom (e.g.
Matth. xiii. 24–30, 31–32, 33, and elsewhere). The existence
of the Kingdom of Heaven as already present on earth is
thus clearly taught. On the other hand, it is no less definitely
taught that the Kingdom is to be looked for in the *future.*
Thus, in *Mk.* ix. 1 (cp. *Matth.* xvi. 28, *Lk.* ix. 27) it is said:
"Verily I say unto you, There be some here of them that
stand by, which shall in no wise taste of death, till they see
the Kingdom of God come with power". The future coming
of the Kingdom is also taught in *Matth.* vii. 21, 22: "Not
every one that saith unto me, Lord, Lord, shall enter into
the Kingdom of Heaven; but he that doeth the will of my
Father which is in heaven. Many will say to me in that
day . . .", cp. also *Lk.* xiii. 23–29. Though spoken of as in
the future, it is not a far distant future that is thought of:
"Verily I say unto you, This generation shall not pass away,
until all things be accomplished" (*Mk.* xiii. 30, *Matth.* xxiv. 34,
Lk. xxi. 31). Similarly, in *Matth.* xix. 28 our Lord says to
His disciples: "Verily I say unto you, that ye which have
followed me, in the regeneration when the Son of Man shall
sit on the throne of his glory ye also shall sit upon twelve
thrones judging the twelve tribes of Israel" (cp. *Lk.* xxii. 30).
Finally, in various passages it is stated that no one can know
when the advent of the Kingdom will take place: "But of
that day or that hour knoweth no one, not even the angels
in heaven, neither the Son, but the Father" (*Mk.* xiii. 32,
cp. *Matth.* xxiv. 36, 50, xxv. 13, and elsewhere). The Kingdom is, therefore, a present reality, and also a future consummation. Very significant in this connexion are our Lord's
words in *Jn.* xiv. 15–20.

It will thus be seen that in so far as the Kingdom of Heaven is spoken of as both present and future, the background of apocalyptic and orthodox Judaism, respectively, again foreshadowed truths. In much, as the Gospels show, our Lord corrected and spiritualized the earlier ideas. Into the details of this we need not go here. It will suffice to say that His outstanding demand was that those who would become members of the Kingdom should live in accordance with the divine will. This is brought out again and again; but nowhere so succinctly and pointedly as in the words: "Thy Kingdom come; thy will be done, as in heaven, so on earth." In connexion with the truth that the Kingdom of Heaven is both present and future, we recall the parallel truth, taught by our Lord, that the true believer in Him is already partaker of eternal life on this earth, and also in the world to come: "He that believeth on the Son hath eternal life" (*Jn*. iii. 36, see also verse 24). The same truth underlies the words of St. Paul in *Rom*. viii. 11: "But if the Spirit of him that raised up Jesus from the dead dwelleth in you, he that raised up Christ Jesus from the dead shall quicken also your mortal bodies through his Spirit that dwelleth in you"; in other words, immortal life is, through the Spirit, both present and future.

Finally, as to the cosmical cataclysm and the "signs" which are to herald the advent of the Kingdom, so prominent in the Apocalyptic Literature, we are faced with a somewhat difficult question. In view of what our Lord taught about the Kingdom as already present on earth, a few illustrations of which have been given, it may well be asked how any account of these "signs" of the coming of the Kingdom could have found a place in His teaching. And yet they are made to figure prominently (e.g. *Matth*. xxiv. 6, 7, 29–31, *Mk*. xiii. 7, 8, 24–27, *Lk*. xxi. 10, 28). It can, of course, be argued that these "signs" are spoken of only in connexion with the Kingdom viewed as future; but this mars the conception of unity between the Kingdom as both present and future, which our Lord taught. It is also worth noting that there is no mention of these "signs" in the Fourth Gospel.

On this question, then, one must have an open mind; the possibility must be reckoned with that these "signs" passages

K

may have been due to the evangelists who were familiar with the Apocalyptic Literature. In many cases the verbal identity between the two is very striking. In writing on the subject of our Lord's teaching on the Kingdom McNeile remarks: "A difficulty presents itself at the outset. It is undeniable that in no case can we be quite confident that we possess the *ipsissima verba* of our Lord. His utterances, which reached their form a generation or more after their delivery, must be largely coloured by passing through successive minds." [1] This applies with special force to utterances about the "signs".

[1] Essay on "Our Lord's Use of the Old Testament", *Cambridge Biblical Essays* (ed. Swete), p. 220 (1909).

CHAPTER X

THE MESSIAH: THE FIRST PHASE OF BELIEF

In dealing with this supremely important subject it is absolutely necessary that we should begin by considering what we learn from the Old Testament; for although this presents us only with the first phase of belief, it contains the foundation upon which the developments were built. The teaching of the later literature is based partly on that of the Old Testament, and partly on extraneous sources. But in this chapter we shall confine ourselves to one aspect only of Messianic belief, that of the human Messiah.

I

THE TEACHING OF THE OLD TESTAMENT

We must begin by emphasizing the fact that various passages have, in times long subsequent to their origin, been interpreted in what is called a " Messianic " sense; but these passages, read in the sense which the writers intended, do not lend themselves to this interpretation. We are far from denying the justification of discerning in the passages in question the foreshadowing of truths; we only affirm that the writers themselves had no knowledge of this, and that it is, therefore, inappropriate to describe such passages as Messianic prophecies.

Further, we are confronted by an initial difficulty in that there is in some cases uncertainty as to the date of the passages in question, and in consequence differences of opinion among expert authorities exist. In this matter, however, we would only urge the recognition of the fact that, granted the probability of most of these passages being post-exilic, in some cases earlier thought is echoed.

For the present, then, we shall ignore the question of dates, and take the passages in question in the order in which they occur in the Old Testament. For reasons which will be obvious as we proceed, we shall avoid the use of the term Messiah; instead we shall speak of the " ideal figure ". The fact must be noted at the outset that this ideal figure is referred to in a way which makes it clear that the conception of him was familiar to those for whom the writers wrote; cryptic and mysterious references to him point in the same direction.

The first reference to the " ideal figure " is of this cryptic nature: " The sceptre shall not depart from Judah, nor the staff from between his feet, until he cometh to whom it belongeth, and him shall the peoples obey . . ." (Gen. xlix. 10–12). The rendering " until Shiloh come " is meaningless; the Septuagint and other ancient authorities have this as just translated, " to whom it belongeth ". Judah is to rule until the advent of him to whom the sceptre and staff, symbols of rule, really belong, i.e. the " ideal figure " who will come as king; and he will inaugurate the return of the " Golden Age " (see pp. 121 ff.). In connexion with this passage Deut. xxxiii. 7 must be read: "Hear, Yahweh, the voice of Judah, and bring him unto his people "; here again there is a cryptic, but well understood, reference to the ideal figure, " him ". The same is true of the next passage, Num. xxiv. 17: " I see him, but not now; I beheld him, but not nigh; there shall come forth a star [1] out of Jacob, and a sceptre shall rise out of Israel. . . ." The context of each of these passages shows that they refer to the reign of peace and prosperity which the " ideal figure " will inaugurate by subduing Israel's enemies. The way in which this mysterious figure is introduced, without any explanation, suggests the existence of some well-known current conception regarding the ruler in the happy time to come. The figure, we venture to believe, was of extraneous origin, and adapted to Israelite expectations (cp. Chap. IX, section i). No eschatological sense, in the later connotation of the term, can be attached to these passages.

Next, we have four passages in which the conception of the " ideal figure " is adapted and made to apply to a ruler of the house of David; he is called the " Branch ", or " Shoot ", " out of the stock of Jesse ". The context of these passages again contains thoughts of the future time of peace and well-

---

[1] For " star " used in reference to a king, see Isa. xiv. 12, though in a very different connexion.

being. These passages are *Isa.* iv. 2–6, xi. 1–10, *Jer.* xxiii. 5, xxxiii. 15; with these some other passages must be read because they, too, have transferred the " ideal figure " and his rule to the Davidic house; they are: *Isa.* ix. 6, xvi. 5, xxxii. 1–8, *Jer.* xxx. 7–9, *Hos.* iii. 5, *Amos* ix. 11–15, *Mic.* v. 2–4.[1] None of these passages, taken as they stand, are eschatological, however they may have been interpreted in later times.

So far, then, it will be seen that in three passages (*Gen.* xlix. 10–12, *Deut.* xxxiii. 7, *Num.* xxiv. 17) the " ideal figure " is pictured as inaugurating the looked-for time of happiness; these, it will not be denied, are of pre-exilic date. Then we have a number of passages in which the functions of the " ideal figure " are transferred to a ruler of the house of David. These, too, may all be regarded as pre-exilic.

We come next to a very striking fact. In a far larger number of passages in which the future time of bliss is envisaged, not only does the " ideal figure " play no part, but the ruler of the house of David likewise disappears. Yahweh, and He alone, is Ruler. In some of these passages the time of peace and prosperity is described, in others the destruction of Israel's enemies, preparatory to the advent of that time, is spoken of. To quote these passages, which are all post-exilic, would take up too much space.[2]

Thus, with but few exceptions, when what we speak of as the " Messianic Era " is referred to, the thought of Yahweh is so central, the expectation of the *divine* rule so fundamental, that there is no place for the " ideal figure ", and no place for a ruler of the house of David. God is all in all. It is no exaggeration to say that, *normally*, in the " Messianic " teaching of the Old Testament, the human ruler recedes into the background, and ultimately disappears.

Before we proceed it must be pointed out that in the Old

---

[1] *Isa.* xxviii. 16, where the " tried stone " is spoken of, does not belong here; the " tried stone " does not refer to an individual. The picture is borrowed by the writer of *Ps.* cxviii. 22, and applied to an individual, but as the psalm itself clearly shows, this individual is the writer of the psalm. A " Messianic " interpretation is grafted on to it in *Matth.* xxi. 42, *Mk.* xii. 10, 11, *Lk.* xx. 17, *Acts* iv. 11, *i Pet.* ii. 6–8.

[2] *Isa.* ii. 2–4, xvii. 4–8 (possibly), xix. 18–25, xxviii. 5, 6, xxix. 18, 19, xxx. 18 ff., xxxv. 1–10; *Jer.* xxxi. 1–7, L. 4, 5; *Amos* v. 18–20; *Hos.* ii. 18–23; *Mic.* iv. 6–8, v. 10–15; *Joel* ii. 18–32, iii. 1, 2; *Zeph.* iii. 19, 20; *Zech.* ix. 10–17, xiv. 1–12; *Mal.* iii. 1–6. The subject is also referred to in some of the later psalms.

Testament the title " Messiah " occurs only in *Dan.* ix. 25, 26.[1]
Elsewhere, with the article prefixed, it is used as a qualification,
but not as a title. Thus, the priest is spoken of as " the anointed
priest " (e.g. *Lev.* iv. 3, 5, 6, and elsewhere). Frequent is the
phrase " Yahweh's anointed " in reference to the king; Saul
is thus spoken of in *i Sam.* xxiv. 6, 10 (7, 11 in Hebr.), xxvi. 16,
ii Sam. i. 14. 16; so, too, of David in *ii Sam.* xix. 21 (22 in
Hebr.), xxiii. 1; and of Zedekiah in *Lam.* iv. 20; in the *Psalms*
the phrase occurs often in reference to the king, e.g. in *Ps.*
lxxxiv. 9. It is also applied to Cyrus in *Isa.* xliv. 1; and
Zerubbabel is called the " Branch ", a synonym for the
anointed one (see above) in *Zech.* vi. 12.

II

THE " MESSIANIC " PERSON

A short digression must now be permitted; but that it is
called for will not be denied. We have seen that in connexion
with that future time of peace and prosperity (what in later
days is thought of as the Messianic Era), there appears a pre-
eminent personality, or ruler, or " king ". First the " ideal
figure "; then a scion of the house of David; finally Yahweh
Himself. In each case that scene of the happy time to come is
placed either in the land of Israel, or, with the growth of
universalistic conceptions, on earth in general. We can understand that after the establishment of the monarchy, the idea
should have arisen later that one of the Davidic line should
rule in that future age of peace and prosperity; such idealiza-
tion of the reign of him who came to be regarded as the greatest
of Israel's kings is quite comprehensible. We can also understand that with the development of conceptions of Yahweh, the
One and only God, during and after the Exile, and with the
disappearance of the monarchy, the recognition of Yahweh as
the Ruler in that time should have prevailed. What is not so
clear is how we are to account for the presentation of the " ideal
figure " in some of the Old Testament writings. It will not
be denied that the introduction of this enigmatical personality

---

[1] In the Authorized Version, but the Hebrew has " an anointed one ",
the reference being to the High-priest Onias iii.

into Israelite belief belongs to early times, certainly long before the beginning of the monarchy (see above, p. 138). It is well known how in many respects Israel's teachers were indebted to foreign influences, and how they accepted concepts and ideas, mythological and others, from outside sources, which they adopted and transformed because they recognized elements of truth in them. The possibility of this having been the case in the present connexion receives support when it is seen that this "ideal figure" appears in some early extra-Israelite sources. Of these there are several, one or two of which may be quoted. Of particular interest is the following from an Egyptian prophetical text belonging to about 3000 B.C.; after a period of calamity in the land has been described, it is prophesied that a king will come and inaugurate an age of happiness and peace and righteousness: "A king from the south will come, the son of a Nubian mother, a child from Chenchen (i.e. Upper Egypt). He shall receive the crown of Upper Egypt, and shall wear the crown of Lower Egypt. . . . The people in his day will be joyful; that exalted one will make for himself a name for all eternity. They who are prone to evil, they who foster enmity, will keep silent for fear of him. The Asiatics will bow down before him in terror, Libyans will fall headlong before his flame; the agitators because of his wrath, the rebellious because of his power (will be subdued). The Uraeus-serpent [1] upon his forehead will appease the revolters. . . . Justice will again come to its own, and wickedness will be cast away. All who behold it will rejoice, whosoever is in the following of the king." [2]

Here we have the advent of a saviour-king, the destruction of the people's foes, the abrogation of evil, and the inauguration of the time of happiness, each of which has its counterpart in one or other of the Old Testament passages referred to above. While it may well be that the Hebrew accounts of the happy time to come were of Egyptian origin, the conception, as already pointed out (p. 121), was world-wide in ancient days. Thus, to give but one other illustration; in a Babylonian text it is told

---

[1] The fire-serpent encircling the sun's disc was worn by the sun-god; it was also assumed by the king as a mark of supreme power, and denoted his divine origin. It was supposed to emit a flaming breath which burned up his enemies (Erman, *Die Religion der Ägypter*, pp. 19, 56 (1934)).

[2] Gressmann, *Altorientalische Texte zum Alten Testament*, pp. 47 f. (1926).

how a king, by the will of the gods, will come forth as the saviour
of his people.   In his time there will be " days of justice, years
of righteousness, abundance of rain, water in plenty, successful
trading (lit. " good prices "). The gods will be kindly disposed, godly fear will be widespread, the temples teeming (i.e.
with worshippers) . . . the old men will leap, the children
sing, the women and maidens (text broken) . . . they marry
. . . they bear boys and girls; bringing forth as it should be.
To him whose sins have delivered unto death, doth the king
grant life.   They that pined long in prison are set free; they
who were sick for many days recover.   The hungry are satis-
fied, the emaciated are filled, the naked are clothed with
garments." [1]

Here again there are points of contact, though perhaps less
striking, with what we read in the Old Testament about the
looked-for time of happiness.   The close relations, however,
which the Hebrews had with Egypt in the early stage of their
history make it likely that Egyptian rather than Babylonian
influence is to be discerned in the Old Testament passages.[2]
It may be added, in passing, as possibly not altogether without
significance, that in the Ras Shamra poems, belonging to the
fourteenth century B.C., which contain such abundant mythological material, and, in various directions, so many points of
contact with the Old Testament, there is not the slightest
allusion to the primeval " Golden Age ", nor any indications of
the expectation of the coming of a time of peace and happiness
ushered in by the appearance of an " ideal figure ".[3]   But, in
any case, the fact of extraneous influence in this matter must
be recognized, for it explains the presence of the otherwise
enigmatical " ideal figure " presented in some Old Testament
passages.   The Hebrew teachers were remarkable for their
insight and their capacity for discerning elements of truth in
the religious thought of other peoples.   Full of significance,
therefore, are the words of the prophet whose apprehension of

[1] Gressmann, *Altorientalische Texte zum Alten Testament*, p. 328.
[2] It is held by some that in ancient Persian religion the Yima legend
(*Vend.* ii) may reflect the conception of a primeval " Golden Age " and its
return.   If so, it may well have contributed in later times to Hebrew
thought (see above, p. 87).
[3] See Claude F. A. Schaeffer, *The Cuneiform Texts of Ras Shamra-Ugarit*
(the Schweich Lectures for 1936), and R. Dussaud, *Les Découvertes de Ras
Shamra (Ugarit) et l'Ancien Testament* (1937).

God taught him to realize that among all peoples in every age divine influence was at work in spite of much that seemed to belie this: " Art not thou from everlasting, Yahweh, mine holy God " (*Hab.* i. 12).

III

THE TEACHING IN THE APOCRYPHA AND OTHER UNCANONICAL WRITINGS

We will consider here first what is taught in the books of the Apocrypha about the personality whom we have described as the " ideal figure ", and about the scion of the house of David who takes his place.   The subject receives but rare mention in this body of literature.   This is, however, to be accounted for owing to the nature of the writings embodied; their contents are such that references to " Messianism " are hardly to be looked for.   One great exception to this is *ii* (*iv*) *Esdras*, which belongs to the Apocalyptic Literature, to be considered in the next chapter.   Nevertheless, there are in this book certain parts which have been taken from an older source; these will be taken into consideration here.   Now, although, as just re-marked, the subject under discussion receives but scant notice in the Apocrypha, there are in five of the books (including *ii* (*iv*) *Esdras*) a few isolated passages which are instructive in the present connexion, and they must receive attention.   What we found to be the case in the Old Testament reappears in these books in so far that they contain descriptions of the happy time to come, but only once or twice do they speak of the " ideal figure ", or of the scion of the house of David; and the *rôle* assigned to him in either case is insignificant.   It is again the Almighty who is the Ruler in the " Messianic Era ".   Thus, in *ii* (*iv*) *Esdras*, after the Seer has recounted the woes which will precede the advent of the time of bliss, he continues: " And it shall be, whosoever shall have survived all these things that I have foretold unto thee, he shall be saved, and shall see my salvation and the end of my world.   And the men who have been taken up, who have not tasted death from their birth, shall appear.[1]   Then shall the heart of the inhabitants

[1] The reference is to Enoch (*Gen.* v. 24), Elijah (*ii Kings* ii. 11), and in all probability to Moses (*Deut.* xxxiv. 6, " no man knoweth of his sepulchre to this day ", cp. *Mk.* ix. 2 f., *Matth.* xvii. 1–18, *Lk.* ix. 28–36).

of the world be changed, and be converted to a different spirit. For evil shall be blotted out, and deceit extinguished; faithfulness shall flourish, and corruption be vanquished; and truth, which for so long a time hath been without fruit, shall be made manifest " (vi. 25–28). Here, then, the " ideal figure " does not appear at all. The words are put into the mouth of the Almighty (" And lo, a voice spake, and the sound of it was as the sound of mighty waters," verse 17); it is, therefore, to be assumed that Yahweh is the Ruler in that time of righteousness and happiness.[1] Similarly, in Tobit's prayer there is a reference to the future time of happiness, but no mention is made of the " ideal figure "; the Almighty is the Ruler; " Many nations shall come from far to the name of the Lord God, with gifts in their hands, even gifts to the King of Heaven; generations and generations shall praise thee, and sing songs of rejoicing " (*Tob*. xiii. 11). The prayer purports to have been uttered in reference to the return of the captives from Babylon: but it was not originally composed in that connexion, as the opening words show: " Blessed be God that liveth for ever, and blessed be his kingdom " (xiii. 1). The time of happiness and righteousness which is to come is further envisaged in verses 13–18: " Rejoice and be exceeding glad for the sons of the righteous; for they shall be gathered together, and shall bless the Lord of the righteous. O blessed are they that love thee; they shall rejoice in thy peace. . . . And they shall be made glad for ever. Let my soul bless God the great King." There follows a description of Jerusalem as it will be in that time, " builded with sapphires and emeralds and precious stones; thy walls and towers and battlements with pure gold; and the streets of Jerusalem shall be paved with beryl and carbuncle and stones of Ophir " (cp. *Rev*. xxi. 10–21). The whole poem combines very beautifully a nationalistic with a universalistic outlook.

Coming now to *Ecclesiasticus*, we have in xlvii. 22 an indirect reference to a Davidic ruler:

" He will not cut off the posterity of his chosen ones,
Nor will he destroy the offspring of them that love him;
And he will give to Jacob a remnant,
And to the house of David a root from him."

[1] For a different view set forth in this book, see p. 157.

More direct is what is said in the Hymn of Praise—it occurs only in the Hebrew—added after li. 12; in *v.* 8 it is said:

" Give thanks unto him that maketh a horn to sprout for the
    house of David,
For his mercy endureth for ever."

The only other reference in this book to the coming of the " Messianic Era " occurs in the section in praise of Elijah (xlviii. 10):

" Who art written as ready for the time,
    To still wrath before the fierce anger of God,
    To turn the hearts of the fathers unto the children,
    And to restore the tribes of Israel."

Ben-Sira thus believes in a Messiah who is purely human, and who belongs to the house of David; but, as implied in the first of these passages, it is the Lord God who is King.   The thought of the Messianic Era is conceivably present in a passage in the book of *Baruch*, though this is not certain; in iii. 24, 25, it is said: " O Israel, how great is the house of God! and how large is the place of his possession! great, and hath none end; high and unmeasurable."

Coming now to *i Maccabees*, it is possible that the thought of the Messiah may be discerned in iv. 46: ". . . so they pulled down the altar, and laid down the stones in the mountain of the House, in a convenient place, until a prophet should come and decide as to what should be done concerning them."   The reference here is probably to *Deut.* xviii. 18, which is not a Messianic passage, however, though it may have been so interpreted in later times.   A somewhat more definite reference appears in xiv. 41: " And the Jews and the high-priest were well pleased that Simon should be their leader and high-priest for ever (i.e. in reference to his descendants), until a faithful prophet should arise."   In *ii Maccabees* there is no reference to the Messiah, but the references in i. 27, ii. 18 to the gathering together of the people may well contain the thought of the " Messianic times ".

We have dealt so far with the teaching of the Old Testament and the Apocrypha, and it will have been seen that the Messiah, the " ideal figure ", when he is mentioned, appears as a purely human personality.   In considering next what is taught in other books belonging to the Jewish literature of the Greek Period, we shall devote attention first to teaching which is in line with what has already been set forth, namely, that which presents the " ideal figure ", whatever his functions, as purely human. A very different conception is presented in some of these writings; but the detailed consideration of this is reserved for the next chapter.

In most of the books in question, but not in all, the " ideal figure ", or the Davidic king, as the case may be, still appears in the comparatively insignificant *rôle* in the era of happiness to come, just as we have seen hitherto. But—and this is the great fact to be noted—in a few of these books there are some passages, and they are of outstanding importance, in which the " ideal figure " is presented in a wholly different manner; for he appears not as an ideal human personality, but, as just hinted, as of divine nature. We draw passing attention to this here— it will be dealt with more fully later—because during the Greek Period there were special reasons why the human " ideal figure ", or the Davidic king, should have receded into the background. We are far from suggesting that the conception of a divine Messiah was prompted by these special reasons; there were far deeper causes at work which created this conception; but it is well that all the factors should be taken into consideration. Divine purposes are often, by the will of God, furthered by human means. It will, therefore, we feel sure, not be thought out of place if we indicate what these special reasons were. There were two; and both have a distinct bearing on our main subject, as the weighing of them will show.

The first of these reasons is the wider world-view gained by the Jews during the Greek Period, which receives increased expression in the eschatological teaching of the Apocalyptists. Special emphasis in this connexion is laid on the great final world-catastrophe to be brought about by the absolute will of God; the conception of a prodigious working of a divine wonder; this comes more and more to the fore and is the presage of the approach of the time of bliss. When one considers the circumstances of the times, the might of the empires founded by Alexander's successors, the power and influence of Greek culture affecting the whole world of those days, and, later, the domination of the Roman empire, all of which were to be done away with in the world-catastrophe looked for in the near future, one can understand the conviction held by the Apocalyptists that here the intervention of the Almighty himself could alone avail; what significance could the action of a king of the seed of David have! We cannot be surprised to find that in the circumstances of the times the thought of an earthly Messiah should have receded into the background.

Then there is the second reason, which applies, however, only to part of the period with which we are concerned, namely, the conditions brought about by the Maccabæan rising. During the Maccabæan times there existed a powerful princely house, which at some periods during this era was looked upon as presaging the approach of Messianic times; this was held to be the case even by many belonging to the " pious ", or orthodox circles. Thus, during the latter part of the rule of Jonathan, the Maccabee, and during that of his brother Simon, and of Hyrcanus i, and then again during the reign of Queen Alexandra (Salome)—all periods of prosperity—it was believed by many that a truly Messianic era was developing. But even though great and wonderful occurrences were looked for in the near future, to be brought about through divine intervention, these Maccabæan rulers did not belong to the house of David. And during this time, the glory of the tribe of Levi, to which the Maccabæans belonged, increased, to the detriment of the tribe of Judah—to which the Davidic house belonged—in spite of all the Old Testament prophecies. And to crown all, these prophecies were now interpreted as applying to the Maccabæans! (cp., e.g., *Test. XII Patr.*, *Levi* xviii, *Judah* xxiv. 1–3). It cannot be wondered at, therefore, that the traditional belief in the advent of a ruler of the house of David, identified again with the " ideal figure ", should have received but scant attention during the Greek Period; not that this is altogether wanting, as will be seen.

We shall now consider some of the passages in other Jewish literature of this period, but also some belonging to the Apocalyptic Literature, in which the Messiah is presented as a purely human personality. In the book of *Jubilees* xxi. 18–20 the blessing on Judah runs as follows: " May the Lord give thee strength and power to tread down all that hate thee. A prince shalt thou be, thou and one of thy sons (i.e. the Messiah), over the sons of Jacob. May thy name and the name of thy sons go forth and traverse every land and region. Then shall the Gentiles fear before thy face, and all the nations shall quake. In thee shall be the help of Jacob, and in thee shall be found the salvation of Israel. And when thou sittest on the throne of honour of thy righteousness, then shall be great peace for all the seed of the sons of the beloved (i.e. Abraham). . . ." Here we have, then, one of the exceptional passages in this literature; and it presents the Messiah as belonging to the house of Judah; a human ruler endowed with strength from on high; in this case, moreover, he is represented as being himself the ruler in the Messianic Age. Very different from this is the account given in the *Sibylline Oracles* III. 652 ff. Although this begins with the mention of a king who will bring a time of peace on earth, in the long description of that time, which follows, the figure of this king recedes altogether; the Ruler is the Almighty. A few verses may be quoted; the passage opens thus: " And then from the sunrise God shall send a king, who shall give every land relief from the bane of war; some he shall slay, and with some make a sure agreement. Nor shall he do all these things by his own will, but in obedience to the good ordinances of the mighty God." In all that follows this king is never again mentioned; it is the Almighty who rules and directs all things. A few verses will serve as an illustration: " Then shall all the sons of the great God dwell peaceably round the Temple, rejoicing in that which the Creator, the righteous sovereign Judge, shall give them. For he himself shall stand by them as a shield in his greatness, encircling them, as it were, with a wall of flaming fire. Free from war shall they be in city and country. No hand of evil war shall stir against them, for the Eternal himself shall be their champion, and the hand of the Holy One." And there is much else to the same effect.

Next, attention must be drawn to an interesting passage in the *Testaments of the XII Patriarchs* in which the priesthood of the Messiah is proclaimed; the *rôle* assigned to him is a very high and powerful one; but he appears as one who is purely human. This book was written during the latter part of the second century B.C., after the successful conclusion of the Maccabæan struggle. The passage in question is from the *Testament of Levi* xviii. 2–14, and is in the form of a Messianic hymn: [1]

" Then shall the Lord raise up a new priest,
And to him all the words of the Lord shall be revealed;
And he shall execute a righteous judgement upon the earth
for a multitude of days.
And his star (cp. *Num.* xxiv. 17) shall arise in heaven as
a king,
Lighting up the light of knowledge as the sun the day;
And he shall be magnified in the world;
He shall shine forth as the sun on the earth,
And shall remove all darkness from under heaven,
And there shall be peace in all the earth.
The heavens shall exult in his days,
And the earth shall be glad. . . .
And the glory of the Most High shall be uttered over him,
And the spirit of understanding and sanctification shall
rest upon him.
For he shall give the majesty of the Lord to his sons in
truth for evermore;
And there shall none succeed him for all generations for
ever.
And in his priesthood the Gentiles shall be multiplied in
knowledge upon the earth,
And enlightened through the grace of the Lord;
In his priesthood shall sin come to an end. . . ."

This is a Messianic conception utterly different from that of a Davidic king ruling over the Jewish nation. It will be noted that the supremacy of the Almighty is emphasized, and the Messiah is in no way described as other than human; it is " the glory of the Most High " that makes him a pre-eminent ruler. The mention of " a new priest " points to the Seer's expectation of the abrogation of the Maccabæan priesthood which was regarded by him as an usurpation; for the Hasmonæans did not belong to the high-priestly family. That the Messiah is spoken of as a priest is thus an interesting point. It will be noted that he is clothed with the priesthood, not the kingship; the words, " And his star shall arise in heaven as a

---

[1] Charles' edition of the *Testaments*, pp. 62 ff. (1908).

king ", express a comparison, and do not mean that this ideal priest would be a king.

One more illustration, of a later date, must be given, for it echoes the older belief in a Messiah of the seed of David, and the Messianic hopes are purely nationalistic. It is from the *Psalms of Solomon*. For the popular conception of the Messiah and his rule during the half-century immediately preceding the birth of our Lord, they constitute the most valuable document that has come down to us. The length of the following quotation will be pardoned on account of its interest; it is from the seventeenth psalm, verses 23–32: [1]

" Behold, O Lord, and raise up unto them their king; the son of David,
>At the time in the which thou seest, O God, that he may reign over Israel thy servant.
>And gird him with strength, that he may shatter unrighteous rulers,
>And that he may purge Jerusalem from nations that trample her down to destruction.
>Wisely, righteously, shall he thrust out sinners from (our) inheritance;
>He shall destroy the pride of the sinner as a potter's vessel;
>With a rod of iron shall he break in pieces all their substance,
>He shall destroy the godless nations with the word of his mouth;
>At his rebuke nations shall flee before him,
>And he shall reprove sinners for the thoughts of their heart.
>And he shall gather together a holy people, whom he shall lead in righteousness,
>And he shall judge the tribes of the people that hath been sanctified by the Lord his God.
>And he shall not suffer unrighteousness to lodge any more in their midst,
>Nor shall there dwell with them any man that knoweth wickedness,
>For he shall know them, that they are all sons of their God.

---

[1] The quotation is from Gray, in Charles' *The Apocrypha and Pseudepigrapha of the Old Testament*, ii, pp. 649 f. (1913).

And he shall divide them according to their tribes upon the
land,
And neither sojourner nor alien shall sojourn with them
any more.
He shall judge peoples and nations in the wisdom of his
righteousness;
And he shall have the heathen nations to serve under his
yoke. . . ."

There is much more in these psalms to the same effect. We
have thus a picture of the Messiah of the seed of David, that
is, a purely human ruler, whose kingdom will be a kingdom of
righteousness; and this Jewish ruler will subdue all nations,
and rule over them; so that the outlook is wholly nationalistic,
in the sense that the Jewish nation will be pre-eminent. The
teaching that the Almighty will Himself rule in that time of
triumph and happiness finds no place here; but it is said that
the Messiah will be made mighty by God through His holy
spirit (verse 43). He is called " the king of Israel " (verse
47); but the psalm ends with the words: " The Lord himself
is our King for ever and ever ", thus guarding against any
danger to monotheistic belief.

These illustrations will suffice; they represent one aspect of
Messianic belief; another will come before us in the next
chapter. For the bearing of what has so far been said on the
teaching of the New Testament, see the final section of the
following chapter.

L

CHAPTER XI

THE MESSIAH: THE DEVELOPMENT OF BELIEF

THE character and work of the " ideal figure " in the Old Testament and other Jewish literature, which we have so far considered, show that the beliefs and ideas concerning him underwent changes. It may be said that four stages are discernible; first there appears the mysterious figure the origin of the conception of whom is probably extra-Israelite; in the second stage he is described as belonging to the house of David; then he almost disappears from the prominent position assigned to him, and the King who will rule in the happy time to come is the Almighty; and in the final stage the " ideal figure " comes to the fore again as a scion of the house of David.

What is, therefore, of primary importance in all that has so far been said is that the " ideal figure " appears always as a purely human personality. This is the normal conception of him. All the more remarkable, therefore, is the fact that in certain of the writings belonging to the Greek Period he is represented as superhuman. This is the subject of the present chapter.

I

THE SON OF MAN

The supreme importance of this title demands that we should begin by a brief examination of its meaning and use. We must distinguish, it need hardly be said, between the term " a son of man ", and the title " The Son of Man ".

In the Old Testament the term " son of man " occurs in various passages. The earliest of these is *Num.* xxiii. 19, belonging to the Elohistic document. In all the passages in question the term, in its Hebrew form, is *ben' adam*, lit. " a son of man "; and this means simply " man ", a member of the human race. In the book of *Ezekiel* it occurs over ninety times, always in reference to the prophet. Whether or not in this book its use is intended to express the prophet's sense of humility and his feelings of insignificance in the sight of God, there can be no doubt that the term means again " man " in the ordinary sense of the word. This is all simple and straight-forward. But when we come to the book of *Daniel* (166 B.C.) it is rather different. In *Dan*. vii. 13 the term occurs for the first time in literature in Aramaic. The form there is *bar 'enash*, which is the precise equivalent of the Hebrew *ben' adam*, and means, therefore, again " man " in the ordinary sense of the word. Now it is important to note that in the *earlier* Aramaic literature *bar 'enash* (בַּר אֱנָשׁ) always means a " man ", i.e. a human being; but neither the Hebrew *ben ha'adam* (בֶּן הָאָדָם) nor the Aramaic *bar 'enasha'* (בַּר אֱנָשָׁא), " the man ", occurs in the early Hebrew or Aramaic literature; there " the man " is always *ha-'adam* (הָאָדָם) and *'enasha'* (אֱנָשָׁא). It is a *late* and *new usage* in Aramaic when the expressions *bar 'enasha'*, or *bar nasha'* (בַּר נָשָׁא) " *the* man ", are found. These terms expressed a special description of a particular person, and are both Jewish-Aramaic and Christian-Aramaic. When rendered in Greek, ὁ υἱὸς τοῦ ἀνθρώπου, " the son of the man ", is not a proper equivalent; ὁ υἱὸς ἀνθρώπου, " the son of a man ", would be no better. The Aramaic cannot be adequately expressed in Greek, as ἄνθρωπος is not a collective abstract word, which can be the case both with *'enash* and with the Hebrew *'adam*.[1] But to return to *Dan*. vii. 13; when we read: " Behold, there came with the clouds of heaven one like unto a son of man ", it means that, so far as his appearance was concerned, he looked like a man in the ordinary sense of the word. But if this mysterious figure comes with (better " on ") the clouds of heaven, he is not an ordinary man, though he looks like one (cp. *Sib. Orac.* v. 414). He is a supernatural personal-ity. Here arises, then, the question as to who, in the mind of the Seer, this mysterious supernatural being was. On this point the opinions of scholars differ.[2] Now, in the Seer's own interpretation of his vision (*vv.* 15–17), he says that the four beasts whose dominion was taken away (*v.* 12) are four kings (*v.* 17). Then he continues: " But the saints of the Most High

---

[1] See, further, Dalman, *Die Worte Jesu*, pp. 191 ff. (1898).
[2] See, e.g., Rowley, *Darius the Mede . . .*, pp. 62 f. (1935).

shall receive the kingdom, and possess the kingdom for ever, even for ever and ever " (*v.* 18). But in the account of the vision itself, where " one like unto a son of man ", coming on the clouds of heaven, is spoken of, it is said : " And there was given him dominion, and glory, and a kingdom, that all the peoples, nations, and languages should serve him ; his dominion is an everlasting dominion, which shall not pass away, and his kingdom that which shall not be destroyed " (*vv.* 13, 14). If this supernatural being, coming on the clouds of heaven, is to be the ruler in the kingdom, how can the saints of the Most High be the rulers too ? How can these two manifestly contradictory statements be reconciled ? Various efforts have been made to reconcile the irreconcilable ; but we venture to believe that it is best to take the text as it stands, to recognize the contradiction, and to explain the reason of it rather than to attempt to explain it away. The writer of the book of *Daniel* was perfectly aware of what he was writing about, and perfectly aware of the contradiction. But he had before him what he believed to be two truths regarding the Kingdom of God in the " Last Times ", and the ruler in that Kingdom. We must remember that he was, on the one hand, a Jew, with Jewish expectations regarding the Messiah and His Kingdom ; but he was also an Apocalyptist, with a wider mental horizon ; interested in religious ideas with which the ordinary narrow prejudice of the Jews would have nothing to do—not that they can be blamed for this in those days—but the Apocalyptists discerned gleamings of truth outside of Judaism, and they were right, as the sequel proved. So this writer had Jewish national conceptions about the Kingdom and its ruler ; but he had also universalistic conceptions ; and he had learned that the ruler in that Kingdom would be One who was far higher than a Davidic king— there is no sort of doubt that he was indebted to Persian eschatology for this. But here were things which were frankly irreconcilable, and of course the writer knew it ; his compromise was that the elect of Israel should inherit the Kingdom, that is, a Jewish kingdom, and that they should thus in a certain sense partake of rulership ; but the *real* Ruler would be a heavenly one, and yet " like unto a son of man " ; a combination of the human and divine which is somewhat startling. Obviously the Seer does not mention the Messiah, in the

Jewish sense of a Davidic ruler, because his place is taken by this supernatural being; for in saying that He comes on the clouds of heaven, he means that He comes from heaven, an entirely non-Jewish conception of the Messiah.

Thus, the writer of the book of *Daniel* sets forth two incompatible ideas regarding the end of the present world-order: a Jewish kingdom, with the " saints " as rulers, on the one hand; and, on the other, a non-Jewish supernatural Ruler of that kingdom, who is " like unto a son of man ", but who comes from heaven, and whose pre-existence is, therefore, taken for granted.

We come next to the very important section of *i Enoch* known as the " Similitudes " (chaps. xxxvii–lxxi belonging to 105–64 B.C.).[1] The first thing to note here is that the designation " Messiah " is applied to the wondrous figure to whom various other titles are given (xlviii. 10, lii. 4). The first of these titles is " the Elect One ", he who is foremost among those who are loyal to God, and who are called " elect ones ". Thus, in reference to the Day of Judgement it is said:

" On that day mine Elect One shall sit on the throne of glory,
And make choice of their works; and their resting-places
    shall be without number.
Their spirit shall grow strong within them when they see
    mine Elect One,
Even those that have called upon my glorious name.
In that day will I cause mine Elect One to dwell among
    them (cp. *Rev.* vii. 17),
And I will transform the heaven (cp. *Rev.* xxi. 1), and make
    it an eternal blessing and light;
And I will transform the earth and make it a blessing,
And I will cause mine elect ones to dwell upon it,
But the sinners and evil-doers shall not set foot thereon . . ."
    (xlv. 2–6).

The righteousness of the Elect One is such that he receives also the title of the " Righteous One " (liii. 6), who is " mighty in all the secrets of righteousness " (xlix. 2, also lxxi. 14).

[1] The quotations are partly from Charles' edition (1912) and partly from Beer in Kautzsch's *Die Apokryphen und Pseudepigraphen des Alten Testaments* (1900).

But the most striking title by which he is known is that of the
" Son of Man "; thus, in xlvi. 1–3 we read as follows:

" And there I saw him who hath a head of days (see *Dan.*
vii. 13),
And his head was white like wool,
And with him was another whose countenance had the
appearance of a man,
And his face was full of graciousness, like one of the holy
angels.
Then I asked the angel who went with me and showed
me all the hidden things, concerning the Son of Man, who
he was, and whence he came, and why he went with the
Head of Days?   And he answered me and said unto me:
This is the Son of Man who hath righteousness,
With whom dwelleth righteousness,
And who revealeth all the treasures of that which is hidden
(cp. *Col.* ii. 3),
For the Lord of Spirits hath chosen him,
And his lot hath the pre-eminence before the Lord of
Spirits in uprightness for ever."

When it is said (xlvi. 2) that the Son of Man " went with the
Head of Days ", his pre-existence is implied; and this is
definitely stated in xlviii. 2, 3, 6:

" And at that hour the Son of Man was named
In the presence of the Lord of Spirits,
And his name in the presence of the Head of Days.
Before the sun and the signs (i.e. of the Zodiac, see *Job*
xxxviii. 32) were created,
Before the stars of the heaven were made,
His name was named in the presence of the Lord of
Spirits . . .
For this purpose [1] hath he been chosen and hidden in the
presence of him (i.e. the Almighty),
Before the creation of the world, and for evermore."

Again, in lxii. 7 it is said:

---

[1] I.e., as " a staff to the righteous ", and " the light of the Gentiles "
(*v.* 4).

" For from the beginning was the Son of Man hidden,
And the Most High preserved him in the presence of his
might,
And revealed him to the elect."

Mention must also be made of the function of the Son of Man
as Judge, sitting on the throne of the Almighty; the reference
is to the Day of Judgement in the last times:

" And in those days shall the Elect One sit upon my throne,
And his mouth shall pour forth all the secrets of wisdom
and counsel;
For the Lord of Spirits hath given them to him, and hath
glorified him " (li. 3).

The preceding section refers to the Judgement. More definite
is what is said in lxi. 8:

" And the Lord of Spirits placed the Elect One on the throne
of glory;
And he shall judge all the works of the holy ones above in
the heaven,
And in the balance shall their deeds be weighed."

The judging of the wicked is spoken of in xlv. 5, and of the
powers of evil in lv. 4: " Ye kings and mighty ones who dwell
on the earth, ye shall behold mine Elect One, when he sitteth
on the throne of glory, and judgeth Azazel (i.e. Satan) and all
his associates, and all his hosts, in the name of the Lord of
Spirits."

One more passage from this book must be quoted, for it
implicitly imputes divinity to the Son of Man; it is in lxii.
8, 9:

" And the congregation of the elect and holy shall be sown,[1]
And the elect shall stand before him on that day.[2]
And all the kings and the mighty and the exalted, and those
who rule on earth,
Shall fall down before him on their faces,
And worship, and set their hope upon, that Son of Man,
And petition him and supplicate for mercy at his hands."

[1] In reference, as Charles points out, to " the plant of righteousness ",
i.e. the righteous community, spoken of in x. 16.
[2] I.e. the day of Judgement.

This conception of the transcendental Messiah is found also in some later apocalyptic writings. In the *Ascension of Isaiah* we read: "And thereupon the angel who conducted me, said to me, 'Worship this One', (i.e. the Almighty); and I worshipped and praised. And the angel said unto me 'This is the Lord of all praise-givings, whom thou hast seen'. And while he was yet speaking, I saw another Glorious One who was like Him, and the righteous drew nigh and worshipped and praised, and I praised together with them" (ix. 31–33). The striking thing about this passage is that the "Glorious One", i.e. the Messiah, is worshipped, so that he is represented as divine. In this connexion we must also quote from another apocalyptic writing, belonging like the foregoing to the end of the first century A.D., but reflecting earlier conceptions, namely, the *Ezra Apocalypse (ii (iv) Esdras* in the Apocrypha). In the vision recorded in xiii. 1 ff. it is said: "And, lo, there arose a wind from the sea, that it moved all the waves thereof. And behold, and lo, this wind caused to come up from the midst of the sea as it were the likeness of a man. And I beheld, and, lo, that man flew with the clouds of heaven; and when he turned his countenance to look, all things trembled that were seen under him." Then it goes on to describe how this One in the likeness of a man annihilated the wicked with the fire that came forth from his mouth; and how he received a "peaceable multitude" (*v.* 12). He is spoken of as "the Son", i.e. of God, in verse 37; and in xiv. 9 the Almighty is represented as saying to Ezra: "Thou shalt be taken up from among men, and henceforth thou shalt remain with my Son, and with such as are like thee, until the times be ended." Here again, since this "One in the likeness of a man" is called the Son of God, he is thought of as divine (cp. *i Enoch* lxx. 1 f.).

And, once more, in that part of the *Sibylline Oracles* belonging approximately to the same period it is said: "From the clouds of heaven there came a blessed man, holding a sceptre in his hand, (i.e. denoting kingship), which God had delivered to him; and he triumphed nobly over all, and gave back to all the righteous that wealth which aforetime men had taken from them . . ." (*v.* 415 ff.). Here, it is true, we have a strange interminging of exalted and worldly ideas; but the sublime figure of the Messianic king coming on the clouds of heaven (cp. *Dan.* vii. 13, quoted above) is very striking. It will, however, be noted that the title " Son of Man " is not applied to him.

To sum up, then : there is here a conception of the Messiah as one who stands first and foremost in the closest possible relationship to God. He comes from above, and has pre-existed before the creation of the world. He is represented as of divine nature, and, as such, worship is offered to him. On the other hand, as the Son of Man, he is of human nature. He is the Chosen One of God, and acts in all things in accordance with the will of God. He is endowed with divine wisdom, and righteousness is his outstanding characteristic. In divine-human power he will come as Judge of both angels and men at the appointed time, and will annihilate all the powers of evil.

II

THE SEEKING AFTER TRUTH

We have now sought to gain some insight into the Messianic beliefs of the Jews during the Greek Period. Among the mass of detail that which is of central importance is the difference of conception regarding the person of the Messiah held by Jewish teachers belonging to two opposed schools of thought. In the preceding chapter we set forth what was, generally speaking, the orthodox Jewish view, namely, a purely human Messiah whose interest was centred in the Jewish nation. On the other hand, as shown in the present chapter, there were among the Apocalyptists, and, above all, the writer of the " Similitudes " in *i Enoch*, those who believed in a supernatural Messiah to whom divine honours were paid, and who is even conceived of as being on an equality with the Almighty. His rule is not confined to the Jewish nation, but is universal. These two conceptions concerning an earthly and a transcendental Messiah are frankly irreconcilable ; the latter is quite un-Jewish, and there are strong grounds for believing that in this respect the Apocalyptists were in some measure indebted to the religion of ancient Persia (see above, Chap. IX, section i). But however this may be, we must recognize that all these teachers, whether of Jewish or other nationality, were actuated by a sanctified yearning to attain to truth. In what they taught we must discern gropings after realities, and, above all, the adumbration of the supreme and eternal truth to which we refer in the next section. God is from everlasting, and truth, which is from God, is everlasting too; and since God has never left Himself without a witness, the history of mankind tells of man's efforts, of divine prompting, to attain to the goal of truth. Inadequate and halting as man's efforts have been (cp. *Acts* xvii. 23), there was often much that his heart and mind produced which contained the germs of truth; these were to come to fruition in due time.

III

THE FULLNESS OF BELIEF IN THE NEW TESTAMENT

Jewish Messianic belief, as handed down in the sources with which we have dealt, formed the background of Christian teaching. Both the Jewish and non-Jewish elements which composed it contained in some respects erroneous views, in others, inadequately formulated truths. But, taken as a whole, it must be recognized that Jewish Messianic belief was a foreshadowing of some of the central truths of Christianity. This we must briefly illustrate.

First, there is the close relationship between the Messiah and the Lord of Spirits, emphasized especially in the " Similitudes". This sets forth a truth which is, of course, self-evident; but it receives a significant development when we read in the Gospels of our Lord's communing with the Father; for example, in *Lk*. vi. 12 we read that " he went out into the mountain to pray, and he continued all night in prayer to God ", cp. *Mk*. i. 35, *Lk*. v. 16, x. 21, 22, and elsewhere; but especially in the Fourth Gospel do we find the full nature of such communing; and there is much reason to believe that this Gospel tells more fully than the Synoptic Gospels the thoughts and spiritual experiences of our Lord. " It has created a portrait of the divine-human personality which has sunk deeply into the mind of the Church as the supremely true interpretation of Jesus Christ." [1] And in the words of Westcott, his narrative is " the

[1] Inge's esasy on " The Theology of the Fourth Gospel ", in *Cambridge Biblical Essays* (ed. Swete), p. 288 (1909).

mature expression of apostolic experience perfected by the teaching of the Holy Spirit in the writer's own life and in the life of the Church ".[1] Nothing could be more convincing than the beautiful seventeenth chapter.   Then we have such sayings as: " I and the Father are One " (x. 30); ". . . and yet I am not alone because the Father is with me " (xvi. 32, see also xiv. 6, 10, 11); " I came out from the Father, and am come into the world " (xvi. 28).   This last suggests the thought of the pre-existence of the Messiah, taught, as we have seen, in the Apocalyptic Literature.   It is definitely stated in xvii. 5: " And now, O Father, glorify thou me with thine own self with the glory which I had with thee before the world was "; so too, in verse 24.

These passages, like many others throughout the New Testament, teach the great central truth of Christianity: the divine and human nature of Jesus the Messiah, and thus the fullness of truth adumbrated in the Apocalyptic Literature.

We have seen, further, that in this Literature the Messiah is portrayed as Judge.   Here it is important to note that apart from one passage in the Fourth Gospel, which is, however, modified in others, our Lord never speaks of Himself as Judge in the sense in which the Apocalyptists describe the Messianic function at the final consummation.   In *Jn.* v. 27–29 we read: ". . . and he gave him authority to execute judgement because he is a son of man (the definite article is not used), but the Syriac Version has " seeing that he is the Son of Man ". " Marvel not at this; for the hour cometh . . . and they that have done evil unto the resurrection of judgement."   On the other hand, in xii. 47 our Lord says: " And if any man hear my sayings, and keep them not, I judge him not, for I came not to judge the world, but to save the world."   More striking still are the words in iii. 17: " For God sent not the Son into the world to judge the world; but that the world should be saved by him " (Syriac Version, " should live in him "); the judgement that is spoken of in what follows is not in reference to the final judgement.   We have thus, on the one hand, an affirmation of judgement in reference to our Lord, and, on the other, a denial of this.   The contradiction is explained, we believe rightly, by E. F. Scott: " John, with all his originality

[1] *The Gospel According to St. John*, I, p. lxxxv (1908).

of thought, was still partly bound to the past. Along with his own conception he strove to make room for the belief that impressed itself on the Church at large." [1] So far as the teaching of our Lord was concerned, it may be definitely stated that, on this subject, He rejected what the Apocalyptists taught. With what is said in other books of the New Testament we are not concerned, for they reflect the influence of the Apocalyptic Literature in this matter.

On the other hand, however, it is difficult to resist the conclusion that our Lord accepted from the Apocalyptists the designation of the Messiah as the " Son of Man ", and applied it to Himself. This is a much-debated question, and raises a number of subsidiary matters. Into these we cannot enter here. It must suffice to say that in the Gospels the title occurs only in the mouth of our Lord; the use of the third person in reference to Himself is certainly strange, and differs from His ordinary mode of speech. But this use may be due just to the very significance and uniqueness of the title. We have seen that, according to apocalyptic teaching, the conception of the transcendental Messiah and the human Messiah centred in the person of the " Son of Man ". Herein we believe that we are justified in discerning an adumbration, all unconscious, of the central truth of Christianity; if this be so, then the reason of our Lord's use of the title " Son of Man " in reference to Himself becomes clear.

Our Lord, it is said in *Jn.* iv. 22, uttered these memorable words: " Salvation is of the Jews "; they were spoken to a Samaritan woman. The Samaritans, as is well known, were to the Jews at least as objectionable as the Gentiles. But in connexion with these words there was a further utterance by our Lord: " Jesus saith unto her, Woman, believe me, the hour cometh, when neither in this mountain,[2] nor in Jerusalem, shall ye worship the Father. . . . The woman saith unto him, I know that Messiah cometh (which is called Christ), when he is come, he will declare unto us all things. Jesus saith unto her, I that speak unto thee am he."

If the words here recorded mean anything, they mean that

---

[1] *The Fourth Gospel*, p. 216.

[2] I.e. Mount Gerizim on which a rival temple had been built in earlier days, but which had been destroyed by Hyrcanus i more than a century previously.

Christianity was to become a world-religion. Obviously, when our Lord spoke of salvation being from the Jews, He was referring to the Jewish religion; but it must be emphasized that, while He accepted the fundamentals of the Jewish faith, He did not accept the orthodox Judaism of his day. Why—until the end—was our Lord's ministry carried on, in the main, in Galilee? [1] Why did the people in the synagogue of Nazareth want to kill Him (*Lk.* iv. 24–29)? Why did He say: " Think ye that I am come to bring peace on earth? I tell you, Nay; but rather division " (*Lk.* xii. 51)? Why did the Pharisees hate Him? Why did the Jewish religious leaders encompass His death? The answer to all these questions, and to others that could be put, is the same: Because our Lord did not accept the orthodox Judaism of His day, but did accept a form which was not orthodox—and which He perfected in his teaching; the Jews who were orthodox sought to kill Him because He " called God his own Father, making himself equal with God " (*Jn.* v. 18); but the form of Judaism which Christ accepted recognized the truth of this (see above, p. 158).

Everyone knows how much of our Lord's teaching dealt with the Kingdom of Heaven; this is the subject which is central in the Apocalyptic Literature; His familiarity with this literature and His acceptance of much of its teaching appear again and again in the Gospel records. That our Lord was not cognizant of the fact that this literature contained non-Jewish elements is unthinkable, nor can we suppose that He was unaware of their origin. Our Lord's teaching was *sui generis*; nobody would question that; and it differed in important respects from the apocalyptic form of Judaism, as well as from the orthodox form. But our Gospel records make it clear that He was more in sympathy with the teaching of the Apocalyptists than with that of the Pharisees, the representatives of orthodox Judaism. When, therefore, we find in writings belonging to the Apocalyptic Literature truths adumbrated which Christ accepted, we are justified in recognizing among the Apocalyptists instruments of divine revelation, in so far as they were able to apprehend those truths. Therefore we may

---

[1] This is denied by some authorities, but, we venture to believe, on insufficient grounds; see, e.g., *Mk.* i. 28, 39, *Lk.* iv. 14 ff., 44, xxiv. 6, cp. *Acts* ii. 7.

without hesitation say that in much of the teaching of our Lord there are gathered up uncut gems of partial truths handed down from various sources through untold generations; these He took and shaped—and, behold, the crown of the fullness of revelation which was with God from all time: " Jesus Christ the same yesterday, to-day, and for ever " !

CHAPTER XII

THE DOCTRINE OF SIN AND RETRIBUTION

BRIEF reference has been made in the chapter on the Law and the Oral Tradition to the doctrine of justification by works. That this played an unduly prominent part in Judaism is seen from much that is said about it in the New Testament. But it must be recognized that this doctrine did not preclude a very real apprehension of the existence of Sin and its evil results. How fully this exercised the minds of Seers and Sages is abundantly shown in their writings. That the dreadfulness of Sin lay, as the prophets had taught, in its being the cause of separation between the sinner and his God (cp. *Isa.* lix. 2), was fully realized by the religious teachers; hence the reiterated exhortations in their writings to men to refrain from sinful acts.

Obviously, the fact of the existence of Sin was a matter of vastly greater concern than speculations regarding its origin. Nevertheless, it will be well to begin by pointing out the different theories held to account for the existence of Sin.

I

THE ORIGIN OF SIN

It was inevitable that the conclusions arrived at regarding this should have differed; but their very variety shows how the subject must have been deeply pondered over by the Jewish religious teachers. A dualistic theory such as that taught in Persian theology was excluded, since this would, in effect, have denied monotheistic belief.[1] Other theories

[1] In one of the *Gathas* it is said: " In the beginning there were these two spirits, the Twins, who, according to their own words, are the Good and the Bad, in thought and word and action. And between these two the wise chose aright, but not so the foolish " (*Yasna* xxx. 3). These spirits are, respectively, Ahura-Mazda, the " Wise Lord ", and Angra-Mainyu, the " Evil Spirit ", later known as Ahriman.

appearing in the post-Biblical literature are as follows. In
certain passages the origin and prevalence of Sin are imputed
to Adam; thus, in *ii* (*iv*) *Esdras* vii. 118 the Seer says: " Oh
thou Adam, what hast thou done? For though it was thou
who sinned, the fall was not thine alone, but ours also who
are thy descendants! " Similarly in *ii Bar.* xxiii. 4 it is said
that " Adam sinned and death was decreed against those
who should be born "; and more fully in the same book,
lvi. 6: " For owing to his transgression untimely death came
into being, and grief was named, and anguish was prepared,
and pain was created, and trouble perfected. . . ." The
origin of Sin, but not its results, is also implied in *i Enoch*
xxxii. 6: " Then Raphael, the holy angel who was with me,
answered me, and said, This is the tree of wisdom, of which
thy father, old (in years) and thine aged mother, who were
before thee, ate, and they learned wisdom, and their eyes
were opened, and they knew that they were naked, and they
were driven out of the garden." These passages must be
balanced by what is said in *ii Bar.* liv. 15, 19: " For though
Adam first sinned, and brought untimely death upon all, yet
of those who were born from him each one of them hath
prepared for his own soul torment to come; and again, each
one of them hath chosen for himself glories to come. Adam
is, therefore, not the cause, save only of his own soul, but each
one of us has been the Adam of his own soul." Here again
the *origin* of Sin is ascribed to Adam. With the exception of
the first of the passages quoted, it is taught that, while Adam
was the first to sin, this did not involve hereditary sin in the
human race, though it was the cause of universal death. As
to the first passage quoted, *ii* (*iv*) *Esdras* vii. 118, its meaning
must be gained by what is said below on *ii* (*iv*) *Esdras* iii. 21, 22.

We have next the theory that the origin of Sin is to be
sought in Eve. In *ii Bar.* xlviii. 42 her name is coupled with
that of Adam; but this is quite exceptional. In the *Life of
Adam and Eve* xliv. 2–5 Adam puts the whole blame on Eve:
" And Adam said to Eve, What hast thou done? A great
plague hast thou brought upon us, transgression and sin for
all our generations; and this which thou hast done tell thy
children after my death, for those who arise from us shall toil
and fail, and they shall be wanting, and curse us, and say,

All evils have our parents brought upon us, who were at the beginning. When Eve heard these words she began to weep and moan." This theory regarding the origin of Sin must have been long current, for it occurs in *Ecclus*. xxv. 24: " From a woman did Sin originate, and because of her all must die." That this quaint idea should have found acceptance in the Christian Church must indeed cause surprise: " For Adam was first formed, then Eve; and Adam was not beguiled, but the woman, being beguiled, hath fallen into transgression " (*i Tim*. ii. 13, 14).

Another theory: fairly frequent is the attribution to fallen angels of the origin of Sin; in *i Enoch* xvi. 3, for example, Enoch is made to say to the angels (the " Watchers "): " Ye have been in heaven, but all the mysteries had not yet been revealed to you, and ye knew worthless things (i.e. mysteries),[1] and these in the hardness of your hearts ye have made known to women, and through these mysteries women and men work much evil on earth " (cp. ix. 6–9, x. 8, cvi. 13, 14). Elsewhere it is said of the demons, as the offspring of fallen angels, that they are the cause of Sin (*i Enoch* xv. 8, 9, 11, 12, lxix. 6 ff.).[2] In *Wisdom of Solomon* iii. 23, 24 the origin of Sin is attributed to the Devil: " Because God created man for incorruption, and in the likeness of his own proper being made he him; but by the envy of the Devil death entered into the world, and they that belong to him experience it (i.e. death)." Sin is not specifically mentioned here, but it is implied, Sin and death being inseparable.

In contrast to all these ideas we have the definite assertion that man, and man alone, is the cause of Sin: " I have sworn unto you, ye sinners, as a mountain hath not become a slave, and a hill doth not become the handmaid of a woman, even so sin hath not been sent upon the earth; but man of himself hath created it, and under a great curse shall they fall who commit it " (*ii Enoch* xcviii. 4, cp. *Tob*. iv. 5). An interesting passage in this connexion occurs in *Ecclus*. xv. 11 ff.; here the writer combats the argument, urged by some in his day, that as man is created by God, and is by nature prone to sin, he cannot help himself; if he sins it is the fault of the Almighty:

---

[1] The reference is to sexual intercourse, see ix. 8.
[2] See further on this below, p. 288.

M

" Say not, ' From God is my transgression '; for that which he hateth made he not. Say not, ' It is he that made me to stumble ', for there is no need of evil men. Evil and abomination doth the Lord hate, and he will not let it come nigh them that fear him. God created man from the beginning, and placed him in the hand of his *Yetzer*. . . . Poured out before thee are fire and water, stretch forth thine hand unto that which thou desirest. Life and death are before man, that which he desireth shall be given him " (cp. *James* i. 13–16). The mention of the term *Yetzer* here demands a few words of explanation, especially as it is directly connected with the subject of Sin. That it is spoken of by Ben-Sira shows that the thought which it expresses existed long before Christian times; so that although we do not meet with details of the more fully developed doctrine until we find these in the Rabbinical writings, it cannot be doubted that discussions on the subject had for long been in vogue. The word comes from the root meaning " to form ", or " frame ", in reference to what is formed or framed in the heart, i.e. the mind, thus, imagination, purpose, and the like. This may be either good or bad; hence the two kinds of *Yetzer*: the *Yetzer ha-ra*ʻ, " the evil Yetzer ", and the *Yetzer ha-tob*, " the good *Yetzer* ". Ben-Sira, it is true, seems to recognize only the former; the same applies also to the much later book *ii* (*iv*) *Esdras*, where the " evil heart ", and " the evil germ ", and " the grain of evil seed " are spoken of (iii. 20, 22, iv. 30, cp. vii. 92), all undoubtedly in reference to " the evil *Yetzer* ". On the other hand, we have this striking passage in the *Test. XII Patr.*, *Asher* i. 3–9: " Two ways hath God given to the sons of men, and two inclinations . . . for there are two ways of good and evil, and with these are the two inclinations in our breasts discriminating between them. Therefore if the soul take pleasure in the good inclination, all its actions are in righteousness; and if it sin it straightway repenteth. . . . But if it incline to the evil inclination, all its actions are in wickedness, and it driveth away the good, and cleaveth to the evil. . . ." The opening words of this passage would seem to suggest that since both inclinations are given to man from God, the origin of Sin, like that of righteousness, is due to the Almighty. This, of course, is not what the writer meant; for over and above the capacity to do right or wrong is the will of man, without which man would be an automaton. Again, in *ii (iv) Esdras* iii. 21, 22 there is also a reference to the two *Yetzers*, but the evil one is ascribed to Adam: " For the first Adam, clothing himself with the evil heart (= *Yetzer*), transgressed, and was overcome; and likewise also all who were born of him. Thus the infirmity was made permanent. The Law indeed was in the heart of the people, but together with the evil germ (= *Yetzer*); so what was good departed, and the evil remained." This is against orthodox Jewish teaching, according to which man by the act of his will can keep the Law and thus overcome evil. What lies behind such passages as these, and indeed behind the whole doctrine of the two *Yetzers*, is the thought of human free-will. Where it fails is in its inadequate conception of divine grace. But so far as the teaching of the origin of Sin is concerned we are brought back to the theory that this is to be sought in man, not in fallen angels. From all that has been said the great fact emerges that during the period with which we are specially dealing Sages and Seers were intensely imbued with the sense of Sin. This merits a little further illustration.

II

THE PREVALENCE OF SIN

This cannot be better set forth than by showing how insistently the need of repentance is enjoined. The Hebrew word for repentance, *Teshubah*, means literally a " turning ", i.e. turning from Sin to God, thus echoing again the prophetical dictum: " Your iniquities have separated between you and your God." This is brought out in the beautiful words of Tobit: " If ye turn to him with your whole heart and with your whole soul, to do truth before him, then will he turn unto you, and will not hide his face from you " (*Tob.* xiii. 6; see also iii. 3–5, *Judith* vii. 28, *i Bar.* i. 15 ff.). In the same way, Ben-Sira says: " To them that repent doth he grant a return, and comforteth them that lose hope. Turn unto the Lord, and forsake sins, supplicate before his face and lessen offence. Turn unto the Most High, and turn away from iniquity, and vehemently hate the abominable thing " (*Ecclus.* xvii. 24–26, cp. also v. 7, xviii. 21, xxi. 6). Forgiveness to the righteous for their sins when they repent is expressed in the *Psalms of Solomon* ix. 15: "Thou blessest the righteous, and dost not reprove them for the sins that they have committed; yea, thy goodness is upon them that sin, when they repent." But the most striking passage occurs in the *Prayer of Manasses*, verse 4: "Thou, O Lord, according to thy great goodness, hast promised repentance and forgiveness to them that have sinned against thee; and of thine infinite mercies hast appointed repentance unto sinners, that they may be saved. Thou, therefore, O Lord, that art the God of the just, hast not appointed repentance to the just, to Abraham, and Isaac, and Jacob, which have not sinned against thee; but thou hast appointed repentance unto me that am a sinner. . . ." The pronounced recognition of divine grace here is exceptional; but though human free-will receives more emphasis in Jewish theology than divine grace, this latter is by no means wanting. The Jewish character of the whole Prayer makes it certain that it is not a Christian composition. Its pre-Christian date is generally recognized. Then, once more, we have in *ii* (*iv*) *Esdras* vii. 48 this whole-hearted recognition of the prevalence of sin: "For an evil heart hath grown up in us which hath estranged us from God, and brought us into destruction; and hath made known to us the ways of death, and showed us the way of perdition, and removed us far from life; and that not a few only, but wellnigh all that have been created."

It is unnecessary to give further illustrations; what has been said will have shown how fully the wide prevalence of Sin was realized.

III

RETRIBUTION

This subject must be dealt with from two points of view. For the present we are concerned with the teaching that punishment for sin is meted out to the sinner in this life. All suffering, sickness, and calamity are the marks of divine retributive justice; such things, therefore, are the lot of the wicked. The righteous, on the other hand, enjoy prosperity.

Directly contradicted as this belief was by the experience of life, it was still persisted in. Nowhere is this more fully illustrated than in many of the later psalms, where unconvincing arguments are put forth to account for the prosperity of the wicked.[1] The protest against this belief which is the burden of the book of *Job* took long to come to fruition.

The traditional belief is expressed, for example, by Ben-Sira thus: " Who ever trusted in the Lord, and was put to shame? Or who did abide in his fear, and was forsaken? Or who called on him, and was overlooked? " (*Ecclus.* ii. 10, 11). On the other hand, in reference to the wicked: " Woe unto fearful hearts and faint hands, and to the sinner that goeth two ways. Woe unto the faint heart, because it believeth not; therefore it shall not be sheltered .' (ii. 12, 13). Again, in the *Psalms of Solomon* ix. 9 it is said: " He that doeth righteousness layeth up life for himself with the Lord; but he that doeth wrongly forfeiteth his life to destruction." Sometimes the belief is expressed that the sinner's punishment corresponds with the nature of the sin he has committed; thus, in *Jub.* iv. 31, in recording the death of Cain, it is said " his house fell upon him and he died in the midst of his house, and he was killed by its stones; for with a stone he had killed Abel and by a stone was he killed in righteous judgement ". For a similar principle, see *Ps.* cix. 17, 18. It occurs again in *ii Macc.* v. 9, 10, where the death of Antiochus Epiphanes is referred to: " He who had driven so many into exile, died himself in exile. . . . He who had flung out many a corpse to lie unburied had none to mourn for him, nor had he a funeral of any kind or place in the sepulchre of his fathers." With this *i Macc.* vi. 10–15 does not altogether agree, which is not surprising in the more accurate book. See also *ii Macc.* vii. 37, ix. 18, 28, xiii. 8. In the *Wisdom of Solomon* this idea of sin finding a corresponding punishment receives special emphasis; a good illustration occurs in xi. 15, 16, in reference to the Egyptians: " But in requital of the foolish imaginings of their unrighteousness, by which they were led astray, they worshipped senseless reptiles and wretched vermin, thou having sent upon them for vengeance a multitude of senseless animals, in order that they might know that by

---

[1] See the present writer's commentary on the *Psalms*, i. pp. 86 ff. (1939).

what things a man sinneth by these he is punished " (similarly in xv. 18–xvi. 1, and the whole of xvii–xviii. 4).

These illustrations will suffice, though others could be given. The teaching is, therefore, very definite that punishment for sin is meted out in this life. But with the developed belief in the After-life, taught especially by the Apocalyptists, retribution hereafter is set forth in great detail. This subject, however, belongs to our next chapter.

IV

THE OBLITERATION OF SIN

A brief preliminary reference to the Old Testament teaching is demanded because in the later literature there is silence on some points, for the simple reason that they were axiomatic.

Sin being that which separates from God, it can be obliterated only by reconciliation with God followed by forgiveness on His part. Therefore the means whereby to bring about reconciliation with God was that upon which thought and action centred.

Mention must be made first of some elements in the teaching of the Old Testament which are exceptional. There are some rare instances in which the intercession of a righteous man procures divine forgiveness for sinners. Thus, in *Gen*. xviii. 23–32 we read of Abraham's intercession for the people of Sodom; similarly, in the case of Lot, who intercedes for the city of Zoar (*Gen*. xix. 18–21). Again, there are the intercessions of Amos, who appeals to the Almighty on behalf of his people: " O Lord, Yahweh, forgive, I beseech thee; how shall Jacob stand? for he is small. Yahweh had compassion concerning this: It shall not be, saith Yahweh " (*Amos* vii. 2, 3, see also 5, 6). Then there is the very rare instance of vicarious suffering for the sins of others in *Isa*. liii. 4–6, 12: ". . . But he was wounded for our transgressions, he was bruised for our iniquities; the chastisement of our peace (i.e. which procured our peace) was upon him; and with his stripes we are healed . . ."; " for transgressors he made intercession." The foreshadowing of a great truth! Further, there are various passages in which it is taught that God of His mercy and love forgives freely; in *Hos*. vi. 1, for example, it is said: " Come, and let us return unto Yahweh; for he hath torn, but he will heal us; he hath smitten, but he will bind us up "; other passages of similar import are found in a number of the psalms.

It was necessary to draw attention to these three points because they contain the germs of eternal truth; but it cannot be too strongly emphasized that they are wholly exceptional. Normally, the teaching is that man, the sinner, must do something on his part whereby divine forgiveness of sin can be obtained; and what he does is to offer sacrifices. It is unnecessary to go into details here; but all sacrifices, whether involving the outpouring of blood, or not, effect reconciliation with God (cp. *Ezek.* xlv. 15, 17), i.e. they are the means of obtaining divine forgiveness. The term *le-kappēr*, " to effect atonement ", expresses the basic idea, and the sin-cleansing power of blood becomes very marked (see, e.g., *Lev.* iv. 5, 7, 16–18). The ritual of the Day of Atonement (*Lev.* xvi) represents the full development here. Ideally, it may be presumed, repentance, confession, and the resolution of amendment of life, were demanded (cp. *Prov.* xxviii. 13); but with the belief in the efficacy *per se* of sacrifice, it may well be doubted whether anything beyond the gift to the Deity was popularly regarded as necessary. In any case, sacrifices atoned for sin, and were thus the means of obliterating sins.

As is to be expected, the teaching in the later literature is in accordance with traditional belief and practice. One exception, it is true, occurs, viz. angelic intercession; but apart from *i Enoch* [1] this is very rare, and it is directly combated in *ii Enoch* liii. 1: " And now, my children, do not say, Our father stands before God, and prays for us (to be released) from sin; for there is no person there to help any man who has sinned." Otherwise there is again and again the reference to sacrifices commanded in the Law; and that their purpose is atonement for sins needs no insisting on. Ben-Sira makes frequent mention of the subject (e.g. vii. 31, 1–11, l. 5–15, and elsewhere). In *Jub.* vii. 3–5 it is said that sacrifices " make atonement "; and various details about sacrifices are given in *Test. XII Patr., Levi* ix. 7, 11–14. But

[1] E.g., ix. 3, xv. 2, xl. 6, see also *Test. XII Patr., Levi* iii. 5, 6, *ii Macc.* xv. 13, 14.

it is unnecessary to give further illustrations; a few references out of a large number are the following: *i Enoch* lxxxix. 50, *i Macc.* iv. 42–56, especially 53, *ii Enoch* xlv. 3, lix. 2, 3, lxi. 4, 5, lxvi. 2, *ii Bar.* lviii. 5, *Assumption of Moses*, iv. 8. As in the Old Testament, in all this literature it is taught that sacrifices make atonement for sins.

v

OUR LORD'S TEACHING ON SIN AND FORGIVENESS

Our purpose is not to deal here in any way exhaustively with this profoundly important subject; but only to point out how in some particulars the Jewish teaching formed a background recognized by our Lord, and to indicate, on the other hand, its inadequateness. As to the origin of Sin, it is not recorded that our Lord held any theory regarding this. But He implies that Sin is innate in man: " Woe unto the world because of occasions of stumbling; for it must needs be that the occasions come, but woe to that man through whom the occasion cometh! " (*Matth.* xviii. 7). But that there is an evil principle external to man is recognized by what is said in the account of the Temptation (*Matth.* iv. 1–11, *Lk.* iv. 1–13). The universality of sin among men is expressed, e.g., by the words: " Repent ye, for the Kingdom of Heaven hath drawn nigh " (*Matth.* iv. 17), which is of universal application. Once more, our Lord accepted the prophetical teaching that every sin is an act of rebellion against God (*Isa.* lix. 2), for this is implied, e.g., in his words: " If thou wouldest enter into life, keep the commandments " (*Matth.* xix. 17). But our Lord sets forth in another direction an element in the conception of Sin not hitherto held, in teaching that the lack of positive righteous acts constitutes sin; this seems to be brought out, e.g., in his words to the young man who claimed to have observed all the commandments: " One thing thou lackest yet; sell all that thou hast, and distribute unto the poor, and thou shalt have treasure in heaven; and come, follow me " (*Lk.* xviii. 22). Then, again, our Lord rejects the traditional teaching that sickness and infirmity are divine visitations owing to sin; thus, when asked in reference to the man born blind: " who did sin, this man, or his parents, that he should be born blind? " the answer is: " Neither did this man sin, nor his parents; but that the works of God should be made manifest in him " (*Jn.* ix. 2, 3). We recall also the case of Lazarus, a beggar and full of sores, who was carried by the angels into Abraham's bosom, i.e. Paradise (*Lk.* xvi. 20–22). But the most notable and fundamental difference in the teaching of our Lord from that of traditional Judaism was that of the means of the obliteration of sin. He tolerated the temporary continuance of the sacrificial system— that we can understand, for therein centred the traditional conception of the worship of God—but that the offering of sacrifices could in any way atone for sin was wholly foreign to his teaching. The blotting out of sins demanded something very different from that. It will suffice to recall such sayings as these: " The Son of Man hath power on earth to forgive sins " (*Matth.* ix. 10, *Lk.* v. 24); " This is my blood of the new covenant which is shed for many unto remission of sins " (*Matth.* xxvi. 28). It is true that the words " unto remission of sins " occur only in *Matth.*, but as Allen well points out, " Matthew, by adding ' unto remission of sins ', shows that he understood the covenant to be a covenant between God and the many by which remission of sins was secured to them, the sign of this covenanted forgiveness being the shed blood." [1]

We purposely refrain from dealing with St. Paul's teaching on this subject because of his pronounced Jewish standpoint; for the origin of Sin see *Rom.* v. 12–14; the relation between the Law and Sin is dealt with, e.g., in *Rom.* vii. 7–14, and elsewhere. Then he frames a theory of his own about " flesh " being that in which Sin is inherent (*Rom.* viii. 3), as though man being in the flesh, can do no other than sin. With these and other matters we need not concern ourselves here; but whatever St. Paul's ideas on the subject were, he comes back to the basic truth, e.g., *Rom.* v. 6: " For while we were yet weak, in due season Christ died for the ungodly ", see also iv. 25, *Gal.* i. 4, and elsewhere.

[1] *A Critical and Exegetical Commentary on the Gospel according to St. Matthew,* p. 276 (1907).

CHAPTER XIII

BELIEF IN IMMORTALITY: THE OLD TESTAMENT

EVERYONE with knowledge of the facts will endorse the words of J. G. Frazer, in writing: " The question of whether our conscious personality survives after death has been answered by almost all races of men in the affirmative. On this point sceptical or agnostic peoples are nearly, if not wholly, unknown. Accordingly, if abstract truth could be determined, like the gravest issues of national policy, by a show of hands, or a counting of heads, the doctrine of human immortality, or at least of life after death, would deserve to rank among the most firmly established of truths; for were the question to be put to the vote of the whole of mankind, there can be no doubt that the ayes would have it by an overwhelming majority." [1] These words apply with special force to the belief held in ancient Egypt, and, what concerns us more nearly, to that of all branches of the Semitic race. Did space permit, it would have been of great interest to set forth the beliefs regarding the After-life held by the ancient Babylonians, Syrians, and Arabs; for of all of these much information is available, and it throws a great deal of light on what we read in the Old Testament. Our main concern is, however, with the beliefs of later times, namely, with those of the Jews during the Greek Period. Nevertheless, a brief reference to Old Testament teaching is demanded because this forms the background of all that was held on the subject in subsequent times. [2]

We will begin, then, with the earliest stage of belief, which centres in conceptions about the departed. The first matter to be dealt with here is that of consulting the dead, for this obviously presupposes the continued conscious life of the departed hereafter. Most of the references in the Old Testament to this practice consist of prohibitions, and belong to the later literature; they witness therefore to its continued existence.

[1] *The Belief in Immortality*, i. 33 (1913).
[2] The whole subject is dealt with in detail in the present writer's *Immortality and the Unseen World* (1921).

The earliest reference to it, however, is fairly full, and is not a prohibition.   It is contained in *i Sam.* xxviii. 3–25, the narrative about Saul and the witch of Endor.   It is an important illustration of the belief of the early Israelites concerning the departed; space does not permit of our dealing with the details of the narrative; but it is a clear indication of Israelite belief, viz. the departed continue to live in some way after death; they remember; they foresee; they can leave whatever place it is in which they abide; and they can return to this world, in a certain sense.   Further evidence of belief in the continued life hereafter of the departed is afforded by the practice of Ancestor-worship, and the cult of the dead; while there are distinct indications in the Old Testament that both were in vogue among the Israelites, they are but scanty, because, owing to later belief, references to these things were avoided, or in some respects altered.

The analogies of Babylonian and ancient Arab belief, and especially the belief and practice in Palestine at the present day among the Bedouin, make it absolutely certain that Ancestor-worship and the cult of the dead played an important part in the life of the ancient Hebrews.   But the most striking evidence that we have regarding this earliest stage of Hebrew belief in the After-life is the archæological; for this gives us in concrete, tangible form signs of the relations between the living and the dead in ancient Israel, thus witnessing in the most conclusive manner possible to the belief in life hereafter. Here again space forbids our giving many details; but the evidence consists mainly in the presence of cups, bowls, platters of various kinds, necklaces, jewelry, weapons, etc., in graves which have been opened; all these things were intended for use in the next world by those who had departed from this one; they were placed by the side of the body to be used in its new life just as it had used them in this.   In one case the hands of the dead body had been placed in a dish; in another there was a three-legged stone fire-dish for cooking placed near the body.   Very gruesome were the remains of a sacrifice to the dead discovered in a burial-cave in Gezer; it was a case of human sacrifice.[1]   When we ask how the people of

---

[1] See the *Quarterly Statement* of the Palestine Exploration Fund, for 1902 and onwards.

those days conceived of the dead partaking of food, and so on, the answer is simple: they thought of them as they thought of themselves; just as on this earth they required food and drink and clothing and trinkets, so in the life hereafter they would require the same. If it be asked, further, why they did not spend time by the side of the departed to see them partake of what had been prepared for them, the answer is equally simple: they did—but experience taught them that the dead would not eat or drink or move, if watched! In those early days, and doubtless in very much later days, too, there were family tombs in which it was believed that the family gathered together in the After-life, hence the expressions occurring in the Old Testament: "being gathered to the fathers", and "sleeping with the fathers".

Then there is the subject of the *Rephaim*, which offers further evidence of the vivid belief of the Hebrews in the After-life. This is a term applied to the departed; it occurs in several passages (e.g. *Isa.* xiv. 9, 10, xxvi. 14), also on Phœnician inscriptions,[1] as a name of the departed; strange as it may at first appear, an ancient race of giants are similarly named, (e.g. *Gen.* xiv. 5, *Deut.* ii. 20, 21, *Josh.* xvii. 15); but with the connexion between the two we cannot concern ourselves here.[2] Of more importance, as further illustrating belief in the activity of the departed, is the meaning of the name. On the basis of what is said in *Isa.* xiv. 9, 10, it has been held that the word *Rephaim* comes from the root *raphah*, "to be weak", and thus the "weak ones". But in view of what is said about them, and about the departed in general, in other passages, such a term applied to them would be very inappropriate. Far more probable is Lagrange's contention that the name comes from the somewhat similar root *rapha'*, "to heal", and thus the "healers"; he says: "If one bears in mind the close ties which united divination and therapeuty among the ancients, and ʌhat men sought from the gods, above all things, the revelation of the remedies required, one will not be disinclined

---

[1] G. A. Cooke, *A Text-book of North Semitic Inscriptions*, pp. 26, 30 (1903). The name occurs in the Ras Shamra poems, where they appear as the servants of Baal under a leader named Rapha-baal, cp. the name of the angel Raphael in *Tob.* xii. 15.
[2] It is dealt with in the present writer's *Immortality* . . ., pp. 73 f.

to regard the *Rephaim* as the ' healers ' *par excellence*, an extension of the ἥρως 'ιατρός of Athens." [1]

What has so far been said represents the first stage of belief in Immortality, or at any rate in life hereafter, among the Hebrews; and it must reach back to a time of immemorial antiquity. But there was much in connexion with this ancient belief which was quite incompatible with the worship of Yahweh as taught by Moses; indeed, did we not know the tenacity with which traditional beliefs and customs were clung to, we might well wonder at the long period which elapsed between the beginning of the worship of Yahweh among the Hebrews and the first attempts which were made to eradicate those traditional beliefs. The evidence goes to show that these attempts were first made in the ninth or eighth century with the advent of the great prophets. These attempts were necessitated, as we have said, because those old-world beliefs were found to be incompatible with the worship of Yahweh; and there is a passage which gives the fundamental reason why this was so; that passage is *Isa*. viii. 19, which is held, no doubt rightly, to be a later insertion; but that only shows how the ancient beliefs and practices persisted; it runs: " And when they shall say unto you, Seek unto them that have familiar spirits, and unto the wizards that chirp and mutter; should not a people seek unto their God? on behalf of the living should they seek unto the dead? " Slightly corrupt as the Hebrew text of this passage is, the general sense is clear enough: recourse was had to the departed instead of to God. Whatever truth there was in the old belief regarding the reality of life hereafter, this putting of the departed in the place of God was sufficient to condemn it. Hence arose the efforts of the religious leaders, urged on, as we may well believe, by the prophets, to eradicate the old beliefs, and to substitute for them the *Sheôl* doctrine. That brings us to the second stage of belief in the After-life. There is a good deal that could be said about this *Sheôl* doctrine, did space permit. But one or two points must be mentioned. In the pre-exilic literature the references to *Sheôl* are very scanty; its existence is taken for granted, which

[1] *Études sur les religions Sémitiques*, p. 273 (1905). This derivation is confirmed by the Ras Shamra texts, see Lods, in *Comptes Rendus de l'Académie des Inscriptions et Belles Lettres*, p. 639 (1939).

seems to show that by the time the pre-exilic books were written the official *Sheôl* doctrine had been put forth; though, as we know, the old beliefs continued to be held. The passages are only about a dozen in number, and they do not tell us much about the future state. It is mostly in the later literature that conceptions about *Sheôl* occur: it is a land of darkness and dust [1] (*Job* x. 21, 22, xvii. 16, xx. 11, xxi. 26; *Ps.* xxx. 10 [9]); it is far below in the earth (*Job* xi. 8, xxvi. 5, cp. *Deut.* xxxii. 22; *Ps.* lxxxvi. 13, lxxxviii. 7 [6]); there is no return from it (*Job* x. 7; *Prov.* ii. 19); it is described as a city with gates (*Isa.* xxxviii. 10; *Ps.* ix. 13 [14], cvii. 8; *Job* xxxviii. 17); and elsewhere it is compared with a monster, all-devouring (*Isa.* v. 14, cp. *Hab.* ii. 5; *Prov.* xxvii. 20, xxx. 15, 16); and there is the farthest distance between *Sheôl* and Heaven (*Isa.* vii. 11; *Amos* ix. 2; *Ps.* cxxxix. 8). In some of these passages, and certain others, there are indications of development in the *Sheôl* doctrine; with these we cannot deal now.

But the whole conception is lugubrious, and offers nothing but a hopeless outlook.

As already pointed out, the *Sheôl* belief was taught first, in all probability, in about the ninth or eighth century among the Hebrews as a more or less official doctrine; it continued so well into the Greek Period, when a great development took place regarding belief in the Future Life—above all, belief in the resurrection. Now it cannot be too strongly insisted on that the stages of belief regarding the life hereafter cannot be divided off into, as it were, water-tight compartments. The earliest stages of belief continued to be held by many, not only through the whole period during which the official *Sheôl* doctrine was taught, and in spite of it, and not only after the fully developed Jewish belief in the resurrection had been put forth, but it exists to some extent even at the present day among the Syrians and Arabs.[2] The *Sheôl* belief, again, continued long after a far more developed belief had become dominant. On the other hand, there are indications in certain Old Testament passages that even prior to the Greek Period—or in its

---

[1] Cp. the Babylonian conception of *Sheôl* as portrayed in " The Descent of Ishtar "; it is spoken of as " the land without return . . . the house of darkness . . . where dust is their food . . . where dust is spread on door and bolt ".

[2] See Curtiss, *Primitive Semitic Religion To-day*, passim (1902).

earliest beginnings—a developed belief in the future life is to
be discerned. One or two other passages belong to the later
part of this period; but as we are dealing at present with the
Old Testament, we shall refer to all these passages, irrespective
of date, as, in any case, they belong to the Greek Period.

It will not be questioned that a necessary condition for a
developed belief regarding the life hereafter is a deeper apprehension of the nature and personality of God. Of special importance in the present connexion is the recognition of the truth
of the divine omnipresence. This conception of the Almighty
is not met with in the pre-exilic literature; [1] but it occurs in
one of the later psalms belonging to the Greek Period; in
Ps. cxxxix. 7–12 it is said: " Whither shall I go from thy spirit,
or whither shall I flee from thy presence? If I ascend up into
heaven, thou art there; if I make my bed in Sheôl, behold,
thou art there. . . ." In the earlier belief there was no such
thought as that of the presence of God's spirit among the
departed in *Sheôl*; that this idea of His presence should be
contemplated was the necessary first step towards the thought
of God being interested in departed spirits. The belief in
God's omnipresence occurs also in *Job* xxvi, especially (for our
present point of view) verses 5, 6: "The Rephaim tremble
beneath the waters and the inhabitants thereof; Sheôl is
naked before him, and 'Abaddôn hath no covering (from him)";
'Abaddôn, lit. "destruction", is a synonym for *Sheôl*. The whole
chapter must be read to see that the divine omnipresence is its
subject (cp. also *Job* xi. 7–9).

We turn next to a passage which demands some more detailed
examination; it is *Ps.* lxxiii; it is a long psalm, but need not
be quoted in full; we will give the salient passages. In conscious innocence the psalmist says (verse 2): " And as for me,
my feet had almost slipped, my steps had wellnigh stumbled ";
in spite of his conviction that he is righteous, he sees that
misfortune has overtaken him; then he goes on to contrast his
sorry plight with the much more fortunate lot of the wicked
(verses 3–5): " For I am envious at the arrogant, when I see
the prosperity of the wicked; for they have no worries, but
are perfect and settled in their strength; they are not in trouble
as other men are, neither are they plagued like others." The

---

[1] In *Amos* ix. 2, *Isa.* vii. 12, the divine omnipresence is not contemplated.

wicked and their ways are then described up to the end of verse 12, concluding with the words: " Behold these are the wicked, and being always at ease, they increase in wealth." Upon this follows a hypothetical statement; that is to say, the psalmist, for the purpose of his argument, *assumes* a wrong attitude; he says: " Surely in vain have I cleansed my heart, and washed my hands in innocency! For all day long have I been plagued, and chastened every morning." And then he makes it quite clear that this attitude has been taken up only for argument's sake; for he goes on: " If I had said, I will speak thus, behold, I should have dealt untruly with the generation of thy children." And he proceeds to describe the utter destruction of the wicked at their latter end, while in regard to himself, who has sought to lead a godly life, he says (*vv.* 23–25): " Nevertheless, *I* am continually with thee; thou holdest me by my right hand; thou guidest me by thy counsel; and afterward thou wilt take me to glory. Whom have I in heaven but thee? And having thee (i.e. being with thee), I desire nought else on earth." The fuller belief in this beautiful passage is the more striking in that the thought-development manifests itself in three directions: first, regarding the belief in God; for it will have been seen at once that God's relationship to man is apprehended in a far fuller way than in earlier days; it is realized that His power and activity among men are not restricted to this earth, as taught in the old *Sheôl* belief; but that His interest in man is just as great in the Hereafter as in this life; then, as to the belief concerning the future life, the passage expresses the conviction that it is a glorious life, inasmuch as in the Hereafter God is man's portion for ever. And finally, the psalmist is brought to understand that the solution of the perplexities, and of what seemed to be the incongruities and inconsistencies of the divine rule on earth, is to be seen in the reward laid up for the righteous in the world to come.[1]

Our next passage is *Isa.* xxvi. 19. It is necessary to point out here that this passage, which is merely a fragment, is one of the very latest in the Old Testament, belonging almost certainly to the end of the second century B.C., somewhere within

---

[1] Other passages in the *Psalms* which are held by some commentators to present a developed belief in the future life are: xvi. 10, 11; xlix. 15 (Hebr. 16); cxviii. 17; but this is very doubtful; they are quite susceptible of a different interpretation.

the period 113–105 B.C.—we cannot here go into the reasons
justifying this statement, but it is the conviction of most modern
commentators. For our present purpose, however, the exact
date is not of importance as, in any case, the passage comes
within the Greek period. The Hebrew text of the passage is
corrupt; it is ungrammatical, and differs in part from the
Septuagint. This, however, is again not of great consequence,
because there is no shadow of doubt about the main sense of the
passage. We will give, first, the rendering of the Revised
Version, and then the translation of the emended Hebrew text:
" Thy dead shall live; my dead bodies shall arise. Awake and
sing, ye that dwell in the dust; for thy dew is as the dew of
herbs, and the earth shall cast forth the dead." The emenda-
tions of the corrupt Hebrew text are fairly obvious, so that the
following translation may be regarded as reliable: " Thy dead
men shall arise; the inhabitants of the dust shall awake, and
shout for joy; for a dew of lights is thy dew, and the earth shall
bring forth *Rephaim*." The first thing to note here is that belief
in the resurrection of the dead is spoken of without a word of
explanation, which proves that this belief was familiar and had,
therefore, been long in existence. And the second point to
note is that there is here a mixing-up of very old-world
conceptions with an advanced belief regarding the After-life.
That is an interesting illustration of what has already been
pointed out, that stages of belief cannot be divided off into
water-tight compartments, as the older stages always overlap
into the more advanced; this passage sets forth that fact very
strikingly. To explain now what the passage means: " Thy
dead men ", refers to the Jewish martyrs who had laid down
their lives for their faith; that does not, of course, mean that
others who were not martyrs would not rise too. An interesting
subsidiary point is that after the words " Thy dead men " the
Targum adds " the bones of their corpses ", implying that the
flesh had gone to corruption, and that the bones were the
nucleus of the resurrection body; that is the remnant of a very
antique idea regarding the durability of the human bones and
their ultimate function; it is possible that the quaint idea
contributed in its way to the *formulation* of the belief in the
resurrection of the body; nearly a century earlier Ben-Sira,
who did not, apparently, believe in the resurrection, could yet

N

say, in commemorating the Judges of old: " May their bones flourish again out of their place " (*Ecclus*. xlvi. 12), and similarly of the Twelve Prophets: " May their bones sprout beneath them " (*Ecclus*. xlix. 10). Whether or not Ben-Sira had in his mind the remarkable vision of the dry bones that became alive, in *Ezek*. xxxvii. 1–14, one cannot say; but it may well be that the prophetic vision played a part in the development of Jewish ideas of the resurrection. The chapter in question clearly deals with national restitution, but it describes this in terms of the revivification of dead individuals. Though the prophet was not thinking of the resurrection of dead individuals, he must by this vision have familiarized men with such a conception. But to return to our *Isaiah* passage; it goes on to say: " the inhabitants of the dust shall awake "; there we have the echo of the *Sheôl* belief, according to which the departed lie in dust (cp. the expressions " they that go down to the dust ", and " the dust of death ", *Ps*. xxii. 15, 29 (Hebr. 16, 30)). Finally, there are the curious words: " a dew of lights is thy dew, and the earth shall bring forth *Rephaim* "; this means that just as the dew at nights comes down to refresh and give renewed life to the vegetation of the soil, so a heavenly dew descends to re-animate the bodies of the dead lying in the earth; it is a " dew of lights " because it comes down from the heavenly spheres which are illuminated by the stars. As a result of this " dew " the earth " brings forth ", just as by means of ordinary dew the soil brings forth vegetation; only in this case the earth begets *Rephaim*, i.e. departed spirits.

The whole passage is of extreme interest; the intensely materialistic ideas show that in spite of real advance of conception men were still far from envisaging the spiritual character of a risen body; not that that is to be wondered at.

We deal, finally, with the only other passage in the Old Testament which comes into consideration: *Dan*. xii. 2; it runs: " And many of them that sleep in the dust of the earth shall awake, some to everlasting life, and some to everlasting rejection." Here, too, it will be seen that we have the idea of the body abiding in the dust of the earth until the Resurrection. But what is particularly striking about this passage is that it envisages the resurrection of the wicked as well as of the righteous.

The reason why we have devoted more attention to the Old Testament in dealing with the subject of Immortality than has been the case with other subjects will have been evident. Indeed, this persistence of the earlier ideas through the ages will involve reference in the next chapter to one or two passages already considered.   Such repetition cannot, however, well be avoided.

We turn next to consider the belief in Immortality as this appears in the Apocalyptic Literature.

CHAPTER XIV

BELIEF IN IMMORTALITY: THE APOCALYPTIC LITERATURE

IN the Apocalyptic Literature the whole great subject of Immortality is seen to have assumed the form of a completed system of beliefs. It differs in this respect from the isolated passages which refer to the After-life in the Old Testament. Individual Apocalyptists, it is true, differ in various particulars from one another; but this does not affect the completeness of the picture presented.

In view of the largeness of the material at our disposal, it will be readily understood that we can do no more here than offer a general conspexus of the mass of detail contained in this literature. In order to present the beliefs set forth in a clear and simple form, we shall discuss the subjects under the following heads: The Judgement, the Resurrection and the nature of the risen body, Heaven, Hell; concluding with a final section on the teaching of the New Testament; incidental references to an intermediate state between death and resurrection will also be noted.

I

THE JUDGEMENT

The thought of a Judgement at the end of the present world-order is directed in the first instance, as we have seen, against the enemies of the people of Israel; e.g. *Joel* iii. 12: " Let the nations bestir themselves, and come up to the valley of Jehosha-phat; for there will I sit to judge all the nations round about." But this soon becomes developed, and in the Apocalyptic Literature a world-judgement, not only a judgement of the enemies of Israel, is that which is usually presented. In a few cases an individual note seems to be struck; thus, in a book of late date, but one which echoes earlier thought, we have such a passage as this: " And concerning death the teaching is: when the decisive decree hath gone forth from the Most High that the man should die, as the soul parteth from the body that it may return to him who gave it, to adore the glory of the Most High first of all . . ." (ii (iv) Edsras vii. 78; the individual is here first spoken of, the sequel envisages the judgement of the wicked and the righteous in general. Something similar is found in Persian belief: " In that assembly every one sees his own good deeds and his own evil deeds; and then, in that assembly, a wicked man becomes as conspicuous as a white sheep among those which are black " (Bund. xxx. 10); in Yasna xlviii it is said that the good man's dwelling-place shall be in the house of Ahura. But as a rule the individual is lost in the great mass. One of the most striking accounts of the Judgement occurs in i Enoch i. 1-9, part of which may be quoted: " The Holy Great One will come forth from his dwelling, and the eternal God will tread upon the earth, even on Mount Sinai, and appear in the strength of his might from the heaven of the heavens. . . . And the earth shall be wholly rent in sunder, and all that is upon the earth shall perish, and there shall be a judgement upon all men. But with the righteous he will make peace, and will protect the elect, and mercy shall be on them . . . . And behold He cometh with ten thousands of his holy ones to execute judgement upon all, and to destroy all the ungodly, and to convict all flesh of all the works of ungodliness which they have ungodly committed, and all the hard things which ungodly sinners have spoken against him."

Many other illustrations could be given from the apocalyptic writings; we shall offer but one other, which for vividness and terseness of expression is unsurpassed: " And the Most High shall be revealed upon the throne of judgement; and then cometh the End, and compassion shall pass away, and long-suffering be withdrawn. But judgement alone shall remain, truth shall stand, and faithfulness triumph. Then shall recompense follow, and the reward be made manifest. Deeds of righteousness shall awake, and deeds of iniquity shall not sleep. And then shall the pit of torment appear, and over against it the place of refreshment; the furnace of Gehenna shall be made manifest, and over against it the Paradise of delight " (*ii* (*iv*) *Esdras* vii. 33–36). Not only men, but also the angels shall appear before the Judgement-seat: " There shall be the great eternal Judgement, in the which he will execute vengeance amongst the angels " (*i Enoch* xci. 15, cp. xc. 24, and often elsewhere). Frequently mention is made of the books wherein are recorded the good and evil deeds of men: " In those days I saw the Head of Days when he seated himself upon the throne of his glory, and the books of the living were opened before him . . ." (*i Enoch* xlvii. 3, cp. *Dan.* vii. 10, *Asc. of Isa.* ix. 21–23, *ii Bar.* xxiv. 1).

It is, of course, the Almighty Who is Judge in that day, but it must be noted that sometimes the Messiah appears as deputed to fulfil this function; thus in *i Enoch* lxi. 8 it is said: " And the Lord of Spirits placed the Elect One on the throne of his glory; and he shall judge all the works of the holy above in the heaven, and in the balance shall their deeds be weighed " (see also xlv. 3, lxii. 2–5, lxix. 27–29, *Apoc. of Baruch* lxxii. 2). See, further, p. 157.

II

THE RESURRECTION

As has already been pointed out, the conceptions of the Apocalyptists concerning the life hereafter differ in certain directions. This applies to what we are now about to consider. There is, of course, general agreement as to the closest connexion between the Judgement and the Resurrection; that ethical conception is not specifically Jewish, but was taken over by the Apocalyptists; they differ, however, as to which precedes the other. In *i Enoch* xxii. 3, 4 it is said: " These hollow places have been created for this very purpose, that the spirits of the souls of the dead should assemble therein, yea, that all the souls of the children of men should assemble here. And these places have been made to receive them till the day of their judgement, and till their appointed period,—till the great judgement cometh upon them." Some of these " hollow places " are for the righteous, others for the wicked. Here, therefore, there is an intermediate state between death and the Judgement; the Resurrection is not yet mentioned; so presumably it occurs after the Judgement. In *Dan.* xii. 2, 3 it is different; an intermediate state is not mentioned, the dead abide in their graves until the Resurrection, after which the Judgement takes place: " And many of them that sleep in the land of dust shall awake, some to everlasting life, and some to everlasting rejection . . ."; clearly the final destiny here, as decided by the Judgement, refers to the risen. Then, further, we read in the *Test. XII Patr., Benj.* x. 5–9, again a slightly different account, for there is no mention of an intermediate state after death, as in the *Daniel* passage, but perhaps that state may be taken for granted; at any rate, it is simply said: " Keep the commandments of God, until the Lord shall reveal his salvation to all Gentiles. . . . Then shall we also rise, each one (i.e. of the patriarchs) over our tribe, worshipping the King of heaven. Then also all men shall rise, some unto glory and some unto shame. And the Lord shall judge Israel first, for their unrighteousness. And then shall he judge all the Gentiles." So that here again the Resurrection precedes the Judgement. A fuller account appears in *ii (iv) Esdras* vii. 32–36; here three places seem to be distinguished in which the dead abide until the Resurrection: " And the earth shall restore those that are asleep in her; and so shall the dust (i.e. *Sheôl*) those that dwell therein in silence; and the secret places (cp. the " hollow places " in *i Enoch* xxii. 3) shall deliver those souls that are committed unto them. And the Most High shall be revealed upon the seat of Judgement, and the end shall come. . . ." These few passages represent many others; but they are as important as any. The normal sequence is thus: Death, Intermediate state (though this is not always mentioned), Resurrection, Judgement.

This would seem to imply that all men, good and bad, partake of the Resurrection; but this is by no means always taught. In the *Enoch* passage just quoted (xxii. 3 ff.) it is said (*v.* 13) that the wicked will not rise, but that they will be left in the " hollow places ". What happens to them there is that they will be in " great pain till the great day of judgement and punishment and torment ", and that they shall be bound there for ever " (*v.* 11). In *ii (iv) Esdras* vii. 32 ff., on the other hand, all, both good and bad, will rise, after which will come the Judgement. Then it is said further, as we have seen, that the places of torment, and bliss, will appear. Again, in *i Enoch* xci. 9, 10, it is taught that only the righteous will rise; the heathen, it is said, " shall perish in wrath and grievous judgement for ever "; but " the righteous shall arise from their sleep, and wisdom shall arise, and be given unto them ". So, too, in the *Psalms of Solomon* iii. 13–16, it is said of the wicked man: " He falleth—very grievous is his fall—and riseth no more; the destruction of the sinner is for ever. . . . This is their portion for ever. But they that fear the Lord shall rise to life eternal; and their life shall be in the light of the Lord, and shall come to an end no more." On this subject, too, many passages could be quoted; it is unnecessary, for the few which have been given illustrate the teaching of the whole literature. It may be added that, according to Persian belief, the Resurrection is general: " All men rise, both the righteous and the ungodly; every human creature will rise on the spot on which his life left him " (*Bund.* xxx. 7).

Finally, there is the question of the nature of the risen body. Here again, as we should naturally expect, diversity of belief is expressed. In one of the earliest portions of *i Enoch* (xii–xxxvi) it is taught that both the spirit and the body rise; but they rise to an earthly Messianic Kingdom which will last for ever. Belief in the resurrection of the spirit, pure and simple, however, occurs in the later part of this book; it is expressed, for example, in *i Enoch* ciii. 4 and 8: " And the spirits of you who have died in righteousness shall live and rejoice; and their spirits shall not perish, nor their memorial from before the face of the Great One." Similarly of the wicked it is said: " And into darkness and chains and a burning flame where there is grievous judgement shall your spirits enter." The same belief occurs in the words: ". . . when they shall be separated from the corruptible vessel ", i.e. the body (*ii* (*iv*) *Esdras* vii. 88). But in the " Similitudes " of *i Enoch* (xxxvii–lxxi) there seems to be the belief in a spiritual body, for it is said that the righteous will be clothed with " garments of glory and these shall be your garments of life from the Lord of Spirits " (lxii. 16). In the *Ascension of Isaiah* ix. 9, again, it is said: " And there I saw Enoch and all who were with him, stripped of the garments of flesh, and I saw them in their garments of the upper world, and they were like angels standing there in great glory " (see also *ii Enoch* xx. 8). It is interesting to note that according to Persian belief, it is the body that rises, no mention being made of the spirit: " When, then, the whole bodily world receives back its bodies and form, there will be but one grade " (*Bund.* xxx. 8), i.e. there will be no distinction of classes.

These divergent views are of deep interest, showing, as they do, the ardent seeking for truth on the part of good and earnest-minded men, to which they could attain in part only.

III

HEAVEN

Here it must be recognized at the outset that two conceptions have been combined; not that they are by any means always combined in the Apocalyptic Literature; but that is because the individual writers utilized different elements in the traditions, whether indigenous or extraneous, in a somewhat haphazard manner; in the final issue, however, they are combined. These two conceptions are what we designate as Paradise and Heaven. The former is in the first instance conceived of as situated somewhere on this earth (the word means an enclosed space, a garden); the latter lies far away, above the skies. Ultimately Paradise becomes transferred to the heavenly spheres, and is thought of as a department of Heaven. Thus, the two conceptions of Heaven and Paradise are finally combined. We must consider each a little further. It was natural enough that the dwelling-place of the Almighty, i.e. a special department of Heaven, should have been conceived of as one in which the divine presence abode alone, unapproachable. One of the most vivid descriptions of this is given in *i Enoch* xiv. 17–23; here the Seer is accorded, in vision, a sight of God's dwelling-place: " Its floor was of fire, and above it were lightnings and the path of the stars, and its roof also was flaming fire. And I looked, and saw therein a lofty throne; its appearance was as crystal, and the wheels thereof as the shining sun; and there was the vision of the cherubim. And from underneath the throne came streams of flaming fire, so that I could not look thereon. And the Great Glory (i.e. the Almighty) sat thereon, and his raiment shone more brightly than the sun, and was whiter than any snow. None of the angels could enter or could behold his face by reason of the magnificence and glory, and no flesh could behold him. The flaming fire was round about him, and a great fire stood before him, and none around could draw nigh him. Ten thousand times ten thousand stood before him (i.e. outside of the divine dwelling-place), yet did he need no counsellor. And the most holy ones who were nigh to him did not leave by night nor depart from him." The incongruities here are probably due, not to the Seer, but to faulty transmission. Elsewhere it is said, in reference to the dwelling-place of the Almighty, that "there is no need of any light other than that of the unspeakable splendour from the light of thy countenance" (*Apoc. of Abraham* xvii). Sometimes Heaven is thought of as a great building with windows and portals; its length and height none can discern; in it are stored up the stars, the rain, and the dew (*i Enoch* xxxiii. 3, etc., *ii (iv) Esdras* iii. 19); and the Almighty has his own temple there (*Test. XII Patr., Levi.* v. 1; *i Enoch* lxxi. 5). In various passages different heavens are spoken of, seven altogether, and it is in the highest of them that the "Great Glory" dwells, "far above all holiness" (*Test. XII Patr., Levi* ii. 7–iii. 8; *Apoc. of Abraham* xix.; *Ascension of Isaiah* vi. 13, vii. 7 ff., viii. 1 ff., 6 ff.; *ii Enoch* xi. 1–5, xix). The idea of the seven heavens may originally have come from Babylonia; in the ancient Persian Scriptures three heavens are spoken of (*Vend.* vii. 52). This idea of a multiplicity of the heavens was taken up by the Rabbis and much developed (e.g. in the Midrash *Bereshith Rabba*, Parasha 1, lxviii). Various other details about the heavens and their attractiveness, often of a materialistic character, occur in the Apocalyptic Literature; there is every reason to believe that Persian influence is to be discerned in these; it is unnecessary to deal with them here, for it cannot be said that they are of a very edifying character.

Coming now to consider what is said about Paradise, it is necessary to refer first to one or two Old Testament passages. It is there called the "Garden of God" as well as the "Garden of Eden". The belief was widespread that somewhere on earth, but far, far away, there was a wonderful garden in which God was wont to walk; the first man lived in it, but was expelled; since then no man has seen it; but the view of it was granted later to the Apocalyptists in vision. In *Gen.* xiii. 10 it is spoken of as "the garden of Yahweh", and in *Isa.* li. 3 it is

said: " For Yahweh hath comforted Zion; he hath comforted
all her waste places, and hath made her wilderness like Eden,
and her desert like the garden of Yahweh . . .", the two are,
of course, synonymous; cp. also *Joel* ii. 3. But it is in the book
of *Ezekiel* that the most interesting passage occurs; according
to *Ezek.* xxviii. 12 ff., the holy garden of God lies high up on a
mountain where the anointed cherubim walk in the midst of
stones of fire—probably the stars are meant. Clearly some
old-world idea, of Babylonian origin, lies behind this. Then,
when we come to the Apocalyptic Literature we find that this
garden has become the abode of the righteous after death;
but it is still distinguished from Heaven—for example, in such
a passage as *i Enoch* lxi. 12: " All who sleep not above in
Heaven shall bless him; all the holy ones (i.e. the angels) in
Heaven shall bless him; and all the elect who dwell in the
garden of life . . ."; similarly in the *Apoc. of Abraham* xxi:
" And I saw there the Garden of Eden and its fruits, the source
of the stream issuing from it, and its trees and their bloom,
and those who have behaved righteously. And I saw therein
their foods and blessedness. And I saw there a great multitude,
men and women and children. . . ." Above all, here dwell
those few who have never tasted of death, and who abide there
with the Son of God: " And there I saw the first fathers, and
the righteous who from the beginning dwell in that place "
(*i Enoch* lxx. 4); the context implies that Enoch and Elijah
are meant. But foremost among those who dwell in this
Garden is " that Son of Man ". Paradise is thus distinguished
from Heaven. Then we come to the final development,
according to which Paradise is thought of as Heaven itself,
where the Almighty and the Son of Man dwell, and whither
the righteous are gathered:

" And there was great joy among them (i.e. the righteous),
And they blessed and glorified and extolled;

Because the name of that Son of Man had been revealed unto
them.

And he sat on the throne of his glory,
And the sum of judgement was given unto the Son of
Man . . .
For that Son of Man hath appeared,

And hath seated himself on the throne of his glory,
And all evil shall pass away before his face,
And the word of that Son of Man shall go forth,
And be strong before the Lord of Spirits " (*i Enoch* lxix.
26 ff.).

Thus, there is an earthly Paradise and a heavenly Paradise;
they are distinguished in some of the apocalypses, in others
they are identical.

So that, regarding the conception of Heaven; we find that
there is, first, Heaven itself; then there is an earthly Paradise,
and there is a heavenly Paradise. Ultimately all three are
combined as the one glorious dwelling-place of God far away
above the skies. The steps in the development of these conceptions are difficult to follow, partly on account of gaps in the
tradition, and partly on account of the inconsistencies and
contradictions of the apocalyptic writers; but it seems certain
that Heaven, as finally conceived of, is the outcome of this
combination.

IV

HELL

As in the case of Heaven, the conception of Hell, in the
Apocalyptic Literature, is the development of pre-existing ideas.
It will be best to start by considering the two Hebrew words
Sheôl (Greek, *Hades*) and *Ge Hinnom* (Greek, *Gehenna*). According to Old Testament belief, *Sheôl* was thought of as a huge
hollow place under the earth, but pictured as a city; there was
no return from it; the shades of men gathered there after they
died; they dwelt in darkness, forgot all things, and their food
was dust (see further above, pp. 179 ff.). *Ge Hinnom*, " the valley
of Hinnom ", or " of the son (also, sons) of Hinnom ", was a
valley which lay on the west of Jerusalem. It was a place of
ill repute; in *Jer.* vii. 31, 32, it is said: "And they have built
the high places of Topheth (which means "fire-place"), which
is the valley of the son of Hinnom, to burn their sons and their
daughters in the fire. . . . Therefore, behold, the days come,
saith Yahweh, that it shall no more be called Topheth, nor the
valley of the son of Hinnom, but the valley of slaughter; for
they shall bury in Topheth till there be no place to bury "

(see also xix. 6, 12, 13). On account of these evil practices
Ge Hinnom came in later days to be regarded as the symbol of
the place of the wicked departed in the next world, and *Sheôl*
came to be identified with it; the place of punishment in the
next world received the name of the place where wicked deeds
had been perpetrated on earth. We can, then, understand
why, in the Apocalyptic Literature, *Sheôl* is always identified
with *Gehenna*;[1] thus in *i Enoch* lxiii. 8, 10, it is said in reference
to the confession of the wicked: " Our souls are full of un-
righteous gain, but that doth not prevent us from descending
from the midst thereof into the stronghold of Sheôl " (cp.
Gehenna, *i Enoch* xcix. 11, ciii. 7; *Jubilees* vii. 29, xxii. 22).
It is interesting to note that developments regarding the conceptions about *Sheôl* are to be discerned already in the Old
Testament; but with these we cannot concern ourselves now.
In the Apocalyptic books we have a considerable amount of
space devoted to this abode of the wicked departed. Here is a
description of what has now become " Hell " in the ordinary
accepted sense of the word: " And I looked, and turned to
another part of the earth, and saw there a deep valley, with
burning fire. And they brought the kings and the mighty,
and began to cast them into this deep valley. And there mine
eyes saw how they made these their instruments, (namely) iron
chains of immeasurable weight . . ." (*i Enoch* liv. 1–3).[2]
Elsewhere (in *i Enoch* xc. 26, 27), it is said: " And I saw at that
time how a like abyss was opened in the midst of the earth, full
of fire . . . and they were all judged and found guilty, and
cast into this fiery abyss, and they burned; and I saw (them)
burning, and their bones burning." In the *Apoc. of Abraham*
xxxi we read: " And I will give those who have covered me
with mockery to the scorn of the Coming Age; and I have
prepared them to be food for the fire of Hades (here synonymous
with *Gehenna*), and for ceaseless flight to and fro through the air
in the underworld beneath the earth." This last is a curious
idea not often found (see, however, *ii (iv) Esdras* vii. 80);
presumably it is intended to express the utter restlessness of
the wicked hereafter in contrast to the restful repose of the

---

[1] Though, strange to say, that is not quite always the case in the New
Testament.
[2] Note that here " Hell " is situated on the earth; a result of mixing up
the traditional idea of *Sheôl* with the place of punishment.

righteous, but also owing to the old-world idea of the spirit having wings; though how they burn ceaselessly while flying about is not explained. One more illustration of a great number (*i Enoch* iii. 5–8) :

" Woe to you, ye sinners, when ye have died,
    If ye die in the wealth of your sins. . . .
    Know ye that your souls will be made to descend into
        Sheôl (here again synonymous with *Ge Hinnom*),
    And ye shall be wretched in your great tribulation;
    And into darkness and chains and a burning fire,
    Where there is grievous judgement, shall your spirits
        enter. . . ."

Further illustrations are unnecessary; the Apocalyptists simply revel in hell-fire for the wicked. But the idea is not originally theirs; it is borrowed; and did space permit it would be easy to show that it was borrowed from Persian eschatology.

Now, it will be readily realized what an effect these things would have had upon those who listened to the Seers, and who heard their words read. There is no doubt that the bulk of the people believed what the Seers recorded, just as the Seers themselves did. Convinced as they were that by means of vision or trances they were the recipients of the divine revelations, and that they were God's instruments for making known to others what they had received, the Seers could not do otherwise than fulfil what they believed to be their duty among their people. The large amount of the Apocalyptic Literature which has come down to us—and there is every reason to believe that the material was originally much larger—is clear evidence of its wide diffusion and of the popularity of the teaching embodied in it.

v

THE TEACHING OF THE NEW TESTAMENT

Much that is taught in the earlier literature is accepted by the New Testament writers as witnessing to the truth. Taking the subjects in the order followed in the preceding sections, we have first that of the final *Judgement*. Here it must be observed that in the earlier writings we have dealt with the Judge is almost always the Almighty, and only very rarely does the Messiah appear as such. But in the New Testament once or twice our Lord, the Messiah, is the Judge in that Day. Thus, in *Matth.* xvi. 27 : " For the Son of Man shall come in the glory of his Father with his angels; and then shall he render unto every man according to his doing " (cp. xxv. 31, 32). But in the Gospels this is exceptional (see above, p. 161). Again, in *Acts* x. 42 : ". . . that this is he which is ordained of God to be Judge of quick and dead ", see also *ii Tim.* iv. 1. In *Rom.* xiv. 10 it is said that " we shall all stand before the judgement seat of God "; but in the previous verse mention is made of Christ being " Lord of both the dead and the living ", so that it is he, in his divine nature, who sits on the Judgement-seat. Other passages, apart from the Gospels, teach the same truth; but these will suffice.

A good deal is said in the earlier literature of an *intermediate state* after death and before the Resurrection (see above, pp. 188 f.). There is, therefore, some justification for the contention that the very rare reference to an intermediate state in the New Testament is due to the fact that it was taken for granted. It is, in any case, definitely taught in *Lk.* xvi. 19–31, where it is described how the rich man suffered in Hades (not Gehenna, be it noted, the Syriac Version has " Sheôl "), and Lazarus is in bliss in " Abraham's bosom "; no resurrection having yet taken place. Again, an implicit reference to an intermediate state may well be discerned in *Matth.* xii. 32 : ". . . but whosoever shall speak against the Holy Spirit, it shall not be forgiven him neither in this world, nor in that which is to come." It is inconceivable that our Lord could have thought of sinners among the risen righteous in the heavenly spheres whither he was going to prepare abiding-places for them (*Jn.* xiv. 2); the reference must be to where even the wicked underwent amelioration (*Lk.* xvi. 27, 28). Here we recall, further, what is told in 1 *Pet.* iii. 19, iv. 6, where it is said that Christ " went and preached unto the spirits in prison, which aforetime were disobedient, when the longsuffering of God waited in the days of Noah "; so that the Gospel was preached even to the dead.

Belief in the resurrection is so axiomatic that there is no need to illustrate this by quotations. Generally speaking, it is the righteous only who are spoken of as partaking of the resurrection (e.g. *Matth.* x. 28 ; *Mk.* ix. 43–48 ; *Lk.* xx. 35, cp. *Matth.* xxv. 46) ; [1] on the other hand, the resurrection of all men, therefore the evil as well as the righteous, is implied in 1 *Cor.* xv. 22 : " For as in Adam all die, so also in Christ shall all be made alive " ; and in *John* v. 28, 29, it is definitely stated that " the hour cometh, in which all that are in the tombs shall hear his voice, and shall come forth ; they that have done good, unto the resurrection of life ; and they that have done ill unto the resurrection of judgement."

As to the nature of the risen body, it is conceived of not as natural, but as glorious and spiritual (*i Cor.* xv. 42–44) ; they who partake of the resurrection " are as angels in heaven " (*Matth.* xxii. 30). The identity of the risen body with the earthly body is taught, e.g., in such passages as *Matth.* v. 29, 30, x. 28 ; *Rom.* viii. 11, 23 ; *i Cor.* xv. 53 ; a material identity is, however, not meant, see *i Cor.* xv. 44, but rather individual continuity.

The conception of *Heaven* differs from that of the earlier teaching in that it is not conceived of as a circumscribed locality. Human thought and language necessarily fail to express a spiritual truth beyond man's comprehension. The only way in which the realization of what Heaven is, and the only way whereby it can be conceived of as localized, is by describing it as within divine environment. " For now we see in a mirror darkly ; but then face to face ; now I know in part, but then shall I know fully even as also I have been known fully " (*i Cor.* xiii. 12).

The conception of *Hell* as a locality does not differ from that of the earlier literature.

[1] Cp. the *Didaché*, where, in reference to the resurrection, it is said, " but not of all, but as it is said, The Lord shall come, and all the *saints* with him ".

PART IV: WORSHIP

CHAPTER XV

THE TEMPLE

I

In the account of the fall of Jerusalem (586 B.C.) in *ii Kings* xxv. 8, 9, it is said that Nebuzaradan, the commander-in-chief of the Babylonian army, " burned the house of Yahweh ". This did not, however, involve the entire destruction of the sacred edifice; for shortly after we read that " there came certain from Shechem, from Shilo, and from Samaria, even fourscore men, having their beards shaven and their clothes rent, and having cut themselves, with oblations and frankincense in their hand, to bring them to the house of Yahweh " (*Jer.* xli. 5). In itself this would not necessarily indicate that any part of the house of Yahweh had escaped destruction; but we have in *Ezra* iii. 4–6 a passage which shows that, though largely in ruins, some part of the Temple could still be used for worship; for on the return of the exiles from the Captivity, and before the laying of the foundation of the second Temple was begun, it is recorded that " they kept the feast of Tabernacles, as it is written, and offered the daily burnt-offerings by number, according to the ordinance. . . . From the first day of the seventh month began they to offer burnt-offerings unto Yahweh; but the foundation of the Temple of Yahweh was not yet laid."

We need not here go into the reasons why it was so long before the definite rebuilding of the second Temple was begun.[1] What is known for certain is that the rebuilding began in 520 B.C. (*Hag.* i, 14. 15), and that it was completed in 516 B.C.: " And this house was finished on the third day of the month

---

[1] See for details, Oesterley and Robinson, *A History of Israel*, ii, pp. 71ff. (1934).

Adar (= March), which was in the sixth year of the reign of Darius the king."

There can be no doubt that the second Temple occupied, more or less, the site of Solomon's Temple. The building itself, however, would seem to have been of far less grandeur than its predecessor: "Who is left among you that saw this house in its former glory? And how do ye see it now? Is it not in your eyes as nothing?" (*Hag.* ii. 3, cp. *Ezra* iii. 12).

So far as general information about the second Temple is concerned the canonical books give us but scanty details. As to its dimensions, *Ezra* vi. 3 gives a height and breadth which make it far larger than Solomon's Temple (*i Kgs.* vi. 2); this cannot be accepted as reliable. Incidental reference is made in *Neh.* xii. 31, 37, 39, to various gates within the precincts of the Temple, the water gate and the sheep gate and others. Then we have in *Ezra* viii. 29, x. 6, *Neh.* x. 37 reference to the priests' chambers. And, once more, it is said in *Neh.* x. 32 that a Temple-tax of one-third of a shekel was paid annually " for the service of the house of our God ". This, apart from worship, is all that we are told about the second Temple in the canonical books. More, from every point of view, is to be learned from post-Biblical literature, though it is to be recognized that there is not always agreement in the accounts given.

II

First, attention may be drawn to a few historical details. Thus the foundation is referred to in *Ecclus.* xlix. 11, 12, where Ben-Sira commemorates the work of Zerubbabel and Joshua the son of Josedek, " who in their days built the House, and set up on high the holy Temple, which was prepared for everlasting glory "; see also *Tob.* xiv. 4, 5. This is dealt with in greater detail by Josephus (*Antiq.* xi. 106–108), who says that " the Temple was built in seven years' time ". Then we have an interesting passage in *Ecclus.* l. 1–3, where Ben-Sira writes: " Great among his brethren, and the glory of his people, was Simeon, the son of Jochanan, the priest; in whose time the House (i.e. the Temple) [1] was renovated, and in whose days

---

[1] Both *hēkal* (" Temple ") and *bayith* (" House ") are used for the Temple in *ii Kgs.* xxiii. 24 and *Ps.* cxxxviii. 2.

the Temple was fortified; in whose time a reservoir was dug, a water-cistern like the sea in abundance " (from the Hebrew, but the text is somewhat corrupt). In the verses which follow there is also mention of the fortification of the city as well. This is the first reference we have to the fortifying of the second Temple. When this took place it is difficult to determine. But Ben-Sira speaks of it as having taken place in the past, yet he writes as an eye-witness when he describes the appearance of Simeon as he issued forth from the sanctuary (lit. " the house of atonement "). In the former case the reference would be to Simeon i, the son of Jochanan i (about 300 B.C.), in the latter to Simeon ii, the son of Jochanan ii, about a century later. If, as many hold, Ben-Sira had the latter in mind, the fortifying of the Temple and the city was carried out at the instance of Antiochus iii (223–187 B.C.) after his victory over Ptolemy v of Egypt in 199 B.C. During this war, as Josephus tells us, the Jews " suffered greatly, and their land was sorely harassed "; doubtless it was at this time that both the Temple and city suffered damage. After the victory of Antiochus the Jews demonstrated their friendship towards him in various ways; for this they were well rewarded; among other things Antiochus said: " I would also have the work about the Temple finished, and the cloisters, and if there be anything else that ought to be rebuilt " (*Antiq.* xii. 129–144). The further history of the second Temple, its desecration by Antiochus iv Epiphanes in 168 B.C., and its re-dedication by Judas Maccabæus in 164 B.C., have already been described (see p. 28). The only other historical notices that we have are the incidental mention of the " tower near the Temple ", built by Hyrcanus i, in about the year 134 B.C. (*Antiq.* xviii. 91); and the account of its capture by Pompey, the Roman general, in 63 B.C. (*Antiq.* xiv. 337 ff.).

Our next task must be to take a brief glance at the various post-Biblical writings in which details of one kind or another about the second Temple are given.

First, as to the external parts. Josephus, quoting, as he says, the words of Hecatæus of Abdera,[1] has the following account:

---

[1] Most scholars regard this as an error, and believe that Josephus is here quoting an anonymous writer who lived about 200 B.C.; see, e.g., G. A. Smith, *Jerusalem*, ii. 306, 439 (1908).

" There is, about the middle of the city, a wall of stone, the length of which is five hundred feet, and the breadth a hundred cubits, with double cloisters " (*Contra Ap.* i. 198). These cloisters are also referred to by Josephus himself in *Antiq.* xi. 108: " The Jews also built the cloisters of the inner Temple, that were round about the Temple itself." What he says about the interior we shall come to presently. In the *Letter of Aristeas*, 84 ff., the writer tells of the mountain on which Jerusalem stood, and continues: " Upon its crest stood the Temple in splendour, with its three enclosing walls, more than seventy cubits high, and of a breadth and length matching the structure of the edifice. The whole was built with a magnificence and prodigality beyond all precedent. . . . The Temple looks towards the east, and its back is turned westwards."

These references, it is true, give us but a meagre idea of the external appearance of the second Temple. Of greater interest is what is told about the internal arrangements. In the abovementioned quotation given by Josephus the writer describes the interior of the Temple thus: " Therein is a square altar, not made of hewn stone; but composed of white stones gathered together, having each side twenty cubits long, and its height ten cubits." This refers to the outer court. It continues: " Hard by it is a large edifice, wherein there is an altar, and a candlestick both of gold, and in weight two talents; upon these there is a light that is never extinguished, either by night or by day. There is no image, nor any donations, therein; nothing at all is planted there, neither grove, nor anything of the kind " (*Contra Ap.* i. 198 f.).

Another, and a fuller, description is given in the *Letter of Aristeas* 87 ff.: " The altar was built of a size in keeping with the place and with the sacrifices which were consumed by fire, and the ascent to it was on a like scale. The place was approached by a gradual slope from a proper regard for decency (cp. *Exod.* xx. 26), and the ministering priests were clad in coats of fine linen reaching to the ankles " (cp. *Exod.* xxxix. 27). What seems especially to have struck this writer was the abundant water supply with which the Temple was furnished; he says: " The whole floor is paved with stones and slopes down to the appropriate places, so as to admit of its being flushed with water to wash away the blood from the sacrifices;

for many thousand beasts are offered on the feast days. The water supply is inexhaustible. An abundant natural spring bubbles up within the Temple area. . . ." He then goes on to tell of the underground channels through which the water rushes, so that " all the vast accumulation of sacrificial blood is swept away in the twinkling of an eye ". The abundance of water is also mentioned by Ben-Sira (see above). Some details of the Temple furniture occur in *i Macc.* i. 21–23, where it is told how Antiochus iv Epiphanes " took the golden altar, and the candlestick of the light, and all that pertained thereto, and the table of the shewbread, and the cups to pour withal, and the bowls, and the golden censers, and the veil, and the crowns, and the adorning of gold which was on the face of the Temple, and he scaled it off. And he took the silver and the gold and the precious vessels, and he took the hidden treasures which he found." These ornaments were for the most part similar to those described in fuller detail in the Priestly Code (*Exod* xxx. 1–6, xxxv. 31–39, xxxvi. 31–37, xxxvii. 17–24). At the re-dedication of the Temple by Judas Maccabæus there is again mention of the " holy place ", the " altar of burnt offerings ", the " inner parts of the house ", the " courts ", the " holy vessels ", the " candlestick ", the " incense altar ", the " tables ", i.e. of the shewbread, and the " veils " (*i Macc.* iv. 44–51); these last refer to the curtains which separated the Holy of Holies from the Holy Place, and those which hung in front of the Holy Place.

What has been said could be greatly supplemented by the details concerning Herod's Temple given in Josephus, *Antiq.* xv. 391 ff., *War* v. 184 ff., and in the Mishnah and Talmud; but we need not deal with these since the important matters regarding the internal arrangement of the Temple are indicated in the quotations given.

III

We must direct our attention next to such *data* as can be gathered regarding the details of worship. So far as the post-exilic canonical books are concerned there is but little to be learned of such details, let alone anything about the order of service in the Temple. All that is said is of a general character.

Thus, in *Neh.* x. 32–39 we read of the re-institution of the sacrificial system, " the service of the house of our God ", and of the provisions to be made for the support of the priesthood. In the books of *Chronicles* many of the details of worship assigned to the time of David and Solomon reflect the usages of the post-exilic Temple; but these, too, are of a general character. This is natural enough when we think of how familiar to the people all that concerned public worship was. What needs to be specially emphasized is the love of worship, praise and thanksgiving, so often expressed in the psalms of this period; we recall, for example, the psalmist's words : " I wash my hands in innocency, and encompass thine altar, Yahweh, that I may cause the sound of thanksgiving to be heard, and may declare all thy wonder-works; I love the habitation (i.e. sojourning in) of thy house, the place where thy glory abideth " (*Ps.* xxvi. 68, see also *Ps.* xxvii. 4, and various other passages to the same effect).

In turning now to the uncanonical Jewish literature, there are, it must be confessed, but few references to the Temple-worship; but we do get one striking account of the way in which the acts of worship were carried out, namely, the important description given in *Ecclus.* l. 1–21. As this is without parallel for its fullness in the literature of our period, it will be well worth following out the order of service as there detailed; it is the account of one who was himself present; and the service described is that of the Day of Atonement. First he tells of the High-priest coming forth from the holy place to offer the burnt-offering in atonement for himself and the people. He receives the portions of the sacrificial victim from the hands of the attendant priests " the sons of Aaron ". Then, having finished the service of the altar, he pours out the drink-offering at the foot of the altar. Thereupon the priests sound " a mighty blast " on their silver trumpets, and all the worshippers fall down upon their faces " to worship before the Most High ", and offer prayer before " the Merciful ". Then the High-priest comes down from the altar and with uplifted hands gives the blessing. The text of the last verse (21) is somewhat mutilated; but we should probably read : " And a second time they (i.e. the whole body of worshippers) fell down, now to receive the pardon of God from him ", i.e. he pronounces the absolution. Brief as this description is, it gives us a clear picture of one of the services in the Temple during the period with which we are specially concerned. In *Ecclus*. vii. 29–31 Ben-Sira makes an eloquent appeal for the support of the priesthood. Attention may also be drawn to a passage in the *Letter of Aristeas* (92–95), where the writer describes the priests' ministration at the Temple services; he refers, it is true, only to the sacrificial service, as being the central element; but the passage is unique of its kind, and gives the account of an eye-witness; a few sentences from it may therefore be quoted: " Their service is without intermission, some providing the wood, others oil, others fine wheat flour, others the spices; while others again bring the pieces of flesh for the burnt-offering, displaying extraordinary strength. For they grip with both hands the legs of the calves, most of which weigh over two talents, and then with both hands and with wonderful dexterity fling the beast to a considerable height, and never fail to plant it on the altar. . . . There is a place set apart for them to rest, where those who are free from duty take their seats. And thereupon, some of those who have had an interval of relaxation rise up willingly, without any order for their ministration being given." He concludes with a brief reference to the congregation: " The deepest silence prevails, so that one would suppose that there was not a single person in the place, although the ministers in attendance number some seven hundred, not to mention the large multitude of those who bring their sacrifices to be offered; everything is performed with reverence and in a manner worthy of the divine majesty."

As already remarked, we have but rare mention in the literature under consideration of the details of public worship; it may, therefore, be worth while to supplement what has been said by giving in brief outline the order of service offered daily in the Temple, both morning and evening, as recounted in the Mishnah tractate *Tamid*. This service, offered in accordance with what is enjoined in *Exod*. xxix. 38–42, *Num*. xxviii. 1–8, was known as the '*Olath Tamid,* " the continual burnt-offering ", or simply *Tamid*, because continuously offered daily. The account, which is very detailed, given in the Mishnah, undoubtedly records the actual Temple ritual. We give but the briefest possible outline of the main elements. First, there are various preparatory acts, such as setting the altar in order, and cleansing the holy vessels. Then follows the killing of the sacrificial victim, a lamb, and the sprinkling of its blood on the altar; and the seven-branched candlestick is lighted. Thereupon all the officiating priests descend into the court where the worshippers are assembled, and prayers are offered, beginning with the *Shema'* [1] and the saying of the Ten Commandments. This was followed by the incense-offering which introduced the ritual act of laying the flesh of the sacrificial victim on the altar, and offering it up. Then the priests, standing in the *'Ulam*, i.e. the vestibule, before the sanctuary, and facing the congregation, gave the blessing (*Num.* vi. 24–26), mentioned also in *Sota* vii. 1. The ceremony of the meal-offering and the wine-oblation then followed, during which, at the clanging of the cymbal, the Levites sang the psalm for the day, accompanied by instrumental music. This concluded the daily services. It may be added that there was a special psalm for each day of the week; thus, for the first day, *Ps.* xxiv, and for the succeeding days, respectively, *Pss.* xlviii, lxxxii, xciv, lxxxi, xciii, and for the Sabbath, xcii (*Tamid* vii. 4). At the end of each of the three sections into which a psalm was divided when sung liturgically, trumpets were sounded by the priests, and the worshippers prostrated themselves upon the ground.

What has been said refers to the daily morning service; we have not the details about the evening service, but that this, too, was celebrated daily there is ample evidence to show, e.g. *i Chron.* xvi. 40; *ii Chron.* xiii. 11; and Josephus tells of how, even during the siege of Jerusalem the priests " did still twice a day, in the morning, and about the ninth hour, offer their sacrifices on the altar " (*Antiq.* xiv. 65); the evening service is also referred to in the Mishnah (*Pesachim* v. 1).

The worship on Sabbaths and Festivals was the same as the daily services, but many more sacrifices were offered both by the congregation unitedly and by individuals; the former are referred to by Josephus (*Antiq.* iii. 237–239), for the latter see

---

[1] " *Hear*, O Israel; the Lord our God, the Lord is One "; it consists of *Deut.* vi. 4–9, xi. 13–21, *Num.* xv. 37–41. It was recited responsively by the priests and the congregation. Among the prayers were the earliest portions of the *Shemoneh 'Esreh*, the " Eighteen " Benedictions, called also the *Tephillah*, the " Prayer " *par excellence*; see, further, Elbogen, *Der jüdische Gottesdienst in seiner geschichtlichen Entwickelung*, pp. 30 f. (1913).

i Chron. xxix. 21; *ii Chron.* xxix. 31–35, xxx. 24, xxxv. 7–9; see also Josephus, *Antiq.* iii. 237 ff.; in the *Letter of Aristeas* 88 it is said that " many thousand beasts are offered on the feast-days ".

From what has been said, then, it will have been seen that, although sacrifices were of central importance, the elements of praise, thanksgiving, and prayer were by no means wanting in the worship of the Temple. This is, of course, what we should expect. There is no mention of Scripture-reading followed by explanation and exhortation; but that these had their place in the Temple liturgy is convincingly shown by Elbogen (*op. cit.*, p. 239); it seems to be referred to by Josephus when he says: " And the seventh day we set apart from labour; it is dedicated to the learning of our customs and laws " (*Antiq.* xvi. 43). Further proof is afforded by the importance attached to the whole subject in the synagogal liturgy, which was based on that of the Temple. We shall refer to this again in the next chapter.

In conclusion, something must be said about the various Temple officials. At the head stood, of course, the High-priest; he exercised political as well as religious authority, for he was also the president of the Sanhedrin. We read sometimes of High-priests, in the plural; the reason of this is that, owing to the frequent changes in the holders of this office, there were several who, having held the office, were entitled to be called High-priest even though they were no longer such in fact. Next in rank to the High-priest was the *Sagan*, the "chief", i.e. of the priests; his duty was to quell any unseemly disturbance in the Temple courts; when one thinks of the immense concourse of people from all parts during the great festivals, the need of such an official with his retinue of subordinates (*seganim*) is readily understood. Then as to the priesthood; this consisted of twenty-four courses or divisions; the numbers in the divisions seem to have varied (for the whole subject see *i Chron.* xxiv. 3–19; *Antiq.* vii. 367). The daily services were conducted by these courses in turn, each being on duty for a week (referred to, e.g., in the Mishnah, *Sukkah* v. 6–8).

A different body of Temple officials were the singers; as representatives of the congregation in leading the praises of God their position in the Temple worship was of great importance. We read of different guilds of singers belonging to the families of Heman, Asaph, and Ethan (called also Jeduthum), so that the office of Temple-singer was hereditary. In post-exilic times the singers were all Levites, but in earlier days that was not so; this points to the increased importance attached to the office in the second Temple organization (for details see *i Chron.* vi. 16–32, xv. 16–19, xxv; *ii Chron.* v. 12; *Neh.* vii. 44). Of special importance among the duties of the Temple-singers was the service of song during the offering of sacrifices; they accompanied their singing with instrumental music; mention is made of the lyre (*kinnôr*), and the harp (*nebel*); cymbals (*mezaltaîm*) were also sounded at certain parts of the service. On the great festivals pipes (*chalîl*) were also used.

Finally, there were the officials whose duties were not connected with the worship. Great responsibility rested on the Treasurer (*Gizbar i Chron.* xxvi. 20; *Ezra* i. 8, vii. 21), and his subordinates, for they had charge of the many articles of value possessed by the Temple authorities; how considerable these possessions were is evident from what is said in *Ezra* i. 9–11, viii. 26–27. And, once more, there were the Door-keepers (*Sho'arîm*); they, too, were reckoned under the Levites in later times, originally they were laymen. Their duty was to keep watch at the outer gates; the inner gates of the different courts were under priestly oversight. On the subject of the door-keepers see *i Chron.* xxvi. 1–19.

These, then, were the various Temple officials as they existed during the period with which we are dealing, but in each case the office dates back to earlier times.

IV

Coming now to what is said about the Temple in the New Testament, the most notable fact is our Lord's constant visits there for the purpose of teaching. This took place, of course, in the outer court, where men were wont to gather. A number of passages refer to the teaching thus given (e.g. *Matth.* xxi. 23; *Mk.* xii. 35; *Lk.* xx. 1), and it is said that this took place " daily " (*Matth.* xxvi. 25; *Mk.* xiv. 49; *Lk.* xix. 47; *Jn.* vii. 24, etc.). In later days the disciples followed Christ's example in this (*Acts* v. 42).

Of the Temple itself various details are mentioned. The beauty of its structure was a source of wonder: " What manner of stones and what manner of buildings ", says one of the disciples, who also speaks of them as " these great buildings " (*Mk.* xiii. 1, cp. *Matth.* xxiii, 16, xxiv. 1; *Lk.* xxi. 5), bearing out what is said in the *Letter of Aristeas* quoted above. Incidental reference is made to several features; thus, in *Matth.* iv. 5, *Lk.* iv. 9, the " pinnacle " of the Temple is spoken of. Some difference of opinion exists as to the precise meaning of the word; the Greek word means " wing ", i.e. some ornamental projection from the main building; the Syriac Version has *kenpha*, which also means " wing "; but the Old Syriac Version has *qarna*, " horn ", which suggests " pinnacle ", the highest point. Then there is the mention of " Solomon's Porch " (*Jn.* x. 23; *Acts* iii. 11, v. 12); this was the name given to the eastern cloister, presumably because it was built over Solomonic substructures. Further, the " beautiful gate " is spoken of (*Acts* iii. 2, 10); this may have been the gate leading from the court of the women to the court of the men; but this is not certain, it may have been the gate lying more to the east.

In the interior of the Temple we have mention of the " veil "; this was the curtain which separated the outer Temple from the Holy of Holies (*Matth.* xxvii. 51; *Mk.* xv. 38; *Lk.* xxiii. 45); the words " the veil of the Temple was rent in twain from the top to the bottom ", may perhaps be understood as a mystic way of expressing the truth that now what had hitherto separated men from God was removed by the Saviour's sacrifice; cp. the words: " All authority hath been given unto me in heaven and on earth " (*Matth.* xxviii. 18).

Finally, in all four Gospels we have the account of the cleansing of the Temple (*Matth.* xxi. 12; *Mk.* xi. 15; *Lk.* xix. 45; *Jn.* ii. 14); what is here recounted took place in the court of the Gentiles. Whether it belonged to the beginning of our Lord's ministry, according to the fourth Gospel, or at its end, according to the Synoptists, is difficult to decide; authorities differ on the point. We believe that the Synoptists must be followed here, and for this reason: in each, stress is laid on the words, " My house shall be called a house of prayer "; this is quoted from *Isa.* lvi. 7, and it is significant that the words which precede this are, in each case, omitted, namely: " their burnt-

offerings and their sacrifices shall be accepted upon mine altar ".
May it not be that our Lord's action pointed to the abolition of
the sacrificial system? He was about to sacrifice his life upon
the Cross, a sacrifice which atoned for the sins of the world;
the one and only really efficacious sacrifice.

Lastly, as to the Temple officials; the High-priest is very
often mentioned; in *Lk.* iii. 2, two High-priests are spoken of,
and in *Lk.* xxii. 2, 4, 52, the word is used in the plural in reference
to several of them; this we have already explained above.
The "captain of the Temple" is spoken of in *Acts* iv. 1, v. 24;
this was the official called the *Sagan* in the Mishnah; we have
referred to him above; the plural, "captains", in *Lk.* xxii.
52, refers to the subordinates under his immediate command.
In *Lk.* i. 5 we read of a priest named Zacharias, "of the course
of Abijah"; this refers to one of the twenty-four courses into
which the priesthood was divided (see above).

We have now dealt with the references to the Temple in the
New Testament apart from the book of *Revelation*; but the
references to it there belong to a different category.

CHAPTER XVI

THE SYNAGOGUE

THE Hebrew equivalent of the Greek *Sunagōgé* s *Beth ha-Keneseth* (Aramaic *Bē Kenishta*), " House of Assembly " ; it was so called because *keneseth* means a " gathering " for worship. The term does not occur in the Old Testament.

We must distinguish between the Synagogue as a religious institution, and the use of the same word as applied to a building for worship. But before it became an institution it is reasonable to assume that there were antecedent steps which, in course of time, contributed to the formation of a recognized and official organization. Thus, in *Neh.* viii. 1 ff. we read that " all the people gathered themselves together [1] as one man into the broad place that was before the water gate " ; it then goes on to say that Ezra, together with a number of Levites, read the book of the law of Moses, for the people to understand, " from early morning until midday " ; thereupon the people wept, presumably because hitherto they had not understood the Law, and had therefore not observed it. [2] But the Levites told them not to be grieved. As a result, " all the people went their way to eat, and to drink, and to send portions, and to make great mirth, because they had understood the words that were declared unto them." It has been held that the account of this gathering is evidence showing that Ezra had brought the institution of the Synagogue from the Exile, where it is supposed to have originated, and established it in Palestine. But if this were the case, how came it that the returned exiles [3] were wholly ignorant of the Law, as the passage shows? And further, if this gathering was the inauguration of such an important institution as the Synagogue, how are we to explain the fact that it is never mentioned again until at least a couple

---

[1] The word used is *'asaph*, not *kanas*, from which *keneseth* is derived.

[2] One cannot help recalling here *ii Kgs.* xxii. 11, where it is said : " And it came to pass, when the king (i.e. Josiah) had heard the words of the book of the law, that he rent his clothes."

[3] The gathering consisted of those " that went up out of the captivity . . ." (*Neh.* vii. 6).

of centuries later? No, this gathering was one of the steps, of which there must in course of time have been many in various parts of Palestine, which contributed to the ultimate formation of the institution of the Synagogue. Another such step may well be discerned in the procedure adopted by Jehoshaphat in order that the people might be taught the Law; this is recorded in *ii Chron.* xvii. 7–9: " Also in the third year of his reign he sent his princes . . . to teach in the cities of Judah; and with them the Levites . . . and with them the priests. And they taught in Judah, having the book of the law of Yahweh with them; and they went about throughout all the cities of Judah, and taught among the people." The Chronicler wrote some time during the early part of the third century B.C.; had the institution of the Synagogue been in existence in his day he could hardly have failed to make some reference to so important a fact. The probability is that the Chronicler is here intimating the procedure as existing in his day.

It is sometimes maintained that synagogues are referred to in *Ps.* lxxiv. 8; the Revised Version renders this: " They have burned up all the synagogues of God in the land "; but the Hebrew text in this verse is demonstrably corrupt. The word which the Revised Version translates, quite erroneously, " synagogues " is never used in a concrete sense; it means " assemblies " (the R.V. marginal rendering, " places of assembly ", is equally incorrect). So that when the Hebrew text has: " They have burned up all the assemblies . . .", it does not give sense. The Septuagint evidently represents the true text: " We will put an end [1] to all the assemblies of God." The passage is thus very instructive; for it witnesses to the existence of gatherings similar to, though no doubt on a smaller scale than, that recorded in *Neh.* viii, held in open spaces in many centres for the purpose of instructing the people in the Law; it is thus yet another illustration of the steps which contributed to the formation of the Synagogue in the sense of an institution. [2]

---

[1] The equivalent Hebrew would be " cause to cease ", as in *Ezek.* vii. 24, *Dan.* ix. 27. The word rendered " assemblies " is in Greek lit. " festivals ", but in verse 4 of our psalm it is the rendering of the same Hebrew word, *mo'ed,* which is used in the verse under consideration, i.e. " assemblies ".

[2] The Psalm in question was written during the Greek Period, but

As to the question of synagogues in the sense of buildings; that these had not yet come into existence, at any rate, in Palestine prior to the Maccabæan struggle, is suggested by the striking fact that no mention is made of them in the account of the attempt of Antiochus iv to stamp out Judaism (168 B.C.), given, with considerable detail, in *i Macc.* i. 41–57. The synagogues were the places *par excellence* where the rolls of the Law were kept; now we read in verses 56, 57 : "And they rent in pieces the books of the law which they found, and set them on fire. Ane wheresoever was found anyone with a book of the covenant, and if any consented to the law, the king's sentence delivered him to death." The silence here about synagogues makes it, therefore, certain that they were not yet in existence.

Then we have a further significant fact; in the words of Sukenik, " whereas there is archæological evidence of the existence of synagogues in Egypt as early as the third century B.C., and in Greece as early as the second century B.C., the date of the oldest remains of a synagogue found in Palestine is not earlier than the first century A.D." [1] So far as is known at present, the earliest reference to a synagogue occurs on an inscription found at Shedia (an outskirt of Alexandria), belonging to the time of Ptolemy iii, Euergetes (247–221 B.C.). It is called a *Proseuché* ($\pi\rho\epsilon\sigma\epsilon\upsilon\chi\acute{\eta}$ = $o\hat{\iota}\kappa o\varsigma$ $\pi\rho o\sigma\epsilon\upsilon\chi\hat{\eta}\varsigma$), i.e. " House of Prayer " ; [2] to this name for the synagogue we refer below.

There can thus be little doubt that synagogue buildings existed first in the lands of the Dispersion, whence they were introduced into Palestine soon after the Maccabæan wars. In any case, well before the beginning of the Christian Era they were evidently common in Palestine. The first reference we have of their existence in Palestine would appear to be in *i Enoch* xlvi. 8, liii. 6, where the "houses of congregations" is usually taken to refer to synagogues; the date is about the middle of the last century B.C., so that before this there must have been many, since they are referred to as well known.

We must next deal briefly with the subject of worship as

---

before the outbreak of the Maccabæan revolt. The verse in question refers to the destructive action of outside enemies, joined by renegade Jews (for these latter, see verses 18–23).

[1] *Ancient Synagogues in Palestine and Greece* (Schweich Lectures), p. 1 (1934).
[2] *Revue des Études Juives*, xlv. p. 162 (1902).

conducted in the synagogues. For this reference must be made to Philo, Josephus, and the Mishnah; this latter is of later date, but there is no doubt that it often witnesses to traditional usage, though many details mentioned came into use subsequently. To the evidence of the New Testament we shall come later. It may well be that there were differences of usage in minor details as between the Dispersion and the Palestinian synagogues in the matter of worship, but in the main these would not have been of importance. Since, in regard to the Dispersion, the synagogue is called a *Proseuché*, we should have expected that the offering of prayer would have been the outstanding characteristic; but the evidence points to teaching and the reading of the Scriptures as having been the main elements. But the fact is that the term *Proseuché* as applied to the synagogue was borrowed from pagan usage; it was the general name for a place of worship.[1]

While it is not possible to say what the exact order of service was in the earliest times, there is ample evidence as to the central elements. The most important of these was *Teaching*; this is specially stressed by Philo (*Vita Mos.* iii. 216), and Josephus (*Antiq.* xvi. 43, *Contra Apion.* iii. 175); it centred on the *Reading from the Law*, i.e. the Pentateuch, and the *Reading from the Prophets*.[2] As these were read in Hebrew, which was not understood by the bulk of the people, a running translation was added in the vernacular Aramaic; in the Dispersion synagogues the readings were, of course, from the Septuagint Version. Scripture readings were followed by the *Discourse*, which was largely in the nature of instruction, as its technical name (*Derashah*, lit. " Searching ") implies (Philo, *Vita Mos.* ii. 458, iii. 27). It is obvious that *Prayer*, though secondary, was an essential element; under this was included the *Shema'* (" Hear ", viz. *Deut.* vi. 4–9, xi. 13–21; *Num.* xv. 37–41); though not a prayer in the strict sense, it was certainly one of the most ancient features in Jewish liturgical worship; it probably preceded the Scripture readings. In addition to this, there is every reason to believe that at some part of the Service petitions were offered which in later times were included in the

---

[1] For evidence, see Moulton and Milligan, *The Vocabulary of the Greek Testament*, p. 547 (1926).

[2] These were read either standing or sitting, according to the Mishnah tractate, *Megillah*, iv. 1.

prayer known as the *Shemoneh 'Esreh* ("Eighteen" benedictions), called also the *Tephillah*, the "Prayer" *par excellence*. The present form of this prayer is somewhat developed, but in the main it is pre-Christian; [1] it is far more in the nature of a Prayer than the *Shema'*. The importance of the *Priestly Blessing* (*Num.* vi. 22–27) at the conclusion of the Service is strongly stressed in the Mishnah (*Megillah* iv. 5–7), where it is referred to as "the lifting-up of the hands". According to *Meg.* iv. 10, this was uttered in Hebrew, and not translated. The congregational *Amen* was uttered after each of the three sentences of which the Priestly Blessing is composed.

It is certain that the synagogal liturgy was based on that of the Temple; an incidental proof of this is afforded by what is told of Joshua ben Chananiah (he died in A.D. 130); he was a member of the Levitical choir, and records that "the choristers went in a body to the synagogue from the orchestra by the altar, and so participated in both services" (Bab. Talmud, *Sukka* 53 *a*). This points to another element in the synagogal service which we have not yet mentioned, namely, the singing, or saying as the case might be, of psalms. That they occupied a prominent place appears from a number of indications; with these we cannot deal here as this would take up too much space. [2]

We turn now to the New Testament, where further information on various matters is found. First as to confirmation of most of what has already been dealt with. In *Acts* xvi. 13, 16, we read of "a place of prayer"; this probably refers to some spot where the Jews met for prayer, not to a synagogue in the sense of a building, otherwise this word would have been used, as so often elsewhere when a synagogue building is spoken of. At the same time, as already pointed out, a synagogue was often designated *proseuché* ("prayer"); but this is not the case in the New Testament, where *sunagōgē* is always used. In the passage under consideration it is said that the place of prayer was "by a river"; this does not necessarily mean that a synagogue stood there; for although synagogues were often built near water for purification purposes, we often read of the

[1] For details, see the present writer's *The Jewish Background of the Christian Liturgy*, pp. 54–67 (1925).
[2] See the present writer's *The Psalms in the Jewish Church*, pp. 136 ff. (1910).

P

washing before prayer where there is no question of a synagogue (e.g. *Judith* xii. 7; *Letter of Aristeas* 305, 306; *Sib.
Orac.* 591 f.).

But to continue, the element of *Teaching* appears here prominently; thus in *Matth.* iv. 23 we read that " Jesus went about
in all Galilee, teaching in their synagogues "; His method of
teaching creates astonishment, " for he taught them as having
authority, and not as the scribes " (*Mk.* i. 22; *Matth.* xiii. 54;
Lk. iv. 32). The point here is that our Lord did not follow
the ordinary method of the scribes, who appealed to the sayings
of other teachers and to tradition in support of their utterances,
but He made it clear that He was the final authority. From
what is said in *Acts* xvii. 17, it would appear that discussions
sometimes took place in the synagogue; St. Paul, it is said,
" reasoned in the synagogue with the Jews and the devout
persons "; similarly in *Acts* xviii. 4: " he reasoned in the
synagogue every sabbath, and sought to persuade Jews and
Greeks "; so that such discussions were apparently conducted
during the service. The teaching was based on *Readings* from
the Law and the Prophets; *Lk.* iv. 16 ff. is especially instructive.
In this passage only the prophetical reading is referred to;
but in *Acts* xv. 21 it is said: " For Moses (i.e. the Pentateuch)
from generations of old hath in every city them that preach
him, being read in the synagogues every sabbath "; and again
in *Acts* xiii. 15: " And after the reading of the law and the
prophets . . ."; the occasion is the sabbath service in the
synagogue. Of the *Discourse* which followed we have a graphic
account in *Lk.* iv. 16–30, nothing could be more instructive
than this (cp. also *Acts* xiv. 1, 2). In *Acts* xiii. 15 St. Paul is
invited, after the Scripture readings, to put forth some " word
for exhortation for the people ".

Reference has been made above to the designation of the
synagogue as the house of *Prayer*; the only indication which we
have in the New Testament regarding synagogal prayers is in
Matth. vi. 5: " And when ye pray, ye shall not be as the hypo-
crites; for they love to stand and pray in the synagogues . . .";
the attitude of standing during the offering of prayer, though
the reference is not to prayer in the synagogue, is mentioned
also in *Mk.* xi. 25; *Lk.* xviii. 11. The term " house of prayer "
is never used of the synagogue, but only of the Temple (*Matth.*

xxi. 13). As to the *Amen*, important as signifying the participation of the congregation in the prayer offered, we have a reference to this in *i Cor.* xiv. 16: " Else if thou bless with the spirit, how shall he that filleth the place of the unlearned say the Amen at thy giving of thanks, seeing he knoweth not what thou sayest? " It is a question here of Christian worship in a private house, but that only shows that the synagogal practice had been adopted by the early Christians.

Synagogues, as we learn from the New Testament, were used not only for religious, but also for civil, purposes (e.g. *Matth.* x. 17, xxiii. 34; *Mk.* xiii; *Lk.* xxi. 12; *Acts* xxii. 19). The organization of the synagogue, therefore, included secular as well as religious officials, though the distinction between religious and secular was not clearly defined. The highest religious official was the " chief ruler of the synagogue " (e.g. *Mk.* v. 22, 35; *Lk.* xiii. 14; *Acts* xiii. 15, xviii. 8, 17); different from this office was the " ruler of the synagogue ", though in *Mk.* v. 22 Jaïrus is called " chief ruler ", whereas in *Matth.* ix. 1, *Lk.* viii. 41, he is called " ruler "; in the Syriac Version he is called " Rab " in each passage. However, " Ruler " (*archōn*) without the addition of synagogue was a civil official (e.g. *Lk.* xii. 58, the Syriac Version transliterates the Greek *archōn*), and the title was probably another name for " elder "; that is to say, he was the chief of the elders, of whom there were a umber (*Acts* iv. 8, xiii. 15; *Mk.* v. 25; *Lk.* vii. 3–5). A lesser synagogue official was the " attendant " as the Revised Version renders the term in *Lk.* iv. 20, the Syriac Version has " server "; it is, however, used in a much wider sense (cp., e.g., *Mk.* xiv. 54, 65; *Acts* v. 26, etc.). As a synagogue official one of his duties may have been to receive the alms brought for the poor (*Matth.* vi. 2). In the Mishnah a special official for this duty is spoken of (*Demai* iii. 1, *Qiddushin* iv. 5). Once more, though not actually mentioned, it is implied that corporal punishment was inflicted by an official appointed for this purpose (cp. *Matth.* x. 17, and elsewhere; his duties are described in the Mishnah (*Makkōth* iii. 12); in this tractate the various trespasses are enumerated for which scourging was inflicted.

As to the synagogal furniture and the like, there is only the mention of the " chief seats " (*Matth.* xxiii. 6 ; *Mk.* xii. 34 ; *Lk.* xi. 43, xiv. 7, xx. 46); but " the roll of the prophet Isaiah ", spoken of in *Lk.* iv. 17, implies that the chest in which the rolls of Scripture were kept had its place somewhere; [1] it is referred to in *Meg.* iii. 1, where it is called the *Tebah* ("*Ark* ").

In *Jn.* ix. 22, xii. 42, xvi. 2, the term " put out of the synagogue " occurs; this indicated not only the prohibition to enter the synagogue, but also exclusion from the life of the community.

These then are the details given in the New Testament about the synagogue.

[1] Doubtless in front of the congregation as the reader stood before it.

CHAPTER XVII

PERSONAL RELIGION

IN what has been said, first about the Temple, and then about the synagogue, we have seen the prominent place assigned to public worship during the Greek Period. This wholly indispensable expression of religious belief and practice was thus fully provided for. It will be well if we now devote some attention to what we find in our sources about private devotions. That personal religion played an important part in the lives of many is amply shown in the *Psalms*, a number of which belong to our period; many of them are the religious outpourings of devout individuals which were adapted to public worship. Elsewhere, too, in the Old Testament there are incidental allusions to private devotions (e.g. *i Kgs.* iv. 23; *ii Kgs.* xix. 15; *Hab.* iii. 1; *Dan.* vi. 10). But our main concern here is with the evidence provided in the uncanonical literature of the Greek Period on the subject of the intercourse between God and the individual, as distinct from congregational worship. In its essence there is, of course, no difference between the two; but the experience of personal communing with God felt by the individual in isolated solitude generates a sense of intimacy with the Heavenly Father which is not possible in the crowd, uplifted though it be in holy worship, and intensely beautiful as this is. " My God, my God "; " O Lord our God "; they are the same and yet different.

We shall, then, from the point of view of the individual, consider first the subject of *prayer*, as dealt with in the literature of our period. This will be followed by what is said about repentance, confession, and the frequently accompanying act of *fasting*; then there is the necessary sequel of *amendment of life*, often shown forth by *almsgiving*. Finally, something will be said on the subject of *faith*, the great constituent of personal religion, as presented in the literature in question.

We draw attention, then, first to the subject of *private prayer*, the frequent mention of which shows how great a part it must have played in the lives of all right-minded men.   We will begin by noting some of the many instances in which prayer is offered for things spiritual.   Foremost here is the prayer to be kept from evil.   Ben-Sira bids men pray to God that their offences may cease in these words: " Turn unto the Lord, and forsake sin, supplicate before him, and lessen offence " (*Ecclus.* xvii. 25), meaning that offence is lessened by supplicating before Him.   Again, the writer of *Jubilees* reflects his own thought when he says of Abraham: " And he began to pray to the Creator of all things that he would save him from the errors of the children of men . . ." (xi. 17).   Similarly in the *Test. XII Patriarchs* it is told how Levi saw unrighteousness in others, and prayed to be kept from it (*Levi* i. 3, 4); then it is recorded that his prayer was answered: " The Most High hath heard thy prayer, to separate thee from iniquity . . ." (iv. 2). Another passage in *Ecclesiasticus* is worth quoting in this connexion: " O Lord, Father, and Master of my life . . . Give me not a proud look, and turn away lust from me.   May the lust of the belly (i.e. greed) and chambering not overtake me, and give me not over to a shameless soul " (xxiii. 1, 4, 6; as the Greek text stands, verses 1 ff. have got out of order, the Hebrew is not extant).   Prayer for strength in time of temptation appears several times in the *Testaments*, viz. *Joseph* iii. 3, iv. 8, vii. 4, viii. 1; and prayer for forgiveness naturally finds expression, e.g. in *Ecclus.* xxviii. 2 we have these striking words: " Forgive an injury done thee by thy neighbour, and then, when thou prayest, thy sins will be forgiven."   Very poignant is the following passage in the *Prayer of Manasses*, verse 13: " But I humbly beseech thee, forgive me, O Lord, forgive me, and destroy me not with mine iniquities; neither, in thy continual anger against me, lay up evil in store for me; nor pass thou sentence against me, when I am in the lowest parts of the earth."   Then we have the offering of prayer for divine guidance in the right way of life; thus, Tobit urges his son to pray to God that " thy ways may be made straight, and that all thy paths and counsels may prosper . . . the Lord giveth thee all good things . . ." (*Tobit* iv. 19); similarly in *Ecclus.* xxxvii. 15: " But in all these things entreat God, that he may direct thy steps in truth."   This subject of prayer is more fully expressed in *Jub*. xii. 19, 20: "And he prayed that night, and said, My God, God Most High, thou alone art my God . . . deliver me from the hands of evil spirits who have sway over the thoughts of men's hearts, and let them not lead me astray from thee, my God. And stablish thou me and my seed for ever, that we go not astray from henceforth and for evermore."

What we have said so far is in reference to prayer for spiritual needs; a few illustrations may be added in which temporal wants are the subject of prayer. Two of these, exceptional of their kind, but interesting as recording how the sorrowful victim throws himself (or herself) upon God as the one refuge when the outlook is very dark—two of these occur in *Tob*. iii. 1–6, and 7–15. Tobit prays to be saved from the mockery cast on him by his wife, in the first; while, in the second, Sarah, the daughter of Raguel, prays to be delivered from the wrongful accusations of her handmaidens. In the former case the prayer is that Tobit may go to " the everlasting place "; in the latter Raguel's daughter prays to be " released from the earth " that she may " no more hear reproach ". But in each case the prayer is answered without this extreme expedient. The exaggerated pictures are drawn in order to heighten the dramatic element in the story; but the main point is that prayer is addressed to the Almighty for deliverance from cruel wrongs. Again, Ben-Sira utters a prayer for protection against enemies, in the more usual sense, in the following eloquent words: " Save us, O God of all, and cast thy fear upon all the nations. Shake thine hand against the strange people, that they may see thy power. As thou hast sanctified thyself in us before their eyes, so sanctify thyself in them before our eyes; that they may know, even as we know, that there is none other God but thee. . . . Subdue the foe, and drive out the enemy " (*Ecclus*. xxxvi. 1–7, from the Hebrew). Another example of this is the prayer of a certain Eleazar, a priest, recorded in *iii Macc*. vi. 1–15, but the passage is too long to quote. Another subject of prayer is that of recovery from sickness; Ben-Sira exhorts thus: " My son, in sickness be not negligent; pray unto God, for he can heal " (*Ecclus*. xxxvii. 9) ; so shortly put, but how profoundly true! Then he goes on to speak of the physician's prayer: " For there is a time when success is in his power (lit. hand); for he also maketh supplication to

God to make his diagnosis successful, and the healing that it
may give life " (verses 13, 14, also from the Hebrew).

Something must be said next about intercessory prayer,
which is of frequent mention, especially in the *Testaments*;
thus, in *Reuben* i. 7 the patriarch says : " Had not my father
Jacob prayed for me to the Lord, the Lord would have destroyed me "; similarly in iv. 4. Again, in *Gad* vii. 1 it is
said : " If a man prosper more than you, do not be vexed, but
pray also for him, that he may have perfect prosperity " (see
also v. 9). And once more, in *Joseph* xviii. 2 we have this
striking precept : " If anyone seeketh to do evil unto you, do
well unto him, and pray for him, and ye shall be redeemed of
the Lord from all evil " (cp. *Naphth.* vi. 8; *Ben.* x. 1). The
intercession of Moses is spoken of in the *Assumpt. of Moses*, xi.
17, where it is said in reference to his prayers for his people,
" who every hour by day and night had his knees fixed to the
ground praying and beholding him who is omnipotent over the
world. . . ."

Finally, belief in the answer to prayer is often expressed;
Ben-Sira says, for example : " He hearkeneth unto the supplica-
tions of the distressed ; he doth not ignore the cry of the orphan,
nor the widow when she poureth out her complaint " (*Ecclus.*
xxxv. 16, 17). In the *Psalms of Solomon* there are several passages to the same effect, which are well worth quoting; thus,
in ii. 40 the psalmist says : " For the Lord is good to them that
call upon him in patience, doing according to his mercy to his
pious ones, establishing them at all times before him in strength."
And again in vi. 8 : " The Lord heareth the prayer of everyone
that feareth God, and every request of the soul that hopeth for
him doth the Lord accomplish." Once more : " Lord, thy
mercy is over the works of thine hands for ever; thy goodness
is over Israel with a rich gift. Thine eyes look upon them, so
that none of them suffer want; thine ears listen to the hopeful
prayer of the poor " (xviii. 1–3).

These illustrations, then, bear ample witness to the way in
which prayer, in all circumstances of life, was general among
those to whom religion was a reality. We consider next the
subject of repentance. Communing with God, i.e. prayer,
generates the recognition of sinfulness in the suppliant, and
with this comes, through divine grace, the spirit of repentance.

True repentance enforces confession of sin; the two are insepar-able, the former implying the latter, even though confession be not always explicitly mentioned; for the fact is that in Hebrew " to repent ", and " to make confession " have both the same root, *shûb*, " to turn ". The presence of this constituent of personal religion is often made evident in the literature of our period; some quotations illustrative of this must now be given. An exhortation of Ben-Sira runs: " Be not ashamed to confess (lit. turn) sin, and stand not against the stream " (*Ecclus*. iv. 26), meaning that it is just as impossible to stem the current of a river as it is to hide one's sins. Again, in xvii. 25, 26, he urges: " Turn unto the Lord and forsake sins, supplicate before his face and lessen offence. Turn unto the Most High, and turn away from iniquity and vehemently hate the abomin-able thing." Here we have the term " turn " further illu-strated; to turn unto the Lord means to repent, because a man turns from sin; similarly in verse 29: " How great is the mercy of the Lord, and his forgiveness to them that turn unto him." The nature of repentance is thus described in the *Testaments*, *Gad* v. 7, 8: " For true repentance after a godly sort destroyeth ignorance, and driveth away the darkness, and enlighteneth the eyes, and giveth knowledge to the soul, and leadeth the mind to salvation. And those things which it hath not learnt from man, it knoweth through repentance." This is rather a striking passage; its whole import is that where there is true repentance the knowledge of things divine is accorded. In the *Psalms of Solomon* ix. 12–15 the fact of repentance is said, by divine mercy, to obliterate sin: " He cleanseth from sins a soul when it maketh confession, when it maketh acknowledgement; for shame is upon us and upon our faces on account of all these things. And to whom doth he forgive sins, except to them that have sinned? . . . Thy goodness is upon them that sin, when they repent." That men are brought to repentance through the mercy of God is taught in the *Wisdom of Solomon* xi. 23: " But thou hast mercy upon all men, for thou canst do all things, and thou dost overlook the sins of men that they may repent " (cp. xii. 10). The divine patience is beautifully expressed in the *Zadokite Fragments* ii. 3: " Longsuffering is with him, and plenteousness of forgiveness, to pardon those who repent of transgression." But most striking of all the passages which speak of this subject is that in the *Prayer of Manasses*, verses 7–13; it is too long to quote in full, but here are a few of the sentences: "Thou, O Lord, according to thy great goodness hast promised repentance and forgiveness to them that have sinned against thee; and in the multitude of thy mercies hast appointed repentance unto sinners, that they may be saved. . . . For thou, O Lord, art the God of them that repent; and in me thou wilt show forth all thy goodness, for thou wilt save me, unworthy that I am, according to thy great mercy."

The desire to manifest the depth of repentance by some visible act accounts for the frequent connexion of fasting with the expression of repentance; thus, Reuben is represented as saying: "And after this I repented with set purpose of my soul for seven years before the Lord. And wine and strong drink I drank not, and flesh entered not into my mouth, and I ate no pleasant food . . ." (*Testament XII Patr., Reuben* i. 9, 10). In the same book, *Simeon* iii. 4, the patriarch says: "Two years I afflicted my soul with fasting, in the fear of the Lord; and I learned that deliverance from envy cometh by the fear of God"; the envy of which he repents is spoken of in the preceding verses. Again, in the *Psalms of Solomon* iii. 9 it is said of the righteous man that "he maketh atonement for sins of ignorance by fasting and afflicting his soul"; but to counteract what might appear as an undue claim it is added: "But the Lord counteth guiltless every pious man and his house". These few illustrations will suffice. More important is the teaching on amendment of life which follows true repentance; and this is shown forth, above all, by the giving of alms, which came to be regarded as synonymous with righteousness. In the words of Tobit to his son, repentance for past sin is taken for granted, and the paternal advice is given thus: "Give alms of thy substance; and when thou givest alms, let not thine eye be envious. Turn not away thy face from any poor man, and the face of God shall not be turned away from thee . . ." (*Tob.* iv. 7–11; cp. also xii. 8–10). It is unnecessary to quote further passages in illustration of this; the point to emphasize is that where there has been true repentance the penitent cannot do other than prove it by amendment of life; and this could not be more plainly manifested than by almsgiving. It was inevitable that with many the doing of acts of kindness should generate the feeling of self-righteousness, and thus the claim of justification in the sight of God by means of good works. With this perversion of man's true relationship to God we are not here concerned. Where a true and soul-felt personal religion held sway the fulfilling of good works was the outcome of love and loyalty to the Heavenly Father, not a pandering to self-esteem.

What has been said witnesses, in one way or another, to the presence of a living faith. Personal religion without faith would be a contradiction in terms; hence it is not often specifically mentioned, being self-understood. Prayer, as the proof and expression of love for God, would be an empty formula without faith. Repentance, witnessing to the fear of God, would be meaningless without faith. Amendment of life, based on trust in God, would be pointless without faith. Prayer is offered in faith, in the knowledge that it will be answered; true repentance brings with it the conviction of forgiveness; and amendment of life is of real worth only when carried out with a Godward purpose. All this, though not expressed in words, is implicit in many of the quotations which have been given. We may, however, in conclusion, point to a few passages in our literature in which faith, the essence of personal religion, is definitely spoken of. In the *Wisdom of Solomon* iii. 9, for example, it is said: " They that trust in him shall understand truth, and the faithful shall abide in him in love; for grace and mercy are for his elect, and he will graciously visit his sanctified ones." Very finely does Ben-Sira extol faith in the words: " Who ever trusted in the Lord, and was put to shame? Or who did abide in his fear, and was forsaken? Or who called on him, and was overlooked? For the Lord is compassionate and merciful, and forgiveth sins, and saveth in time of trouble " (*Ecclus.* ii. 10, 11). Again, in the *Letter of Aristeas* 234 the question is put: " What is the highest form of glory? " To this the answer is: " To honour God, and that not with gifts or sacrifices, but with purity of soul and devout conviction that all things are fashioned and directed by God in accordance with his will ". And, once more, in the *Apoc. of Baruch* liv. 5, the Seer, in his prayer, says: " Thou lightest up what is dark, and revealest what is hidden, to the pure, who in faith have submitted themselves to thee and thy law." One final quotation, again from the *Wisdom of Solomon* xv. 1–3, we must add, for it is such a whole-hearted confession of faith, though the word is not expressed: " But thou, our God, art loving and true, long-suffering and in mercy ordering all things; for even if we sin, we are thine, knowing thy strength; but we shall not sin, knowing that we are accounted thine. For to know thee is perfect righteousness, and to know thy power is the root of immortality."

These are but a few of the passages that could be cited from our literature showing how real and deep-seated was the faith of those who were God-fearing.

This, then, is some of the witness borne in our literature of the personal religion which ran side by side with public worship.

PART V: TEACHERS

CHAPTER XVIII

THE SCRIBES

In dealing with the subject of the Scribes it will not be without interest if we devote a few words to the question of their origin. The position they occupied during the period with which we are specially concerned was of such outstanding importance that it is worth while enquiring into their antecedents. To say that they originated during the Exile is true only in part; their activity was entirely concerned with the Law; but the Law existed long before the Exile; so that the question naturally suggests itself as to how their activity in this respect was exercised in pre-exilic times. Now the technical term applied to the Scribes in post-exilic times was *Sōpherim*; but this term is never used of teachers of the Law in pre-exilic times. In those earlier days the term was employed often enough, but the *Sōphēr* then was a State official; he occupied an office in the royal household (*ii Kgs.* xviii. 18; *Ps.* xl. 1); thus Shaphan the Scribe appears as a kind of minister of finance (*ii Kgs.* xxii. 3 ff.); and in *Isa.* xxxvi. 3 mention is made of Shebna the Scribe; according to *Isa.* xxii. 15 he was secretary of State; this was in the reign of Hezekiah. According to *Jer.* xxxvi. 12 the scribe had his special chamber in the royal palace; and from *Jer.* xxxii. 14, 15, it is seen that he had charge of legal documents, such as deeds of purchase. That the *Sōpherim* occupied a position of considerable power is evident from *Isa.* x. 1; the actual term does not, it is true, occur in this passage, but they are clearly in the mind of the prophet; in connexion with his words *Jer.* viii. 8 should be read.

Thus, in pre-exilic times the office of the Scribe, or *Sōphēr*, was largely of a secular character. In all the cases just mentioned it is obvious that the prime requisite of the *Sōphēr*

was that he should be able to write; in fact, the term, derived
originally from the root meaning "to count", came to be
applied to one who could put things down in writing, and thus
the man who could write, cp. *Jer.* viii, "the false pen of the
Sōpherim," *Ps.* xlv. I, ". . . the pen of a ready *Sōphēr*". In
days when the art of writing was restricted to comparatively
few, the man who could write was an important person. In
pre-exilic times, then, the term *Sōpherim* was never applied to
those whose concern it was to be occupied with the Law.
Nevertheless, that this demanded the ability to write on the
part of those who taught the Law and handed down copies
of it to their successors, goes without saying. We recall the
work of the codification of the Law in the "Book of the Covenant" (*Exod.* xx. 24–xxiii. 19), belonging in all probability
to the ninth century B.C., and, later, the compilation of the
book of *Deuteronomy*, towards the end of the seventh century B.C.

Why, then, it will be asked, was the term *Sōpherim* not applied
to those who, in pre-exilic times, were occupied with the Law,
and its inculcation among the people? The reason was
because this sacred duty was carried out by the *priests*; they
were the first specialists in, and guardians of, the Law; and
they were thus the spiritual ancestors of the Scribes, so far as
the Law was concerned. The frequent mention of the priests
with the Scribes is, therefore, fully comprehensible, see, e.g.,
Matth. ii. 4, xvi. 21; *Mk.* x. 33, xi. 27; *Lk.* xxii. 2, and elsewhere.

The first post-exilic use of the term *Sōphēr* occurs in connexion with the name of Ezra,[1] who is called "the priest, the
scribe (*Sōphēr*), even the scribe of the words of the commandments of Yahweh and of the statutes to Israel" (*Ezra* vii. 11);
very instructive is what is said in the previous verse that he
"had set his heart to seek the law of Yahweh, and to do it,
and to teach in Israel statutes and judgements". Whatever
other purposes Ezra had in journeying to the home-land, viz.
the settling down once more of the twelve tribes in the land of
their fathers, and the restoration of the national worship,
it would seem that his primary concern was with the Law.
Ezra was thus the originator and father of the *Sōpherim*, or
Scribes, as we now understand the term. Not long after his
time, as Robertson Smith points out, in reference to *i Chron.* ii.

[1] See, in general, Schaeder, *Esra der Schreiber* (1930).

55, " we find them organized in regular ' families ', or, as we should say, ' guilds ', an institution quite in accordance with the whole spirit of the East, which forms a guild or trades-union of every class possessing special technical knowledge ".[1] Thus, *Sōphēr*, or " Scribe ", though used in reference to one who writes, receives a different meaning both as regards writer and subject-matter; the writing has to do with the Law, which, being sacred, occupies the priests, since prophetic activity is now no more what it had been. Such records as we have, belonging to the third century B.C., give us no information about the Scribes. It is not until we come to somewhat later times that we learn from various writings the great activity and development of their work which had taken place during the intervening period. From these it is seen that scribal activity had largely passed out of the hands of the priests, and that the Scribes formed a separate and independent body of legal experts. Their knowledge of the Law constituted them teachers of the people, and made their authority para-mount in this respect. The Law, as interpreted and taught by them, became the standard of life. The subsequent relationship between the Scribes and the priests demands a brief consideration.[2] As the original teachers of the Law, it stands to reason that the priests did not renounce this function even though it was to such a great extent taken over by lay-teachers. Furthermore, although the Scribes undoubtedly attained to a position of predominance among the bulk of the people, the political status of the priests, and more especially their outstanding authority in all that concerned the organiza-tion and conduct of public worship, necessarily invested them with an unique authority. Thus, both Scribes and priests held a commanding position among the people; and this was mutually recognized, hence the frequent mention of them in the Gospels in union (*Matth*. ii. 4, xvi. 22, xx. 18; *Mk*. viii. 31, xi. 18, xiv. 1, 43; *Lk*. xix. 47, xx. 1, xxiii. 10; and else-where). That the Scribes were also closely associated with the Pharisees, who were likewise champions of the Law, is abundantly clear from what we read in the Gospels (e.g. *Matth*. v. 20, xv. 1, xxiii. 2; *Mk*. vii. 5; *Lk*. vi. 7, and elsewhere)

---

[1] *The Old Testament in the Jewish Church*, p. 44 (1895).
[2] For the Scribes as Wisdom teachers, see pp. 234 f.

But that Scribes were also in close touch with the Sadducees is extremely likely, for the Sadducees held strictly to the written Law, though they did not recognize the authority of the Oral Law. The fact, furthermore, that we get such expressions as "the scribes of the Pharisees" (*Mk.* ii. 16, *Acts* xxiii. 9), and "the Pharisees and their scribes" (*Lk.* v. 30), suggests the existence of other scribes, in which case they would necessarily have been scribes of the Sadducees.

The most striking evidence we have of the high respect in which the Scribe was held in pre-Christian times, and of his truly religious spirit, is offered by Ben-Sira. This is so instructive in its contrast to what we know of the later type of Scribe, that the passage is well worth quoting in full: "He (*i.e.* the Scribe, xxxviii. 24) meditateth in the Law of the Most High; he searcheth out the wisdom of all the ancients, and is occupied in prophecies: He preserveth the discourses of men of renown, and entereth into the subtleties of parables; he seeketh out the hidden things of proverbs, and is conversant with the dark things of parables. . . . He applieth his heart to resort early unto the Lord that made him; and before the Most High doth he make supplication, and openeth his mouth in prayer, and maketh supplication for his sins. If the Great Lord will, he shall be filled with the spirit of understanding. He himself poureth forth words of wisdom, and giveth thanks to the Lord in prayer; he himself directeth his counsel and knowledge, and in the secrets thereof doth he meditate. He himself declareth the instruction of his teaching, and glorieth in the Law of the covenant of the Lord. Many praise his understanding, never shall his name (so the Syriac) be blotted out, his memorial shall not cease and his name shall live unto generations of generations . . ." (xxxix. 1–11). A number of interesting points arise here, but want of space forbids us to deal with them. Unfortunately, the Hebrew of the passage is not extant, the above having been taken from the Greek.

Although in the book of *Judith* the Scribes are not mentioned, many details of what they taught are to be found; so that the book is a witness to their activity during the second century B.C.[1]

[1] For details, see the present writer's *The Books of the Apocrypha* . . ., p. 381 (1914).

In another book of the Apocrypha, namely *i Maccabees*, mention is made of the Scribes, and they are identified with the *Chasidim*, the " godly ones "; it is said in vii. 12, 13: " And there was gathered together unto Alcimus and Bacchides a company of scribes to seek for justice; and the Chasidim were the first among the children of Israel that sought peace of them." In a slightly earlier phase of the Maccabæan struggle the *Chasidim*, it is said, willingly acquiesced in the decision of Mattathias and his friends, to fight against the Gentiles even on the Sabbath, a previous experience having shown the futility of refraining from fighting on the Sabbath; and every one of them " offered himself willingly for the Law " (ii. 39–42). The identification of the Scribes with the *Chasidim* is an interesting point to which we shall refer again later (p. 244). Only once elsewhere in the Apocrypha is there a reference to the Scribes; it is quite incidental, and they are not mentioned by name; this is in *ii (iv) Esdras* viii. 29, where they are spoken of as those " that have gloriously taught thy Law ".

As to the other books of the Apocalyptic Literature, from what has been said above about the scant reference to the Law here (p. 59), it is no matter of surprise to find that the Scribes receive no notice. It need hardly be pointed out that the reference to Enoch as " the scribe ", and " the scribe of righteousness " (*i Enoch* xii. 3, 4, xv. 1) has nothing to do with the Scribes of whom we are thinking.

The wisdom of the Scribes is largely embodied in the *Mishnah*, which, though not codified until the end of the second century A.D., contains much in its laws which goes back many centuries, together with additions and amplifications gradually mounting up during the previous five or six centuries. This wisdom consisted of two parts, known as *Halakah* and *Haggadah*. The former of these means " rule ", " binding law ", and is applied to the legal element in the Oral Law, and the Rabbinical discussions and decisions dependent on it. A halakic decision became binding if based on one or more of the following principles: first, if it had been long in existence and was generally accepted; then, if it could be traced back to a recognized authority; third, if it could be shown to be based on Scripture; and fourth, if it was upheld by the majority

Q

of teachers.[1] The term *Haggadah* means " narration ", in reference primarily to Scripture, indicating the teaching contained in the sacred writings, and explaining its meaning. But it includes more than this; " the Haggadah ", says Zunz, " which is intended to bring heaven nearer to the congregation, and also to raise man up to Heaven, appears, in doing so, as glorifying God, on the one hand, and as the comfort of Israel on the other. Therefore the most important contents of the discourses comprise religious truths, moral maxims, discussions concerning just retribution, the inculcation of laws which attest the nationality (i.e. of Israel), descriptions of Israel's past and future greatness, scenes and legends from Jewish history, comparisons between divine and Israelite institutions, eulogies of the Holy Land, encouraging narratives, and comfort of every kind." [2] This Haggadic literature thus constitutes a *thesaurus* of the highest and deepest thoughts of the Scribes and their successors on religion and ethics, embodied in popular form.

Of the influential position of the Scribes fully established before the beginning of the Christian Era we have ample evidence in the Gospels. The most frequent title applied to them is γραμματεύς , the equivalent of the Hebrew *Sōphēr*, but they are also spoken of as " teachers " (*Lk.* ii. 46), as " law teachers " (*Lk.* v. 17), and as " lawyers " (*Lk.* vii. 30, and elsewhere), thus indicating their special characteristics. According to *Matth.* xxiii. 7, they affected the honorific title of *Rabbi*, " my master ", or " teacher ". Their legitimate claims are recognized by our Lord: " The scribes and the Pharisees sit on Moses' seat, all things, therefore, whatsoever they bid you, these do and observe " (*Matth.* xxiii. 2, 3); the words which follow, " but do not after their works, for they say and do not ", must be understood in the light of such passages as *Matth.* xii. 7, xv. 4 ff., xv. 23, 24; they kept the letter of the Law, but ignored its spirit and underlying moral principles. On the other hand, that there were Scribes of a more spiritual type is seen from what is said, e.g., in *Matth.* viii. 19 = *Lk.* ix. 57, and xiii. 52. For the most part, as we have seen, the Scribes are mentioned in close connexion with the

---

[1] Strack, *Einleitung in Talmud und Midraš*, p. 5 (1921).
[2] *Die gottesdienstlichen Vorträge der Juden*, p. 362 (1892).

Pharisees; this was because, while the Scribes were the interpreters of the Law, the Pharisees made it their aim to live according to the letter of the Law. The two are, of course, not to be identified. The Scribes are sometimes connected with the chief priests, without any mention of the Pharisees (*Matth.* ii. 4, xvi. 21; *Mk.* viii. 31). Outside the Gospels there is very rarely any reference to the Scribes; they are mentioned in *Acts* iv. 5, vi. 12, xix. 35; elsewhere only in *i Cor.* i. 20, though conceivably they were in the mind of St. Paul in *ii Cor.* iii. 6.

CHAPTER XIX

THE WISDOM TEACHERS

I

WE are concerned here with the Wisdom teachers who lived
and taught during the Greek Period. But it must be emphasized that these teachers were the spiritual descendants of an
important ancestry, the history of which goes back for centuries
before this period. This is not the place to trace out that earlier
history; but there are one or two things which are worth
drawing attention to because they show the important position
occupied by the Wisdom teachers already in pre-exilic times,
a position which involved something more than the teaching
of Wisdom.

Their technical designation, *Chakāmim*, " Wise ones ", was
familiar in the time of Isaiah (*Isa.* xxix. 14), so that they must
have been a well-known and recognized body long before his
day. Particularly instructive is what is said in *Jer.* viii. 9 :
" How say ye, We are wise men (*Chakāmim*) and the law
of Yahweh is with us? Nay but, the lying pen of Scribes
(*Sōpherim*) hath falsified it " (i.e. the law of Yahweh, lit. hath
made it for a lie). Wise men and Scribes are here identified ;
but, of course, the Scribes here spoken of were of a different
order from the Scribes of later days. At the same time,
it is interesting to note that Ben-Sira seems to imply a similar
identification when he says : " The wisdom of the scribe
increaseth wisdom " (*Ecclus.* xxxviii. 24, Hebr.), and in
describing the activity of the Scribe he says that " he searcheth
out the wisdom of all the ancients " (xxxix. 1). There can
be little doubt that the terms *Chakām* and *Sōphēr* were applied
to one and the same individual, just as among the Egyptians
and Babylonians.[1] But, as among these, so among the Hebrews,
the wise Scribe was originally a State functionary (*ii Sam.* xx. 25 ;

[1] For detailed evidence of this, see the present writer's *The Book of Proverbs* (Westminster Commentaries), pp. lxviii ff., 196 (1929).

i Kgs. iv. 3; *ii Kgs.* xix. 2); according to *ii Kgs.* xxii. 3–7, as we have already seen, the Scribe Shaphan occupied a position of a kind of minister of finance, and *Jer.* xxxvi. 20, 21, suggests that Elishama the Scribe had charge of the State archives. Here again it would seem that in later times there were some Scribes who were both Wisdom teachers and State officials, for Ben-Sira says of the scribe that " he serveth among great men, and appeareth before a ruler, he travelleth in the land of alien nations . . ." (xxxix. 4) ; and Ben-Sira himself, a Wisdom teacher *par excellence,* says: " Hearken unto me, ye great ones of the people." The secular duties of the Wisdom Scribe of these later times would, of course, differ from the function he fulfilled under the monarchy; but what Ben-Sira says would suggest that in his day there were Scribes of outstanding character who were also Wisdom teachers; obviously they were the exception; but it is interesting to see that the original twofold function had not wholly died out in later days. Generally speaking, however, by the beginning of the Greek Period, probably before, the *Chakāmim* and the *Sōpherim* had become two very different bodies of teachers. Two things undoubtedly they had in common: the honour and glory of God, and the good of their fellow-creatures; but their methods of teaching were widely different in spite of the fact that both had practical aims; those of the *Sōpherim* or Scribes, in the later connotation, have been dealt with in the previous chapter. We devote our attention here to the teaching of the Wise men, or Sages.

We shall indicate first the writings in which their teaching is contained; it will be understood that we are restricting ourselves to writings belonging to the Greek Period: A few of the *Psalms,* e.g., i, cxi, cxii, xcix, contain elements which are of the Wisdom type; *Prov.* i–ix, xxxi. 10–31; the *Wisdom of Ben-Sira (Ecclesiasticus)* ; the *Wisdom of Solomon*; *Pirke Abōth* (Sections or " Sayings of the Fathers "; it contains sayings of teachers who lived from 200 B.C. onwards); and the Wisdom section in the book of *Baruch* (iii. 9–iv. 4). To this period belong also *Ecclesiastes,* and, according to some scholars, the book of *Job*; but, as these deal with special themes and are not of the same practical nature as the normal Wisdom writings, we shall leave them aside here. The same applies to *iv Maccabees,* which was written with the object of illustrating and proving the power of " inspired reason ".

II

It must be emphasized that, with all their practical teaching which so often has such a secular ring, the Hebrew Sages were in their heart of hearts religious teachers. Indeed, one of the most admirable *traits* in their teaching is that the affairs of every-day life must not be divorced from religion. It is true that the earlier Wisdom books have but little to say about worship and sacrifices, and the subject of prayer is rarely mentioned; in most of the later writings, however, with which we are here concerned, all these subjects find frequent expression. It is true that, generally speaking, it may be said that the main object of the Sages was to teach men how to live happy lives as long as they were on this earth. This led them to deal predominantly with human character and conduct: the relations between parents and children, between man and wife, friend and foe, rich and poor, high and low; they glorify the beauty of virtue, and contrast with it the hatefulness of vice, and this led them to teach what was right behaviour in every phase and occupation of life, how to accept adverse fortune in whatever guise it might appear, and the fitting attitude of him who enjoys wealth—and so on; in a word, how to live to the best advantage; to do right because it brings its own reward; to avoid wrong-doing because it entails disadvantages. All this may give the impression that the Sages were not greatly actuated by religious motives; but one must look beneath the surface and realize that underlying all these precepts which seem to be purely secular in character there lies a religious foundation. Again and again, directly or by implication, it is insisted upon by the Hebrew Sages that Wisdom, whatever its form, is the gift of God; they show that good fortune as the result of right living, or misfortune as the result of wrong-doing, are not merely processes of cause and effect, but matters of divine intervention in the affairs of men. It is pointed out that true wisdom and godliness are really the same thing, and that the origin and essence of wisdom is the fear of the Lord; and that it is, therefore, incumbent on all men to observe the commandments of God. While this applies to the Sages of all periods, it is not to be denied that those of earlier times did not in their teaching reach the same high level as that of the Sages of the Greek Period. The increasing stress laid on the religious element among the later Sages is seen, for example, in that a more vital difference is recognized between piety and godlessness than between wisdom and folly; and it is significant that Ben-Sira estimates a godly man of limited understanding more highly than a clever man if he transgresses the Law: "Better", he says, "is one that hath small understanding, and feareth (i.e. the Lord), than one that hath much prudence, and transgresseth the law" (*Ecclus.* xix. 24). When, therefore, the Hebrew Sage addressed himself to his people, whether in the market-place (cp. *Prov.* viii. 1–5 . . .) with its crowd of listeners, good, bad, and indifferent, or in the house of learning (*Ecclus.* li. 23—25) with its more serious audience, he spoke as an ethical teacher in the service of God, and never dreamed of such a thing as ethics without religion. And that being the case, he would say many things without any reference to religious thought because to him religion was the basis of his teaching.

III

That the teaching of the Sages was approved by our Lord and the Apostles is shown by the quite evident allusions to the Wisdom literature occurring in the New Testament. To a few of these it will be well worth while drawing attention. We naturally think first of our Lord's words in *Matth.* xi. 19, *Lk.* vii. 35: "Wisdom is justified by her children" (so the Syriac Version); the various readings "by all her children", and "by her works", need not trouble us as they do not affect the main point, viz. the exaltation of Wisdom. The meaning of the saying, in spite of various interpretations which have been proposed, seems straightforward enough: they who, like the Baptist and our Lord Himself, are guided by Wisdom follow the right way; they therefore proclaim by their righteous life that her guidance was of divine ordering. For the personification of Wisdom, cp. *Prov.* viii. 1–36; *Ecclus.* iv. 11–19; *Bar.* iii. 9–iv. 4; *Wisd.* vii. 22–viii. 1. Again, it is

possible that in uttering the parable of the Rich Fool (*Lk.* xii.
16–20) our Lord may have had *Ecclus.* xi. 19 in mind. The
Rich Fool says to himself: " Soul, thou hast much goods laid
up for many years; take thine ease, eat, drink, and be merry.
But God said unto him, Thou foolish one, this night is thy soul
required of thee; and the things which thou hast prepared,
whose shall they be? " With this we may compare what
Ben-Sira says of the man who " waxeth rich "; he is made to
say: " I have found rest, and now will I eat of my goods ";
but, continues the Sage, " he knoweth not what the day will
bring forth; he leaveth (his goods) to another, and dieth."

When we turn to the Pauline epistles we find a number of
instances in which the Apostle quite obviously used the book
of *Wisdom* in his teaching. This is seen, for example, in a
striking manner in comparing *Rom.* i. 18–32 with various
passages in the book of *Wisdom.* Nothing could be more
convincing than the linguistic parallels here; but the two sets
of passages must be read in the original in order to see how
St. Paul made use of the earlier work. To give the quotations
here would take up an undue amount of space; they are set
forth in parallel columns in Sanday and Headlam's commentary on *Romans*, pp. 51, 52 (1914). One or two other
illustrations may, however, be given. In *Rom.* ix. 20, 21,
St. Paul, in the course of his argument on the divine sovereignty,
retorts to a supposed objector: " Nay but, O man, who art
thou that repliest against God? Shall the thing formed say
to him that formed it, Why didst thou make me thus? Or
hath not the potter a right over the clay, from the same lump
to make one part a vessel unto honour, and another unto dis-
honour? " While this simile of the potter probably came
originally from *Isa.* xlv. 9, there can be but little doubt that
Wisd. xv. 7 was in St. Paul's mind: " For the potter laboriously
kneading the soft earth, mouldeth each several thing for our
service; but from the same clay doth he fashion both the vessels
which serve to clean uses, and those of a contrary sort, all in
like manner; but what is to be the use of each of these the
potter is judge." Again, the strange thought expressed by
St. Paul in *i. Cor.* vi. 2, 3: " Know ye not that the saints shall
judge the world? . . . Know ye not that we shall judge
angels? " in reference to departed spirits, echoes what is said

about the souls of the righteous in *Wisd*. iii. 8: "They shall judge nations, and have dominion over peoples."

Once more, a convincing illustration of St. Paul's use of *Wisdom* is afforded by comparing *Ephes*. vi. 10–17, about putting on the whole armour of God, with *Wisd*. v. 17–20; the former is sufficiently well known not to need quotation, but the *Wisdom* passage runs thus: "He shall take his jealousy [1] as complete armour, and make the Creation his weapon for the repulse of his enemies; he shall put on righteousness as a breastplate, and array himself with justice unfeigned as with a helmet; he shall take holiness as an invincible shield, and shall sharpen stern wrath as a sword. . . ." The writer here, following *Isa*. lix. 17, 18, conceives of the Almighty in these terms; St. Paul adapts his thoughts and applies them to the Ephesian converts.

These illustrations will suffice, though many more could be given. It must thus be recognized that the Wisdom teachers in their own sphere had a distinct part to play in the preparation for Christianity.

[1] This word means here God's will-determination on behalf of his people, to whom reference is made in the context.

CHAPTER XX

THE PHARISEES AND SADDUCEES

THE origin of these strongly opposed antagonists, together with the original cause of their antagonism, goes back to a time long before that in which they are spoken of as Pharisees and Sadducees. Apart from the New Testament the earliest mention of the Pharisees by name occurs in Josephus' *Jewish War*, i. 110 ff.,[1] where their close relationship with Queen Alexandra (75/4–67/6 B.C.) is spoken of; but it is in the *Antiquities* (xiii. 288–298) that the first appearance of Pharisees *and* Sadducees under these names is recorded; this was during the reign of John Hyrcanus (135–104 B.C.); and here they are already described as distinct parties. Of their origin Josephus says nothing; but it is clear from the way in which he speaks of each party that they were constituted as opposed bodies both politically and religiously before his time. It is usually held that the differences between the Pharisees and Sadducees are to be traced back to early post-exilic times; that this is true of some of their most outstanding differences is certain; but we venture to believe that the basic cause of what ultimately resulted in the formation of these two parties must be sought in much earlier times. It is a long story, and very involved, but we will endeavour to put the salient points as briefly as possible.[2]

The original priesthood of the Israelites was vested in the house of Aaron, and in very early times we read of the oversight in the worship of the Tabernacle being exercised by Ithamar the son of Aaron the priest (*Exod.* vi. 23, xxviii. 1; *Num.* iii. 2–4, iv. 28, 33).[3] This lasted until the time of Solomon.

[1] The *Jewish War* was written about A.D. 75 or a little later; the *Antiquities* was completed by about A.D. 94. Josephus was born in A.D. 37, and died soon after A.D. 100.

[2] We are indebted here, in the first instance, to Aptowitzer, *Parteipolitik der Hasmonäerzeit . . .*, pp. xxii ff. (1927).

[3] These passages are all from the Priestly Code, but it is recognized by

For reasons into which we need not go (see *i Kgs.* ii. 12–35), the legitimate priesthood, represented now by Abiathar, was thrust out, " and Zadok the priest did the king put in the room of Abiathar ". Of the origin of Zadok nothing is known. For the time-honoured Aaronic priesthood to be thus ousted from fulfilling its functions, and for a house of unknown priestly origin to be installed in its place, could not have failed to produce bitter indignation among the mass of those attached to historical tradition. Solomon's action was, no doubt, dictated by political considerations; but his contempt for traditional religious practice is ominously illustrated by what is said in *i Kgs.* xi. 1–8, where it is told of him that " his wives turned away his heart after other gods "; he worshipped, we read, "Ashtoreth, the goddess of the Zidonians, Milcom the abomination of the Ammonites, and Chemosh the abomination of Moab ". That there is no record of any protest against this alien worship on the part of the Zadokite priesthood is perhaps not without significance.

Thus, from the time of Solomon onwards there were two priestly houses, those of Ithamar and Zadok; the fact that those belonging to the former were precluded from exercising their rightful functions in the worship of the Temple could not, of course, affect their hereditary priesthood (cp. *i Chron.* xxiv. 1–6). Since there is no record of the ancient priesthood having made any attempt to assert their rights, we must suppose that they acquiesced in humble resignation. But that through the centuries which succeeded there were many who regarded the Zadokite priesthood as an usurpation cannot be doubted, since as late as the time of Jeremiah the " old paths " are championed, and the " shepherds ", i.e. the official priesthood, are pilloried; the passage in question is so instructive that it must be quoted: " Thus saith Yahweh, Stand ye in the ways and see, and ask for the old paths, where is the good way, and walk therein, and ye shall find rest for your souls; but they said, We will not walk therein. And I set watchmen over you (saying), Hearken to the sound of the trumpet; but they said, We will not hearken. Therefore hear, ye

---

all authorities that this Code contains very early elements; this certainly applies to passages, such as those referred to, which contain genealogical *data.*

peoples, ye shepherds of the flocks.[1] Hear, O earth: Behold, I will bring evil upon this people, even the fruit of their thoughts, because they have not hearkened unto my words; and as for my law, they have rejected it " (*Jer*. vi. 16–19). Especially to be noted is this stress on the rejection of the Law. On the very eve of the Exile, therefore, we have this prophetical witness to the opposing tendencies of walking in the old paths, i.e. in reference to the upholders of the tradition, and the " shepherds ", i.e. the official religious leaders, who rejected the Law. That this is the correct explanation of the passage the sequel will show. As to conditions during the Exile itself, two tendencies are to be noted: on reading *Ezek*. xiv. 1–8, *Isa*. xl. 18–25, xlii. 17, xliv. 9, 20, it is but too evident that in a section among the exiles reverence for the ancestral religion was at a low ebb. On the other hand, early post-exilic writings show clearly enough that the religion of Yahweh, as taught by priest and prophet, was preserved and handed on. This indicated a cleavage among the exiles, and the echoes of this are heard in such passages as *Zeph*. ii. 1–3; *Mal*. iii. 13–18.

We come now to the early post-exilic period. From the point of view of our present investigation we must note especially the following facts: the High-priest is Joshua the son of Jehosadak (*Zech*. iii. 1–10, vi. 11); so that the official priesthood is still vested in the house of Zadok. In *Ezra* x. 18 we read: " And among the sons of the priests there were found that had married strange women (these): of the sons of Joshua, the son of Jehosadak, and his brethren . . ."; true, it is added that " they gave their hand that they would put away their wives "; but from x. 15 it is evident that this did not apply to all; see also *Neh*. xiii. 28, where we are told that the grandson of Eliashib the High-priest had married the daughter of Sanballat the Horonite, and submitted to expulsion from the community rather than put her away. That this marrying of women of alien race was flagrant contempt of the Law is evident from all that is said in Ezra ix. The next fact to note is that among those who returned with Ezra was " Daniel, of the sons of Ithamar " (*Ezra* viii. 2), showing that the legitimate Aaronic priesthood was still represented. That Ezra himself belonged to this priesthood can hardly be doubted; for he is

[1] This is the reading of the Septuagint; the Hebrew text is corrupt.

often spoken of as " Ezra the priest ", and his attitude towards
the ruling priesthood shows that he did not belong to the
house of Zadok.[1] That Ezra was the great champion of the
Law is sufficiently familiar and needs no further dwelling on.
We have, therefore, in the early post-exilic period opposed
views represented by those lax in legal observance, and those
strict in their loyalty to the Law. The antagonism between
the partisans is recorded as continuing during the century or so
after the Exile; see *Isa.* lvii. 20, lviii. 9, lix. 1–15; *Mal.* ii. 14–16,
iii. 7–iv. 6 (iii. 24 in the Hebrew text).

During the Greek Period this antagonism became more
marked, owing to the exalted position occupied by the High-
priests under Hellenistic rulers; for their necessary contact
with the non-Jewish world had the effect of further weakening
their adhesion to their ancestral faith.

But the High-priestly party were by no means the only
ones affected by contact with Gentile elements. The intermingling of peoples brought about by the conquests of Alexander
the Great was the means of creating a changed outlook on the
part of many Jews not necessarily connected with the High-
priestly following. That this constituted a grave menace to
orthodox Judaism is ominously illustrated by what we read in
i Macc. i. 11–15: " In those days came there forth out of
Israel transgressors of the Law, and persuaded many, saying,
Let us go and make a covenant with the Gentiles that are
round about us; for since we were parted from them many
evils have befallen us. And the saying was good in their eyes.
And certain of the people were forward herein, and went to the
king (i.e. Antiochus iv Epiphanes), and he gave them licence
to do after the ordinances of the Gentiles. And they built a
place of exercise in Jerusalem according to the laws of the
Gentiles; and they made themselves uncircumcized, and forsook the holy covenant, and joined themselves to the Gentiles,
and sold themselves to do evil." Nothing could illustrate

---

[1] In *Ezra* vii. 1–6, which gives Ezra's genealogy, he is a descendant of
Aaron; that " Shallum, the son of Zadok ", is mentioned as one of his
ancestors is, of course, an error; Ezra is not reckoned among his descendants
in the genealogy given in *i Chron.* vi. 1–14 (see verses 12–14); on the other
hand, both Zadok and Shallum appear among the sons of Aaron! But as
Kittel has shown, the text of the genealogy is very faulty (*Die Bücher der
Chronik*, pp. 39–42 (1902)). But there is no reason to doubt that Ezra was
descended from Aaron.

more clearly the tendency, long at work among certain sections
of the Jews, to belittle the authority of the Law as handed
down through the centuries. The result was that Antiochus
Epiphanes, encouraged by such anti-Jewish tendencies among
the Jews themselves, believed that the time had come when he
might attempt to hellenize the whole people by stamping out
Judaism altogether. The Maccabæan revolt resulted; with
this we have already dealt (pp. 24 ff.). What we are here
concerned with is that at the beginning of this revolt we hear
for the first time in post-Biblical literature of the Hasidæans
(the Greek ʾAσιδαῖοι), or *Chasidim*, the "pious", or godly ones:
"Then were gathered together unto them (i.e. Mattathias
and his followers) a company of Hasidæans, mighty men of
Israel, every one that offered himself willingly for the law"
(*i Macc*. ii. 42; they are probably also referred to in i. 62, 63).
That there is no word of explanation as to who the *Chasidim*
were shows that they formed a well-known body within the
community; cp. also the frequent occurrence of the term in
some of the later psalms. They were *par excellence* the upholders
of the Law, though not members of the priesthood; their
ardent love of peace (see *i Macc*. vii. 13, 14), though not peace
at the expense of principle, is further evidence of their religious character. They are not mentioned again for the
simple reason that the Pharisees were their spiritual descendants.

Throughout Israel's history there was an inner division of
both priests and prophets, a division which was fundamentally
religious, though personal considerations, such as the displace-
ment of the house of Abiathar by that of Zadok, would in-
evitably accentuate it. There was a lax party, which was ever
open to foreign influence, and a stricter party, which strove
after religious purity. The stricter party was not confined
to priests or prophets. In the days of Elijah there were 7000
who had not bowed the knee to Baal, who might be regarded
as the spiritual ancestors of the *Chasidim*. In the Greek
period the pressure of Hellenism was welcomed by many
elements in the nation, including many members of the priesthood, but was resisted by others, both priests, such as Mattathias,
and others. It is in the time of acute crisis in the time of
Antiochus iv that we meet the name *Chasidim*, but their
spirit lies deeply imbedded in the history of Israel.

After the successful termination of the Maccabæan wars, resulting in national independence and religious freedom, difficult conditions arose regarding the relations between the Hasmonæan [1] rulers and the legal rigorists. Differing views have been put forth as to the nature and course of the struggle that ensued. We do not propose to discuss these, for the records do not give sufficient information to reach conclusions with any degree of certainty. For our present purpose it suffices to note the final issue, viz., the opposition between the two definitely formed parties of Pharisees and Sadducees referred to at the beginning of this chapter. Mention must be made here of the very different view regarding the origin of the antagonism between the Sadducees and Pharisees held by Finkelstein.[2] He maintains that " the Pharisees were originally an urban, and the Sadducees a country group; but that gradually the Pharisees won to themselves, through their peculiar eschatological teachings and their democratic ideas, the mass of Judæan farmers, so that by the time of Josephus there were left to Sadducæanism only the wealthiest in the nation ". We cannot enter here into a discussion of the arguments, often interesting, if rather discursive, adduced in support of the hypothesis; we must, however, confess that they strike us as far-fetched, sometimes irrelevant, and, in the main, unconvincing.

We come now to consider the names whereby these two parties were known. The English form " Pharisees ", comes from the Greek, Φαρισαῖοι, equivalent to the Aramaic *Perishaya*, Hebrew *Perushim*, from the root *p-r-sh*, both meaning the " separated ones ". When the name was first coined is not known; nor is it known whether the Pharisees assumed the name themselves, or whether it was applied to them by their opponents; in the former case it would imply conscious pride; in the latter it would imply contempt. These uncertainties account for the different theories held regarding the meaning of the name. They are, briefly, as follows: the Pharisees assumed it in order to emphasize their separation

---

[1] So called after Hasmon, the ancestor of the Maccabæan leaders.
[2] See the *Harvard Theological Review*, vol. xxii, pp. 185–261 (1929): " The Pharisees: their origin and their philosophy ", and his large work, *The Pharisees : the sociological background of their faith* (1938).

from the common people; the difficulty in accepting this theory is that the facts are against it. The Pharisees were anything but separated from the ordinary people, they were constantly among them, as the Gospels show, and Josephus records that " the Pharisees have the multitude on their side " (*Antiq*. xiii. 298). If by the " separateness " we are to understand the sanctity or holiness of the Pharisees as compared with the common lot, then we should expect a different term, for the root *q-d-sh* also means " separate " in the sense in which holiness brings this about; but in this case they would have been called *Qĕdoshim*, " holy ones ", " saints ". Once more, it has been held that the " separatedness " is to be understood in the sense that the Pharisees desired the Jews to be separate from the Gentiles; *data* in support of this are wanting; against it is the fact that the Pharisees pursued an active missionary propaganda among the Gentiles, cp. *Matth*. xxiii. 15, where it is said that the Pharisees " compass sea and land to make one proselyte ". The theory which would explain the name Pharisee as " separatist " in any of these senses is thus faced with difficulties (but see below). Another theory, also connected with the idea of " separation ", may be mentioned.[1] This is hinted at by Josephus, who says of the Pharisees (*War*, ii. 162) that " they are esteemed most skilful in explaining the laws with accuracy ". Here we may recall *Neh*. viii. 8, where it is said that the teachers of the law " read in the book, in the law of God, interpreting (this in Hebrew is from the root *p-r-sh*) it; and they gave the sense, and caused the people to understand the reading ". Further, in Rabbinical literature this root, *p-r-sh*, from which the name Pharisee is derived, is constantly used in the sense of to " explain ", " expound ", " interpret ", in reference to Scripture, which is explained in the interests of the Oral Law. So that, while the root *p-r-sh* means both to " separate " and to " interpret ", there is certainly some evidence to show that the name Pharisee had reference to the latter. In this case the term could be understood as " expounders ", i.e. of the Law, which was undoubtedly one of their chief functions.

One other theory may, quite tentatively, be suggested.

[1] Quoted from the present writer's *The Books of the Apocrypha* . . ., p. 132 (1914).

The term may have had a simpler and more prosaic origin. The Zadokites (Sadducees), the official religious leaders, accepted only the written Law as contained in the Scriptures; the Pharisees, on the other hand, differed from this in their insistence on the claims of the oral Law as well, and thereby formed themselves into a separate body of teachers opposed to constituted authority. It is possible, therefore, that the representatives of this latter applied the name of Pharisee in a contemptuous sense to those who had separated themselves in this manner from the priestly teachers.[1] It must be remembered that the Pharisees were laymen; and for laymen to arrogate to themselves the function of religious teaching, which belonged to the priesthood, would naturally have aroused the indignation of the latter.[2]

It is recognized that all these theories are no more than theories, more or less plausible; in no case can proof of correctness be claimed. This is to be regretted; but under the circumstances dogmatism would be misplaced.

We come next to the name " Sadducees ". Here again there is some difference of views regarding the meaning of the name; but they do not call for much discussion. The Greek Σαδδουκαῖοι represents the Hebrew *Zaddukim*; it has been held that this is derived from the adjective *Zaddik*, " righteous "; but in this case the name would be *Zaddikim*; the change of vowel from *i* to *u* cannot be accounted for as no analogy exists. Moreover, to explain " Sadducees " as the " righteous ones " has no basis; they never claimed to be any more righteous than others, nor are they ever described as such. Another explanation advanced with great ingenuity by Cowley, is that the name is a corruption from the Persian *Zindik* (Arabic *Zindikun*, plur. *Zanadîku*), meaning " infidel ". He holds that " it is quite possible that the Persian word was used about 200 B.C. in the sense of " Zoroastrian ", and if so, it might be applied by opponents to a party in Judæa who sympathized with foreign ideas, and rejected beliefs which were beginning to be regarded as distinctively Jewish. It would thus have been

---

[1] This would account for the Hebrew form for " Pharisees ", i.e. *Perushim*, " separated ones ".

[2] The fact, as pointed out in chap. xviii, that the Scribes and Pharisees were in close touch with priests may well point to the antagonism between the Zadokite and Aaronic priesthood.

R

used at first in a contemptuous sense, and, later, when the original meaning was forgotten, was, in the well-known Jewish manner, transformed in such a way as to bear the interpretation ' Sons of Zadok ' (*Bene Zadok*) with a suggestion of ' righteous ' (*Zaddîkim*)." [1] Interesting as this is, there are insuperable objections to the theory, and it has received no acceptance by scholars; Cowley himself puts it forth " with great diffidence ".

Lastly, there is the theory, now generally accepted, that the name was derived from Zadok (see above). The objection here that the double *d* in *Zaddukim* cannot be accounted for, and is therefore not derived from Zadok, is quite beside the mark.[2] We may take it as established that by " Sadducees " is meant the party whose origin was derived from the Sons of Zadok in whom the official priesthood was first invested when their ancestor Zadok was instituted by Solomon: " and Zadok the priest did he put in the room of Abiathar " (*i Kgs.* ii. 35, cp. *v.* 27).

To sum up, then. The original priesthood was vested in the house of Aaron, special duties being assigned to Ithamar, the son of Aaron. In the time of Solomon the legitimate priesthood was replaced by the Zadokites. Two priestly houses thus existed, though it was the Zadokites who occupied the official position. The evidence of Jeremiah shows that as late as his time the usurpation of the priesthood by those who did not walk in the " old paths " is condemned. On the return from the Exile the Zadokites were still in possession of the priesthood; but mention is also made of the house of Ithamar, the true representatives of the Aaronic priesthood. The former are lax in their observance of the Law, and there is antagonism between them and the orthodox, headed by Ezra the priest, belonging, as we must believe, to the Aaronic priesthood on account of his antagonism to the Zadokites. The two parties ultimately became known as the Pharisees and Sadducees, with their respective following.

The specific teaching of the Pharisees and Sadducees, respectively, will come before us in considering what is said

---

[1] *Encycl. Bibl.* iv. 4236 (1903).

[2] There are plenty of instances of *dagesh orthophonicum*, and *dagesh euphonicum* in Hebrew (see Gesenius-Kautzsch, ed. Cowley), 13 *c*, 20 *c*, *g*.

about them in the New Testament, and in the writings of Josephus. To this we now direct our attention.

   .   .   .   .   .

There were elements in the teaching of the Pharisees which had a part in the preparation for Christianity. As illustrative of this it will be well to note, as an important preliminary consideration, some passages which tell of the friendly intercourse between our Lord and the Pharisees. In *Lk.* v. 17, for example, we read of " Pharisees and doctors of the law sitting by " while Christ was teaching; presently, it is true, the Pharisees accuse Him of blasphemy on account of His words to the palsied man, " Thy sins are forgiven thee ". But on the man being healed, we read that " amazement took hold on all, and they glorified God; and they were filled with fear, saying, We have seen strange things to-day ". There is no reason to doubt that the " all " included the Pharisees. In *Lk.* xvii. 20, 21, when the Pharisees ask Him about the kingdom of God, He says to them : " The kingdom of God is within you "; whether we render the Greek by " within you ", or by " in the midst of you ", does not affect the main point that we have here another illustration of friendly intercourse between our Lord and the Pharisees (cp. also *Mk.* x. 1–12; *Jn.* viii. 12–20). Significant, too, is the way in which the Pharisees give warning to Christ of Herod's evil intent against him (*Lk.* xiii. 31). The friendship between Christ and Nicodemus the Pharisee will also be recalled (*Jn.* iii. 1 ff., vii. 50, 51). There are thus good reasons for believing that there was much friendly intercourse between our Lord and the Pharisees. In course of time enmity arose against Him and His teaching; but even so He could say to His disciples : " The scribes and Pharisees sit on Moses' seat; all things, therefore, whatsoever they bid you, these do and observe; but do not after their works . . ." (*Matth.* xxiii. 1 ff.). This leads us to consider the specific teaching of the Pharisees. It goes without saying that at the base of all their teaching was their monotheistic belief; but it is perhaps not always sufficiently realized that this traditional belief was upheld against Hellenistic influences. Attention has already been drawn to the support which Antiochus Epiphanes received from renegade Jews when he attempted to stamp out Judaism (pp. 23, 25); this

showed the tendencies among certain Jewish circles to repudiate the ancestral faith. The Maccabæan rising, political
as well as religious in its aims, was successful in its defence of
the Jewish faith; but we must bear in mind the zeal of the
Chasidim (*i Macc.* ii. 42; *ii Macc.* xiv. 6), those godly ones who
were the staunchest upholders of Judaism; and, as we have
seen, they were, in effect, the Pharisees of a slightly earlier
time. In respect of monotheistic belief, therefore, the Pharisees
took a real part in the preparation for Christianity. Another
element in their belief in God is referred to by Josephus:
" They ascribe all to Providence, that is to say, to God, and yet
allow that to act as is right, or the contrary, is principally in the
power of men, although fate, or Providence, does co-operate
in every action " (*War*, ii. 162, 163). That this teaching
on divine Providence was accepted by our Lord as in accordance with the truth is seen, for example, by His words
in *Lk*. xii. 6, 7: " Are not five sparrows sold for two farthings ?
and not one of them is forgotten in the sight of God. But
the very hairs of your head are all numbered. Fear not;
ye are of more value than many sparrows." Further, in
what Josephus says there arises the doctrine of divine grace
and human free-will; and here again our Lord accepted
Pharisaic teaching as true: on the one hand, we have
such words as: " Apart from me ye can do nothing "
(*Jn*. xv. 5); and, on the other, there is the parable of the
talents (*Matth.* xxv. 14–30), especially verse 15: " And unto
one he gave five talents, to another two, to another one, to
each according to his several ability." Divine grace, on the
one hand, and human free-will in the use of the talents, on
the other.

So far as monotheistic belief was concerned, the Sadducees,
though favourable to Greek influences, did not differ from the
Pharisees; but they were not the propagators and teachers
of the faith in the sense that these latter were.

Next, there is the Pharisaic teaching on the Law and its
observances. This has already been referred to. It will be
sufficient to quote the words of Josephus showing how the
Sadducees differed from the Pharisees fundamentally both
in theory and practice: " The Pharisees have delivered to the
people a great number of observances by succession from their

fathers, which are not written in the laws of Moses; and for that reason it is that the Sadducees reject them, and say, that we are to esteem these observances to be obligatory which are in the written word, but are not to observe what are derived from the tradition of our forefathers" (*Antiq.* xiii. 297).

We come now to the belief in the life Hereafter. So far as the Pharisees are concerned there is but little mention of the subject; this, however, is, no doubt, due to the fact that their belief was common knowledge, for in *Acts* xxiii. 8 it is definitely stated that they believed in the resurrection. Josephus' evidence on the subject is somewhat ambiguous; he deals with it in two passages; these are worth quoting. In *Antiq.* xviii. 14 he says that the Pharisees " believe that souls have an immortal vigour in them, and that under the earth there will be rewards or punishments according as they have lived virtuously or viciously in this life; and the latter are to be detained in an everlasting prison, but that the former shall have power to revive and live again ". Here it is only the righteous who rise, for the wicked there is only the continued existence of the soul. In the *War*, ii. 163, he records that the Pharisees " say that all souls are incorruptible, but that the souls of good men only pass over (μεταβαίνειν) into other bodies, but that the souls of bad men are subject to eternal punishment ". Here we have again belief in the immortality of the soul; if the resurrection of the bodies of good men is meant, there is clearly implied a doctrine of metempsychosis. That the Pharisees did, however, believe in the resurrection of the body cannot be doubted in view of the New Testament evidence, and the frequent expression of this belief in all the Rabbinical literature, where it is axiomatic.

As opposed to Pharisaic belief we have that of the Sadducees. In the Gospels their disbelief in the resurrection is stated in *Matth.* xxii. 23; *Lk.* xx. 27; see also *Acts* iv. 2, xxiii. 8. This is further borne out by what Josephus says, namely, that they hold that " souls die with the bodies " (*Antiq.* xviii. 16); and again in *War*, ii. 165: " They also take away the belief of the immortal duration of the soul, and the punishments and rewards in Hades."

In saying that the Sadducees denied not only the resurrection, but also the immortality of the soul, Josephus goes beyond what is said in the New Testament. Not only so, but he implies that the traditional *Sheôl* belief of the Old Testament was repudiated by the Sadducees. It is impossible to accept his evidence in this matter. Against it we have also the words of Ben-Sira, whose general attitude is Sadducæan: " Whether a thousand, a hundred, or ten years (thou livest), in *Sheôl* there are no reproaches concerning life " (xli. 4, Hebrew text), meaning that in *Sheôl*, the place of all the departed, none can boast of having lived longer than another. In xvii. 27, 28, based evidently on *Ps.* vi. 5, he says: " Who shall give praise to the Most High in Hades, instead of them which live and return thanks? Thanksgiving perisheth from the dead as from one that is not; he that is in life and health shall praise the Lord " (cp. *Isa.* xxxviii. 18, 19); this is from the Greek; the Hebrew is not extant. The *Sheôl* belief is here clearly in line with that of the Old Testament (cp. also xxx. 17, xxxviii. 23: in the latter the soul's departure is spoken of). The " Fragments of a Zadokite Work " are held by a number of scholars to be Sadducæan; it may be so, but they seem to emanate from sectaries who left Jerusalem for Damascus on account of their dissatisfaction with religious conditions in Jerusalem; their loyalty to the Law was more pronounced even than that of the Pharisees; so that, while opposed to them, it is difficult to see how they could have been less opposed to the Sadducees. For this reason we hesitate to regard the " Fragments " as representing the Sadducæan standpoint. However this may be, it is worth giving the following quotation from these " Fragments ": " They who hold fast to Him are for the life of eternity, and all the glory of man is for them " (v. 6); these last words presumably mean all the glory accruing to those " who hold fast by the commandments of God " (v. 1). But whether or not the " Fragments " are Sadducæan in the official sense, what is here said is in accordance with what the New Testament tells us, viz. that the Sadducees did not believe in the resurrection, but which does not mean that they denied belief in immortality.

Finally, we come to the subject of superhuman beings, angels and demons. We devote special chapters to the popular beliefs regarding these during the Greek Period.

Here we are concerned only with the views of the Pharisees and Sadducees.

That the Pharisees believed in the existence of angels needs no insisting on; the reference to angelic ministration in the Old Testament makes this obvious. In the Gospels the references of our Lord to angels never call forth any protest from the Pharisees. In *Acts* xxiii. 8 it is said that they believe in both angels and spirits. While Josephus makes no reference to Pharisaic belief on the subject, he believes in them himself (*Antiq.* i. 73), and presumably takes for granted that the Pharisees believed in them. As little doubt can there be about their belief in demons : " If I by Beelzebub cast out demons, by whom do your sons cast them out? therefore shall they be your judges " (*Matth.* xii. 27; *Lk.* xi. 19); according to the first of these passages the words were addressed to the Pharisees.

Josephus, again, does not refer to Pharisaic belief here, taking it for granted; for his own belief in demons, see *Antiq.* viii. 45; *War*, vii. 185.

As to Sadducæan beliefs things are not so clear. In the *Acts* passage just referred to it is said that the Sadducees believed neither in angels nor spirits.[1] This is difficult to understand in view of the appearance and activity of angels as recorded in the Pentateuch (cp. also *Ps.* civ. 4), which the Sadducees regarded, so far as the written word was concerned, as their final authority. It may, then, be that what is said in *Acts* xxiii. 8 is due to a mistaken inference derived from the Sadducæan disbelief in the resurrection, namely, that the *departed* do not become angels; this does not necessarily deny the existence of angelic beings who have never been in the flesh. In *Ecclus.* xliii. 17 we read : " The holy ones (i.e. the angels) of God have not the power to recount the wondrous works of his might. Yet God hath given strength to his hosts to stand in the presence of his glory " (Hebrew text; the Septuagint has quite misunderstood the meaning of this passage). Ben-Sira, as already mentioned, represents, in the main, the Sadducæan standpoint.

As to Sadducæan belief in demons, this is nowhere denied, and the world-wide belief in them makes it certain that the

---

[1] The distinction between angels and spirits may refer, respectively, to the heavenly hosts and cosmical forces, cp. *Gal.* iv. 3, 9; *Col.* ii. 8, 20.

Sadducees believed in them like the rest of mankind in those days.

From what has been said it will, therefore, be seen that in various ways our Lord accepted the teaching of the Pharisees; and in so far it may be justly said that the Pharisees had a real part to play in the preparation for Christianity. Where they failed Christ rectified it, and taught the better way.

CHAPTER XXI

THE ESSENES. THE THERAPEUTÆ

I

THE voluminous literature dealing with the Essenes which has accumulated during the last century or so bears ample witness to the interest which the subject inspires.[1] Nor is this to be surprised at, for the problems raised by their beliefs and practices are intricate and thought-provoking, while the very mystery surrounding their *raison d'être* is of fascinating interest; as Lightfoot truly remarked, they constitute " the great enigma of Hebrew history ".[2] Inasmuch as the evidence points to their existence during the latter half of the second century B.C. and onwards, some account of them is called for here; but it must be emphasized that they exercised no influence upon their fellow-Jews or on Jewish belief and practice.

The sources of our information regarding the Essenes are very scanty; it will be well to indicate them here. The main source is Josephus, who gives details about them, or brief references, in the following passages: *War*, i. 78–80, ii. 119–161, iii. 11, v. 145; *Antiq*. xiii. 171, 172, xv. 370–379, xvii. 345–347, xviii. 18, 22; *Life*, i. 10, 11.[3] The only other sources are Philo, in various passages in his *Quod omnis probus liber*, xii, xiii, and in his *Apology for the Jews* preserved in Eusebius' *Praep. Evang.* viii. 11, and the Elder Pliny in a few passages in his *Historia Naturalis*, V. xvii. 4. References in early Christian writings are probably based on one or other of these; in any case, they give us but little further knowledge on the subject.

On many topics connected with the Essenes there are differ-

---

[1] Schürer, *op. cit.*, ii. 651–654, gives an exhaustive enumeration. To this we may add the interesting chapter on the Essenes by Guignebert, in *The Jewish World in the Time of Jesus*, pp. 172–190 (Engl. transl. by S. H. Hooke, 1939).

[2] *St. Paul's Epistles to the Colossians and to Philemon*, p. 80 (1886).

[3] In this passage he says that he joined an Essene named Banus and continued with him for three years leading the life of an Essene. His knowledge of them is thus, at any rate in the main, first-hand.

ences of opinion among scholars; to take note of all these would demand too much space; nor are the arguments put forward in support of views always convincing. We shall, in giving some account of the Essenes, be guided by the sources, as indicated above; supplementary matter sometimes demands mention, in such case our indebtedness will be duly acknowledged.

The Essenes were, without exception so far as we know, of Jewish race. There is no evidence that they lived anywhere but in Palestine. The meaning of the name is an unsolved riddle; there is uncertainty even as to its form. Josephus spells it in two different ways (*'Essēnoi* and *'Essaioi*); Pliny has *Esseni*, and Philo *'Essaioi*. That the name is Hebrew, or Aramaic, may be taken for granted; but what the Semitic form was is again a matter of dispute. The most likely theory is that which derives it from the Aramaic equivalent of the Hebrew *Chasid*, plur. *Chasidim*, " holy " or " pious " ones. Schürer shows the justification for this from the linguistic point of view.[1] We may be permitted to add a further argument in its favour. It is generally recognized that the Pharisees were the spiritual descendants of the *Chasidim*, the legal loyalists *par excellence*. Now, the Pharisees, owing to the very fact of their championship of the Law, were drawn into politics. As Schürer points out, " when the worldly powers opposed the observance of the Law, especially in its strict enforcement as demanded by the Pharisees, the latter gathered themselves together in opposition to the rulers, and thus became in a certain sense a political party, meeting the violence offered them by violence. This happened not only at the time of the oppression of Antiochus Epiphanes, but especially during the reigns of John i Hyrcanus (134/3-104/3 B.C.), and Alexander Jannæus (102/1-76/5 B.C.), when the ruling powers opposed the Pharisaic ordinances in the interests of the Sadducæan standpoint." [2] In the reign of Alexandra (75/4-67/6 B.C.) they became the predominant political power: " So Alexandra ", says Josephus, " when she had taken the fortress, acted as her husband had advised her, and spake to the Pharisees, and put all things into their power, both as to the dead body (i.e. of her husband), and as to the affairs of the

---

[1] *Op. cit.*, ii. 655.   [2] *Op. cit.*, ii. 463 f.

kingdom . . ." (*Antiq.* xiii. 405). We suggest, therefore, that the Essenes, who, as will be seen, were, above all things, upholders of the Law, and desired to live strictly in accordance with the Law, consisted of those who were dissatisfied with the political activities of the Pharisees, and formed themselves into a body representing the original *Chasidim,* whose name they appropriated, and of whom the Pharisees were unworthy.

It is possible that this may throw light on the question of the date at which the Essenes first came into existence. The first time Josephus uses the name Essene it is in reference to " a certain Judas who was of the sect of the Essenes ", and who predicted the death of Aristobulus i (103/2 B.C.); the name was clearly familiar by then (*Antiq.* xiii. 310–13). He mentions them again in xiii. 171: " At this time there were three sects among the Jews ", of which the Essenes formed one; " at this time " is in reference to the leadership of Jonathan (161–148 B.C.); but, as he immediately goes on to speak of the defeat of Demetrius in 150 B.C., it is probably about this year that Josephus had in mind. If so, we may put the date at which the Essene body began to be formed as some time soon after the death of Antiochus iv Epiphanes (he died in 164 B.C.).

II

We come next to say something about the organization and practices of the Essenes. The entire membership of the Essene Order numbered 4000, or rather more. They were distributed among the cities of Palestine, and formed independent communities under the head of a president or overseer (*Epimelētēs*); to him implicit obedience was due; Josephus says: " And truly, as for other things, they do nothing but according to the injunctions of their overseers."

A preliminary novitiate of a year was required of anyone desirous of joining the Order. Having satisfactorily endured this test, " he is made a partaker of the waters of purification," ceremonial purity being strongly insisted on. After this there were two more years of preparation; thereupon, " if he appeared to be worthy ", he was admitted to full membership. The vows which he had to make were, as Josephus says, " tremendous ". The nature of these vows gives such a deep

insight into the essence of Essenism that they demand enumeration here: the candidate had to swear that he would exercise
piety towards God, observe justice towards men, harm nobody,
hate the wicked, help the righteous, show fidelity to all men,
especially to those in authority, and if he should be placed in a
position of authority, that he would not abuse his power;
further, that he would ever be a lover of truth, and reprove
liars; that he would never be guilty of theft or of unlawful
gains.   He had, moreover, to swear that he would never keep
anything secret from the members of the Order, nor com-
municate its doctrines to others.   Finally, he had to swear
to take care to preserve the books belonging to the Order,
and to keep secret the names of the angels.   These last two
matters raise interesting points to be referred to again.   It will
thus be seen that the Essene ideals were very exalted; some
writers, therefore, suggest that Essenism influenced primitive
Christianity.   From this we entirely dissent.

Josephus says that the initiates, after their preparatory
trial was over, were divided into four classes; the only
differentiation that he makes, however, is between " juniors "
and " seniors ".   But in another passage he says that the
Essenes " choose out other persons' children while they are
pliable and fit for learning, and esteem them to be of their
kindred, and form them according to their own manner of
living ".   From this it is evident that the first of these classes
consisted of boys, say of the age of sixteen or so, in which case
the third and second classes denoted two further stages, the
second and third years of the novitiate; while the fourth class
comprised the fully initiated.   Philo is obviously mistaken in
saying that the " Essenes are all full-grown men, already
verging on old age ".

The various customs and practices of the Essenes may next
be briefly considered.   All our sources lay stress on their uprightness of life, simplicity of living, and self-control in all
things: " These Essenes ", says Josephus, " reject pleasures
as an evil, but esteem continence, and the conquest over our
passions to be virtue."   Similarly Philo: " As for the love of
virtue, they point us to freedom from the love of possessions,
fame, and pleasure, to self-control, to endurance, and also to
contentment, simplicity, good humour, modesty, regard for

laws, firmness of character, and such-like qualities." No member of the Order was allowed to have individual possessions, they had all things in common; it was a law among them, Josephus tells us, that " those who come to them must let what they have be common to the whole Order, insomuch that there is no appearance of poverty, or excess of riches, but everyone's possessions are intermingled with every other's possessions, and so there is, as it were, one patrimony among all the brethren ". Slavery was, of course, out of the question among them. On the question of marriage our sources are not altogether in harmony. Philo and Pliny say definitely that it was not permitted, while Josephus says in one passage that " they neglect wedlock "; elsewhere, however, that " there is another order of Essenes, who agree with the rest as to their way of living, and customs, and laws, but differ from them in the point of marriage, as thinking that by not marrying they cut off the principal part of human life, which is the prospect of succession; nay, rather, that if all men should be of the same opinion, the whole race of mankind would fail "; an extremely feeble argument, for there was no question of *all* men being celibates! But what Josephus says certainly points to the existence of two types of Essene Orders: the stricter, which was the original and far larger body, and the somewhat laxer, which arose during the later period of the history of the Order.

As to the occupations of the brethren, Josephus' evidence is again not uniform; in *Antiq.* xviii. 19 he says " they entirely addict themselves to husbandry", but in *War*, ii. 129, he speaks of their exercising " those arts wherein they are skilled, in which they labour with great diligence "; similarly Philo says that " they practise such arts and crafts as are consonant with peace, and thereby benefit themselves and their neighbours "; possibly this points to some difference of usage in the communities of the Order. An incidental occupation is referred to by Josephus; medical science of a modest character was evidently pursued since " for the cure of distempers they seek out such roots as may be effective "; he says, further, that " they enquire into the properties of stones "; the belief in the healing virtue of certain stones was widespread in antiquity.[1]

[1] See Frazer, *The Golden Bough : The Magic Art*, i. 161 ff. (1911).

Three minor points may be mentioned as being not without some interest. The first has reference to novices; on their entry upon the first year's novitiate they received a small hatchet, a girdle, and a white garment. The purpose of the " hatchet ", or spade, is explained in *War*, ii. 148, 149; the white garment with the girdle was the dress of the Order, which even the novices wore.

A curious notice of Essene usage occurs in *War*, ii. 147: " They also avoid spitting in their midst, or on the right side "; the former would be avoided lest the spittle should alight on someone and defile him. The latter is more interesting; the right side is the source of light and therefore of purity, so that to spit on that side is an insult to the Deity; the left-hand is the place of darkness and impurity. Thus, right-hand and left-hand, light and darkness, represent good and evil. These ideas are of ancient Persian origin, the outcome of dualism.[1]

III

Of special importance were the religious beliefs and practices of the Essenes; to these we must now direct attention.

Since, as we have seen, the Essenes were Jews, their belief was first and foremost *monotheistic*; the fact that this is never mentioned in any of the sources shows that it was self-evident. In two passages Josephus describes the Essenes as *fatalists* pure and simple: " Fate governs all things ", they say, and " nothing befalls men but what is according to its determination "; they ascribe " all things to God ". This evidence cannot be accepted, for their whole manner of life and practice denies it. What Philo says on the subject is far more likely to be true: " They are taught piety, holiness, justice, the management of affairs, citizenship, the knowledge of what is truly good or bad or indifferent, how to choose the right, and how to shun the contrary . . . regarding the Deity as the cause of all good, but of no evil." That does not sound like fatalism.

In connexion with their *doctrine of God*, Josephus says elsewhere: " And as for their piety towards God, it is very extraordinary; for, before the sun rises, they utter nothing of

[1] For the significance of the right side among the ancient Persians, see Scheftelowitz, *op. cit.*, p. 131.

profane matters, but offer certain prayers, which they have
received from their fathers, as though making supplication
at its rising "; in connexion with this it must be added that
on certain occasions " they cover themselves round with their
garment that they may not affront the rays of God ". With
their monotheistic belief there can be no question of sun-
worship (see further below).

The only reference to the *angelology* of the Essenes occurs
quite incidentally, one of the oaths of the novice being that he
will keep secret the names of the angels. This must have been
due to the supposed efficacy in averting evil which the utterance
of the angelic name effected; but we are much in the dark
on the matter.

Of far greater importance was their belief in *immortality*.
According to Josephus, they believed in the pre-existence of the
soul, which is united to the body as to a prison; but when
set free from the bonds of the flesh, it mounts upwards and
continues immortal for ever. Their belief in the life hereafter
Josephus compares with that of the Greeks: " good souls have
their habitations beyond the ocean, in a region that is neither
oppressed with storms of rain or snow, nor with intense heat,
but that this place is such as is refreshed by the gentle blowing
of a west wind that is perpetually blowing from the ocean ";
on the other hand, " bad souls " abide in " a dark and tem-
pestuous den, full of never-ceasing punishments ".

Nothing shows more clearly the Jewishness of the Essenes
than their reverence for and observance of the *Law*; in this
they went even further than the Pharisees. " What they most
of all honour, after God himself, is the name of their legislator
(i.e. Moses), whom if anyone blaspheme, he is punished
with death "; thus Josephus. The Law of Moses, therefore,
dominated their whole mode of life. Philo refers to this in
saying that " they devote themselves above all things to
Ethics, taking for their guidance the ancestral laws (i.e. the
Pentateuch) which no human soul could have devised without
divine inspiration ". Special mention is made by Josephus
of Sabbath observance, in which " they are stricter than any
other of the Jews . . . for they not only get their food ready
the day before, that they may not be obliged to kindle a fire
on that day, but they will not remove any vessel out of its

place ". Similarly Philo speaks of the seventh day as being held sacred by them; " on it they cease all work ", adding a short account of their attendance in the synagogue. Another illustration of their observance of the Law was the emphasis laid on ceremonial purity. On the other hand, their sacrificial system was not carried out in the traditional way; Josephus says that " when they send what they have dedicated to God to the Temple, they offer their sacrifices, under special conditions of purity which they observe, on which account they are excluded from the common court of the Temple, but offer their sacrifices themselves ". In connexion with this exclusion from the Temple, it is curious that we read elsewhere of " the gate of the Essenes " on the west wall of Jerusalem; that their name should have been given to one of the city gates suggests that they were held in high respect. As their gifts to the Temple were accepted, and as they were good Jews, their exclusion from the Temple is strange.

Their *reading of Scripture* is referred to by Philo; but that they had in addition sacred writings of their own seems to be implied by Josephus when speaking of the oaths of the initiate who has to swear that he will " preserve the books belonging to their sect ".

IV

These beliefs and practices of the Essenes owe their origin to different sources. It will, therefore, be of interest to indicate, or at any rate to suggest, what these sources were. That differences of opinion exist in regard to some of these matters is fully recognized; under the circumstances it could hardly be otherwise. We have pointed out more than once before that during the Greek Period extraneous influences affected the Jews in various directions; this is well illustrated in the case of the Essenes. In spite of their quite obvious fundamental Jewish beliefs, some instances have come before us which are un-Jewish, and which may therefore be regarded as having been taken over from some extraneous source. Attention has been drawn above to the Essene custom of uttering prayers at sunrise, and also to their avoidance of affronting " the rays of God ". This has been thought to refer to sun-worship; had this been the case Josephus would, as a good Jew, assuredly have put in a word of protest; moreover, he would certainly not have sojourned for three years among the Essenes had they been guilty of such an idolatrous practice. The two customs mentioned above can be paralleled by similar ones among the ancient Persians; [1] but while we cannot believe that the Essenes worshipped the sun, it may well be that they adopted the Persian practice in so far that at sunrise they offered prayers to the Creator of the sun. In this connexion it is worth noting that among the Jews at the feast of Tabernacles two priests, standing by the eastern gate of the Temple at sunrise, said: " Our fathers, when they stood on this spot, turned their back to the Temple of the Eternal One, with their faces towards the east, and worshipped the sun towards the east (cp. *Ezek.* viii. 16) ; but as for us, our eyes are turned towards the Lord, yea, towards the Lord." [2] The custom of the forefathers here mentioned may well have been due to Persian influence, which, though especially prominent from the Exile onwards, was in all probability present, mediated through Babylon, in pre-exilic times. Another mark of Persian influence is to be seen in the belief in the pre-existence of the soul; not only so, but also in the conception of the nature of the soul the Essenes seem to have been indebted to Persian thought. Josephus says that they believed the soul to emanate from " the most subtile air "; this is entirely in accordance with what the Persians believed.[3]

As to Greek influence on Essene belief and practice, Josephus, as we have said, sees this in the conception of the life hereafter. Elsewhere he says that the Essenes " live the same kind of life as do those whom the Greeks call Pythagoreans ". Very diverse opinions are held on this subject, some scholars holding that Greek influence on the Essenes was entirely absent, while others see it in many directions; the former seems improbable, for it is generally recognized that Hellenic influences played a considerable part in Palestine; the other view is undoubtedly exaggerated. In a few respects such influence may be postulated, viz. the withdrawal from worldly affairs, communal possessions, the repudiation of marriage, the allegorizing of what was said in the sacred writings, and the future state.

[1] Scheftelowitz, *op. cit.*, p. 125.
[2] Mishnah, *Sukkah* v. 4. Cp. also Tacitus, *Hist.* iii. 24.
[3] Scheftelowitz, *op. cit.*, p. 159.

S

V

A brief consideration of the subject of the *Therapeutæ*
(" Servers " of God, " Healers " of the soul) is called for, since
there were many points of identity between them and the
Essenes. This Jewish sect lived in a community life on the
shores of Lake Mareotis, not very far distant from Alexandria;
though apparently they were not confined to this locality, but
had adherents living in other lands. Our knowledge of them
is gained solely from Philo's *De Vita Contemplativa*; his authorship of this little work is denied by some scholars, but without
sufficient reason. He doubtless idealizes things in some respects, but in the main his account of the *Therapeutæ* must be
regarded as reliable.

It will be instructive if we point out first the ways in which
the *Therapeutæ* showed identity with the Essenes, and then
those particulars which were peculiar to them.

Like the Essenes, they were strict monotheists, and had a
profound contempt for every form of idolatrous worship;
without doubt, too, they believed in immortality, though
this is not directly referred to. They were loyal observers
of the Law of Moses, paying special heed to the sanctity of the
Sabbath. They withdrew from the world, and lived a community life in strict seclusion. They embraced poverty, and
had all things in common. They repudiated marriage.
They were ardent in the study of the Old Testament Scriptures;
and their method of allegorical interpretation was similar to
that of the Essenes. They offered up prayers at sunrise, but
it is specially said that these prayers were addressed to God
and were petitions for wisdom and the knowledge of the truth.
On the other hand, they differed from the Essenes in that
the Order was not confined to men, women being also admitted;
though, of course, the strictest purity was observed. So far as
the evidence goes there was no novitiate or ceremony of initia-
tion. The stress laid on ritual purifications among the Essenes
has no parallel among the *Therapeutæ*; nor is anything said
about their offering sacrifices. Rigid abstemiousness played a
great part in their lives, and absolute fasting was highly
esteemed; for days together they refrained from food of all
kinds. Ordinarily their food consisted of edible plants, bread

with salt, and water; only on Sabbaths did they meet together
for a fuller meal, of a sacred character; on these occasions
the women were separated from the men. On every fiftieth
day high festival was held, and then men and women joined
together; they feasted and danced, and sang sacred songs.
One of the most distinctive differences between the two
Orders was that the *Therapeutæ* devoted no time to labour of
any kind. All day in their cells they gave themselves to
meditation, prayer and the study of Holy Writ. Only on
Sabbaths did they meet together for congregational worship,
and partake of a sacred meal.

Thus, in spite of some differences of a marked character,
there was much affinity of view and practice between the
Therapeutæ and the Essenes; and as among these, there is
reason to believe that extraneous influences are to be discerned
in several directions.

PART VI: BELIEF IN INTERMEDIATE SUPERNATURAL BEINGS

CHAPTER XXII

ANGELOLOGY [1]

BELIEF in the existence of beings other than human forced itself upon the mind of early man owing to multitudinous occurrences for which he could not otherwise account. Just as experience taught him that among his fellow-creatures there were some kindly disposed, and others the reverse, so, he argued, must it be among these invisible beings to whose action he ascribed, respectively, what was favourable to him, and what was harmful. There is no reason to suppose that in origin such beings were in any way connected with religious beliefs. But a time came when, in the history of early man, the beneficent among these invisible beings naturally received greater attention and honour; but the maleficent, on account of their harmful actions, were hated and degraded as the enemies of mankind. All this applies, of course, to many millenniums prior to the rise of religion in any true sense of the word. Of the nature of the gradual steps upward we are able to draw some inferences from what we know of the beliefs and practices of uncivilized man, and of the culturally more advanced races who followed him. The beneficent spirits became gods, and in a natural development arose the belief in high-gods and inferior gods, the latter being the ministers of the former. In the Persian scriptures the equivalent of angels is *Yazatas*, i.e. " those worthy to be worshipped ", and epithets of divinity are applied to them, showing that they were deities of a lesser order.[2] The whole process developed ultimately into the religious dualism such as appears in the religion of ancient Persia.

[1] This subject and that of the following chapter have been dealt with by the present writer also in *A Companion to the Bible* (ed. J. W. Manson), pp. 332 ff. (1939).

[2] Scheftelowitz, *op. cit.*, p. 12.

I

THE TEACHING OF THE OLD TESTAMENT

We are dealing here only with angels in the sense of superhuman beings; in the Old Testament the Hebrew word is
often used of ordinary human messengers. We shall be
restricting ourselves here to the use of the word as applied to
the heavenly messengers of God.

Hebrew religion, in the earliest forms known to us, is already
in a very advanced stage, though the echoes of earlier beliefs
are to be discerned. One of these must be mentioned here on
account of its direct connexion with the subject in hand. The
stage had long been reached in which spiritual beings were
subject to God. They are called *mal'akim*, " messengers "
(*Gen.* xxviii. 12, xxxii. 2), whom we designate, through the
Septuagint, " angels ". Other names are: " the host of
Yahweh " (*Josh.* v. 14, cp. *Ps.* xxxiii); " the sons of God "
(*Gen.* vi. 2, 4; *Job* i. 6); " the holy ones " (*Job* v. 1; *Ps.* xxxix.
6); and " Watchers ", which occurs only in *Dan.* iv. 14 (17)
and in the singular in verses 10, 20 (13, 23), a title which is
frequent in *i Enoch* (see below). Now, we find in several
passages that one of the angels, " the angel of Yahweh ",
is identified with Yahweh Himself. Thus, in *Gen.* xvi. 7–12
" the angel of Yahweh " converses with Hagar; thereupon
in verse 13 it is said: " And she called the name of Yahweh
that spake unto her, Thou art 'El roi (a God of seeing). . . ."
Similarly in *Gen.* xxxi. 11 compared with verse 13, in *Gen.*
xlviii. 16 compared with verse 15, in *Exod.* iii. 2 compared with
verses 4 ff., in *Num.* xxii. 35 compared with verse 38, and in
Judg. vi. 11 ff. compared with verse 16. These passages
may thus well be echoes of an earlier stage of belief in which
there was no clear distinction between God and the angels
(cp. *Ps.* xxix. 1, 2). An intermediate stage seems to be re-
flected in *Exod.* xxiii. 20–22: " Behold, I send an angel before
thee, to keep thee by the way, and to bring thee into the place
which I have prepared. Take ye heed of him, and hearken
unto his voice; be not rebellious against him; for he will not
pardon your transgression; for my name is in him. But if
thou shalt indeed hearken unto his voice, and do all that I
speak, then will I be an enemy unto thine enemies. . . ." The

passage is a very interesting one, since it bridges, as it were, the gulf between the stage in which the angels were gods, and that in which there is a clear differentiation between God and angels, who are His messengers. It is, of course, this last stage which represents the normal teaching of the Old Testament on angels.

As a rule, the angels are represented as visible, and in human form (e.g. *Gen.* xix. 1 ff.; *Judg.* vi. 20 ff., xiii. 9 ff.; *Ezek.* xl. 3, xliii. 6, and elsewhere), though according to *ii Kgs.* vi. 17 they can apparently make themselves invisible to ordinary mortals. In *ii Sam.* xxiv. 15–17 David is said to have seen " the angel that smote the people ". They are spoken of as spirits in *Ezek.* iii. 12–14, viii. 3, xi. 24, xliii. 5. In the pre-exilic biblical writings, however, we have not many references to angels; but it must not be inferred from this that belief in them was wanting, or was regarded as unimportant; even the relatively few references to them show that this cannot have been the case. They are the messengers of Yahweh who carry out His purposes among man, and as such their activity must have been thought of as constant, even if not often apparent to mortals.

But it is in post-exilic times that the ministry of angels receives more frequent mention and becomes altogether a more prominent factor in religious belief. The development of conceptions regarding angels during the post-exilic periods can be accounted for in two ways. As we have pointed out more than once before, the influence of Persian beliefs made itself increasingly felt from the Exile onwards; and in this sphere it was the more likely to be strongly exercised in that the extraneous beliefs were but extensions superimposed on something that was already believed in. In the second place, the apprehension of Yahweh's transcendence and supremacy, which was so prominent an element in post-exilic religion, had the effect of conceiving Him to be too holy and sublime to act directly in the affairs of men; His will was therefore held to be carried out through intermediate angelic agency. This we must illustrate by quoting a few relevant passages.

As heavenly beings, the primary function of the angels is to worship and give praise to God; e.g. *Neh.* ix. 6: " The host of heaven worshippeth thee "; this is brought out especially

in some of the post-exilic psalms (e.g. ciii. 20, cxlviii. 2).
But more frequent is the mention of their action among men.
Thus as the protector of godly men it is said in *Ps.* xxxiv. 7:
" The angel of Yahweh encampeth round about them that
fear him and delivereth them "; here the angel is evidently
thought of as invisible, similarly as in *Ps.* xci. 11, 12: " For he
shall give his angels charge over thee to keep thee in all thy
ways. . . ." Another way in which angels are described as
being helpful to men is set forth in some detail in *Zech.* iv, v,
where an angel interprets to the Seer the visions of which he has
been the recipient [1] (cp. *Job* xxxiii. 23 ff.). At other times
angels appear as punitive agents; in *Isa.* xxxvii. 36, for example,
it is said: " And the angel of Yahweh went forth, and smote
in the camp of the Assyrians a hundred and fourscore and
five thousand. . . ." Similarly in *Ps.* lxxviii. 49: "He cast
upon them the fierceness of his anger, wrath, and indignation,
and trouble, a sending of angels of evil." As to the last two
passages, there is no getting away from the fact that angelic
action is ascribed to occurrences which can be explained
as due to more prosaic causes; but it was, nevertheless, in
accordance with the belief of the times that such things should
be thought of as acts brought about through supernatural
agencies. Prior to the Greek Period angels appear only as
messengers of God; they occupy no independent position,
and exercise no authority of their own.

II

ANGELOLOGY DURING THE GREEK PERIOD

The most developed angelology is met with in the Greek
Period. We will deal first with the books of the Apocrypha.
Very instructive here is what is recounted in the book of
Tobit. A leading *rôle* is assigned to an angel named Raphael
(iii. 17, xii. 15); he is a healer, as his name implies, the
guardian of Tobit's son during his journey, and, above all, he
describes himself as " one of the seven holy angels, which
present the prayers of the saints, and go in before the glory of
the Holy One " (xii. 15). The privilege of the angels to appear

[1] For the angelology in Zechariah as due to Babylonian influence, see
Gunkel, *Schöpfung und Chaos in Urzeit und Endzeit*, pp. 122 ff. (1895).

in the presence of the Almighty is spoken of in *Ecclus.* xlii. 17 :
" The holy ones of God have not the power to recount the
wondrous works of his might; but God hath given strength to
his hosts to stand in the presence of his glory." [1] A very
different function is that of the angel who punishes one who
bears false witness: " For even now the angel of God hath
received the sentence of God and shall cut thee in two "
(*Susanna*, v. 55). A similar function of punishing the wicked,
though under very different circumstances, is that described
in *ii Macc.* iii. 24–26, where it is told of how Heliodorus was
smitten by angels who " scourged him unceasingly, inflicting
on him many sore stripes ". This punishment was inflicted
because Heliodorus attempted to rob the Temple treasury.

We must turn now to the Apocalyptic Literature, for it is
here that angelology in the fullest form is presented. It is in
this literature that we find crystallized what had gone before
and elaborated under the influence of Persian beliefs; not
that earlier thought was free from that influence, but the
Apocalyptists made fuller use of that extraneous source. In
our illustrations from this literature we shall restrict ourselves
mainly to quotations from pre-Christian writings, but it will
be understood that those of slightly later date reflect earlier
conceptions and beliefs. As one of the most important
apocalyptic writings the book of *Daniel* will receive attention
here, though included among the canonical books.

The first point to note is that some of the angels are known
by name, thus making their individuality more definite.
Raphael has been mentioned above, but in *i Enoch.* xx. 1–7
the names of seven are given : Uriel, Raphael, Raguel, Michael,
Saraqael, Gabriel, and Remiel; of these, two occur in the
book of *Daniel*, viz. Gabriel in viii. 16, ix. 21, and Michael
in x. 13, xii. 1. That the names of these angels, or rather
archangels, were of Persian origin, corresponding to the
Ameshaspentas, or archangels, in the Persian angelic hierarchy,
can hardly admit of doubt.[2] The celebrated third-century
Rabbi, Simeon ben Lakish, says that such names came from
Babylon (Midrash, *Bereshith Rabba* on *Gen.* xviii. 1), which is

---

[1] Grades in the angelic host seem to be implied here.

[2] Cp. Kohut, *Über die jüdische Angelologie und Dämonologie in ihrer Abhängigkeit vom Parsismus*, pp. 24, 25 (1866). Other names of angels occur
in *Yasht* x. 51, 68, 79.

likely enough; but there is no doubt that the Babylonians, by the middle of the first millennium B.C., if not before, were influenced by Zoroastrian belief.

Next, as to the appearance of angels. According to the original Hebrew conception, angels are in form similar to men, but in later times, even pre-exilic, they are pictured as having wings; this, again, was due to the Persian belief that angels flew (*Yasht* xiii. 49, 70, 84). In *ii Enoch* i. 5, for example, we read of angels whose " faces shone like the sun . . . their wings were brighter than gold ". Elsewhere stress is laid on the whiteness of their appearance, symbolizing purity (*i Enoch* xc. 21, 22, cp. cvi. 10 and *vv.* 1, 2).

The outstanding feature of the nature of angels is their holiness; thus in the passage referred to above (*i Enoch* xx. 1–7) each of the angels mentioned is called " one of the holy angels "; but this applies also to all the angels; in the book of *i Enoch* they are frequently referred to as " the holy ones " (e.g. xii. 2, xlvii. 2), or " the holy ones of heaven " (ix. 3, lxi. 12); so, too, in *Dan.* iv. 13: " A watcher and an holy one came down from heaven "; in the book of *Jubilees* mention is made of " the angels of sanctification" (ii. 2, 18, and elsewhere); and in the *Test. of the XII Patriarchs, Levi* xviii. 5, we read of " the angels of the glory of the presence of the Lord ". There is every reason to believe that this element was due to Persian influence, for it is characteristic also of Persian angelology (e.g. *Yasht* xiii. 1; *Yasna* lxiv. 4, 8). Another element of the angelic nature is expressed by the term " watchers ", which is often applied to them. This may well have arisen from the early conception which identified the angels with the stars; the appellation was very appropriate as applied to those who watched when all men slept (cp. *i Enoch* xxxix. 12); the identification is expressed, for example, in *i Enoch* xviii. 13, 14: " I saw there seven stars like great burning mountains, and to me, when I enquired regarding them, the angel said, This place is the end of heaven and earth; this has become a prison for the stars and the host of heaven " (cp. also lxxii–lxxv). Then, once more, the angels are identified with the elements of Nature, see especially *i Enoch* lx. 11–21, lxxv, lxxx, and *ii Enoch* xvi. 7; but the most instructive passage on this subject occurs in the book of *Jubilees* ii. 2; this tells of

the first day of Creation, when in addition to the heavens
and the earth God created "the angels of the spirit of fire
and the angels of the spirit of the winds, and the angels of the
spirits of the clouds, and of darkness, and of snow, and of hail,
and of hoar-frost ", also of thunder and lightning, of cold and
heat, of winter, spring, autumn and summer, etc.

Turning now to the functions of the angels. Primarily,
of course, this centres in their ministry in heaven: " thousand
thousands ministered unto him, and ten thousand times ten
thousand stood before him " (*Dan.* vii. 10, cp. *i Enoch* xiv. 22).
In *i Enoch* xxxix. 12, 13, it is said: "Those who sleep not
bless thee; they stand before thy glory and bless, praise and
extol, saying, 'Holy, holy, holy, is the Lord of spirits; he
filleth the earth with spirits' . . . Blessed be thou, and blessed
be the name of the Lord for ever and ever "; see also xl. 1 ff.;
and often in other writings of the period the same is expressed.
But still more frequently is the function of angelic ministration
among men spoken of. Here we may mention first the idea
that the Almighty uses an angel to give a message to men;
thus Uriel is instructed to go to Noah and tell him that the
flood is about to come; also to explain to him how he may
escape (*i Enoch* x. 1–3). So, too, in *ii (iv) Esdras* vii. 1 ff. the
Seer tells of the angel who was sent unto him, and who says:
" Up, Esdras, and hear the words that I am come to tell
thee." Elsewhere we read of angels interpreting visions,
Dan. viii. 16 ff., ix. 23 ff. A further function is that of interceding on behalf of men with God; thus, in *i Enoch* ix. 3 we
read: " And now to you, the holy ones of heaven, the souls of
men make their suit, saying, Bring our cause before the Most
High." Again, it is told how Enoch heard an angelic voice
praying and interceding for those who dwell on the earth,
and supplicating in the name of the Lord of spirits (xl. 6, see
also xlvii. 2). In the *Test. XII Patr.*, *Levi* iii. 5, we read that the
archangels " make propitiation to the Lord for all the sins of
ignorance of the righteous "; and in v. 6 it is said: " I am
the angel who intercedeth for the nation of Israel that they may
not be smitten utterly, for every evil spirit attacketh it "
(cp. v. 7). This intercessory act on the part of angels finds
frequent expression elsewhere too. Then, once more, the
mention of guardian-angels likewise occurs often. We have

seen how Raphael acted as guardian-angel to Tobias: similarly
in the *Test. XII Patr., Jud.* iii. 10, Judah says that "an angel
of might followed me everywhere, that I should not be overcome". A graphic picture is presented in the *Apoc. of Abraham*
x; Abraham lies prone, overcome with fear at the voice of the
Almighty; but an angel is sent to him, then it continues:
"And the angel came, whom he had sent to me, in the likeness
of a man, and grasped me by my right hand, and set me up
upon my feet, and said to me: 'Stand up, Abraham, Friend
of God, who loveth thee, let not the trembling of man seize
thee. For lo! I have been sent to thee to strengthen thee
and bless thee in the name of God, who loveth thee, the Creator
of the celestial and the terrestrial. . . .'" A great many other
illustrations of this angelic function could be given; but these
will suffice. It seems probable that the belief in guardian-
angels came originally from Persia, for they are frequently
mentioned in the Persian Scriptures as protectors of the true
believers; in *Yasht* xiii. 1, for example, Ahura-Mazda says to
Zoroaster that he will tell him concerning "the swiftness
and might, the beauty, the helpfulness, the friendship of the
powerful, pre-eminent guardian-angels of the true believers".[1]

But it is not only individuals who have their guardian-
angels; nations, too, were believed to have these celestial protectors. This is referred to in *Ecclus.* xvii. 17: "For every nation
he appointed a ruler, but Israel is the Lord's portion"; the
"ruler" here refers to a guardian-angel, i.e. Michael according
to *Dan.* x. 13, 21, xii. 1.[2] In *i Enoch* lxi. 10 reference is made
to "all the angels of the principalities". That angels help
in battles is clear from the *Daniel* passages (see also *ii Macc.* iii.
23–26, v. 2, 3); this idea may also be due to Persian influence
(*Yasht* xiii. 23, 37, 43). Lastly, there is the teaching about the
guardianship of angels over the departing souls of the righteous,
and about their punishing the souls of the wicked in the next
world. Regarding the former we have in the *Test. XII. Patr.,
Benj.* vi. 1, the statement: "The inclination of the good man

---

[1] The subject of the *Fravashis* (guardian-angels) is fully dealt with by
Scheftelowitz, *op. cit.*, pp. 152 ff. The *Fravashi* is the imperishable, purely
spiritual, prototype, of deities, but also of men who are true believers; it
was worshipped as divine.

[2] In the Septuagint of Deut. xxxii. 8 it is said: ". . . he set the bounds
of the nations according to the number of the angels of God."

is not in the power of the deceit of the spirit of Beliar, for the angel of peace guideth his soul "; the reference here is to the soul after death. Then we have a remarkable narrative in the *Test. of Abraham*[1] xvi–xx about the death of the patriarch. There is a long discussion between Abraham and Death, personified, i.e. the angel of death. Abraham refuses to follow him; ultimately, however, "Death deceived Abraham; and he embraced his hand, and straightway his soul clave to the hand of Death". Then it goes on to say that "Michael the archangel stood by him with a host of angels and they raised his precious soul in their hands in a cloth divinely woven . . . and the angels escorted his precious soul, and ascended into heaven singing the hymn of the Thriceholy to the Lord God of all . . ." (xx).

On the other hand, there are angels to whom is assigned the task of punishing the souls of the wicked hereafter; in *i Enoch* lxii. 11, for example, it is said: "And he (i.e. the Almighty) will deliver them to the angels for punishment, to execute vengeance upon them because they have oppressed his children and his elect" (so, too, liii. 3, lvi. 1–4, and elsewhere).

In conclusion, a word must be said about the *Cherubim* and *Seraphim*. In their origin these imaginary supernatural beings do not come within the category of angels; but the idea concerning them went through a process of development, and they came ultimately to be regarded as orders of angels. The *Cherubim*, half-human and half-animal in form, were of Babylonian origin; they were looked upon as the guardian-spirits of temples, etc., an idea which was adapted by the Hebrews who represented them as guardians of the Tree of Life (*Gen.* iii. 24), and of the Mercy-seat (*Exod.* xxv. 18–20); they appear also as guardians in the innermost chamber of Solomon's temple (*i Kgs.* vi. 23–29). The most fully developed ideas about them occur in *Ezek.* i. x. Finally, in *Ps.* xviii. 10 we have the anthropomorphic conception of Yahweh riding on a *Cherub*, which, in the other half of the verse, is paralleled with the wind; so that here the elemental character of angels is applied to the *Cherubim*. Very different in origin were the *Seraphim*; in *Num.* xxi. 6, cp. *Deut.* viii. 15, they appear as "fiery serpents", i.e. demons; but later they were conceived

---

[1] First half of the first century A.D.; it is a Jewish writing.

of as angels (*Isa.* vi. 2–4). Both *Cherubim* and *Seraphim* are described as winged. How deep-seated was the popular superstition about these supposed supernatural beings is seen by the references to them in the later literature. In *i Enoch* lxi. 10 they are mentioned with the addition of another order, the *Ophannin*, " wheels ", i.e. of the divine chariot (*Ezek.* i. 15); but nothing is said as to the special characteristics of this order. In several of the apocalyptic books, notably in *i* and *ii Enoch*, there is a good deal said about the *Cherubim* and *Seraphim*, but the subject is not of sufficient importance to need further consideration.

It will thus be seen that Jewish angelology had become greatly developed by the time of the Greek Period. We have given but a few illustrations of the many contained in the literature of the last three pre-Christian centuries; but the salient points have, it is hoped, received notice. In the Rabbinical literature a great deal is said about angels; in many cases this, no doubt, represents earlier beliefs; but it does not contribute anything further that is essential; that may, therefore, be left aside.

The angelology of the period with which we have been specially concerned presents a background to what we read in the New Testament on the subject. To this we must now turn.

<h2 style="text-align:center">III</h2>

<h3 style="text-align:center">THE BELIEF IN ANGELS IN THE NEW TESTAMENT</h3>

In the main, what is said about angels in the New Testament coincides with that of the earlier literature. Without going into too much detail we may note the chief points of identity between the two.

In two instances the angels are named: Gabriel in *Lk.* i. 19, 26, and Michael in *Jude* 9 and *Rev.* xii. 7. Angels appear in bodily form, presumably like men, e.g. in *Acts* viii. 26, xii. 13, and often elsewhere, cp. *Acts* vi. 15; but sometimes their appearance is supernatural, as in *Matth.* xxviii. 3: " His appearance was as lightning, and his raiment white as snow " (cp. *Lk.* xxiv. 4, 5; *Jn.* xx. 12; *Acts* i. 10). Although not as prominent as in the earlier literature, it is doubtless taken for granted that the primary function of angels is to give praise to God (*Lk.* ii. 13–15 and often in *Rev.*). Far more frequent are the references to their ministry among men (*Acts* v. 19, viii. 26, xii. 7 ff., in *v.* 15, it is evidently St. Peter's guardian-angel that is meant; xxvii. 23, 24).

One cannot help being struck by the way in which the angelic ministration is sometimes described as a dream or vision. In such passages as *Lk.* i. 11–20, spoken of as a vision in verse 22, and *Matth.* i. 20, ii. 13, 19, *Acts* x. 3, xii. 9, there is no real appearance in the ordinary sense. Then, again, the lengthy conversations with angels recorded in *Matth.* xxviii. 2–7, *Lk.* i. 11–20, 26–38, give the impression of artificiality; it is difficult to regard such accounts as historical; they read rather like elaborations on the part of the evangelists. In contrast with the earlier literature, in the New Testament the angels are very rarely thought of as intercessors; it seems to be implied in *Acts* x. 3, 4, where an angel says to Cornelius: " Thy prayers and thine alms are gone up for a memorial before God " (cp. *Tob.* xii. 12, " I did bring the memorial of your prayer before the Holy One "). More definite is *Rev.* viii. 3, 4: " And another angel came and stood at the altar, having a golden censer; and there was given unto him much incense, that he should add it unto the prayers of all the saints. . . . And the smoke of the incense with the prayers of the saints went up before God out of the angel's hand." But we can understand why this so very rarely receives mention, cp. *Rom.* viii. 34: " It is Christ Jesus that died, yea rather, that was raised from the dead . . . who also maketh intercession for us ", and *Hebr.* vii. 25: ". . . seeing that he ever liveth to make intercession for us." As in the earlier literature, there are one or two instances where it is told how angels take the soul to Paradise; thus, in *Lk.* xvi. 22 we read: " And it came to pass, that the beggar died, and that he was carried away by the angels into Abraham's bosom ", cp. *Acts* i. 10, 11, and the quaint legend echoed in *Jude* 9, of Michael contending with the Devil about the body of Moses.[1] Once more, the identification of angels with the elements occurs in *Col.*

[1] According to some of the Church Fathers this was preserved in the *Assumption of Moses*; the form in which this has come down to us ends in the middle of a sentence; the concluding portion doubtless contained the legend.

i. 16, 17; *Rev.* vii. 1, the worship of whom is condemned, *Col.* ii. 8, 18; *Rev.* xix. 10, xxii. 8, 9.[1]

Finally there are some utterances on the subject of angels by our Lord which demand special notice. In *Matth.* xviii. 10 there is the beautiful saying about the guardian-angels of children always beholding the face of their Father in heaven. Then in *Lk.* xv. 10 we have the words: " Even so, I say unto you, there is joy in the presence of the angels of God over one sinner that repenteth " (cp. *v.* 7). And once more, in *Matth.* xxvi. 53: " Thinkest thou that I cannot beseech my Father, and he shall even now send me more than twelve legions of angels? " See also *Matth.* xxii. 29, 30; *Lk.* xii. 8, 9. Such sayings, with their ring of genuineness, are plain evidence of our Lord's belief in the ministry of angels. On the other hand, there are a number of passages of an eschatological character about which, owing to their similarity with passages in the Apocalyptic Literature, doubts are sometimes felt as to their having been uttered by our Lord (*Matth.* xiii. 39, 41, 49, xvi. 27, xxiv. 31; *Mk.* viii. 38, xiii. 27; *Lk.* ix. 26; *Jn.* i. 51). In these cases it is possible that the evangelists, being familiar with the traditional Jewish teaching about angels, may have attributed sayings to our Lord which they felt to be appropriate. This is a possibility, but not a matter on which to be dogmatic. Upon the whole, it may be said that while our Lord witnesses to the ministry of angels, He does not teach that they are concerned with the affairs of men in this world. On the other hand, it can of course be justifiably urged that this belief was so axiomatic that it did not call for special mention on His part.

Of the epistles it need only be said that the writers, being devout Jews, held the traditional belief. The book of *Revelation*, as belonging to the Apocalyptic Literature, is full of references to angels.

· · · · ·

Jewish angelology of the Greek Period thus presents us, in this domain, with a background to Christian belief; and though in various respects fantastic and unacceptable, it contained the germs of truth, and in so far offers its quota to the preparation for Christianity.

---

[1] It will be remembered that the Sadducees, according to *Acts* xxiii. 8, did not believe in the existence of angels.

CHAPTER XXIII

DEMONOLOGY

As compared with the belief in angels and their ministry, the belief in demons and their activity has played by far the greater part in the history of mankind. Much space would be required were we to deal in any way exhaustively with the subject. Though full of quaint interest from the point of view of folklore, the subject is not an edifying one. Nevertheless some account of it is demanded.

There are reasons for believing—but we shall not go into them here—that so far as Old Testament demonology of pre-exilic times is concerned, Babylonian and Egyptian influence in this domain predominated,[1] while in post-exilic times, and especially during the Greek Period, the influence of Persian demonology made itself felt in the strongest possible way. The marks of Persian influence were such that we have thought it well to devote a section to a brief outline of Persian demonology, for this will help to show how Jewish demonology of the Greek Period borrowed many ideas from that of ancient Persia.

I

THE DEMONOLOGY OF THE OLD TESTAMENT

It is a striking fact that in the pre-exilic literature of the Old Testament the mention of evil spirits is rare. This cannot be accounted for on the assumption that belief in them was not held; Semitic demonology was far too deeply ingrained in the popular conception for that to have been the case. The rarity of such references is to be explained by the ardent belief in Yahweh on the part of the religious teachers to whom we owe the Old Testament records. Monotheism was not yet

---

[1] Ungnad, *Die Religion der Babylonier und Assyrier*, pp. 243 ff. (1921); Meissner, *Babylonien und Assyrien*, ii. pp. 198 ff. (1925); Wiedemann, *Magie und Zauberei im alten Ägypten*, in " Der Alte Orient " vi. 4 (1904).

established, and any spiritual beings which might be thought
to rival in any degree the power of the One God were ignored
as much as possible. In post-exilic times it was different.
By then monotheistic belief was so strongly entrenched that the
mention of rival spiritual powers did not constitute any danger
to this.

But that the belief in them existed in the earlier times is clear
enough. In common with Semitic belief in general certain
animals were held to be the incarnations of demons; serpents
especially come within this category; [1] thus, in *Num.* xxi. 6
we read of fiery, or *seraph* (from the root meaning " to burn "),
serpents who bit the people; they are not called evil spirits
or demons, it is true, but the universal belief among the ancient
Semites that serpents were demons makes it certain that demons
were thought of here. In *Deut.* viii. 15 the *seraph* serpents
are again referred to, together with scorpions; and the *seraph*
serpent is spoken of as flying, in *Isa.* xiv. 29, xxx. 6. A different
order of demons were the *Se'irim*, or " hairy ones ", e.g. *Lev.*
xvii. 7, *Isa.* xxxiv. 14, who were supposed to take up their
abode in desolate places and among ruined sites (*Isa.* xiii. 21);
they were equivalent to the Greek satyrs. [2] At the head of this
type of demons there was, it would seem, the demon named
'Azazel (*Lev.* xvi. 7–28); but in *i Enoch* lxix. 2 he is reckoned
among the fallen angels, and in x. 8 all sin is ascribed to him;
but if one of the fallen angels, he must originally have been
one of the angels of God; this would explain the name '*Azazel*,
which means " God hath strengthened ". Other animals
of a demonic nature mentioned are *Ziyyim*, " wild beasts ",
'*Ochim*, " doleful creatures ", or " howlers ",[3] '*Iyyim*, " hawks ",
and *Tannim*, possibly " wolves ", but the meaning is uncertain;
all these occur in *Isa.* xiii. 21, 22. Then there are the *Benōth
Ya'anah*, " daughters of greed ", probably " ostriches " (*Isa.*
xiii. 21).

All these types of demons were, of course, believed in throughout post-exilic times; but the occurrence of the word *Shēdim*
(*Ps.* cvi. 37), the inclusive expression for every kind of demon,

---

[1] Wellhausen, *Reste Arabischen Heidentums*, pp. 152 f. (1897).

[2] On these see Frazer, *The Golden Bough : Spirits of the Corn and the Wild*,
ii. 1 ff. (1912).

[3] Cp. the expression " howling wilderness " (*Deut.* xxxii. 10); demons
were believed to congregate in the wilderness.

T

shows that a great development had now taken place. A few demons of special type are also mentioned: *Lilith*, the " night-hag " (*Isa.* xxxiv. 14), '*Aluqah*, a flesh-devouring ghoul [1] (*Prov.* xxx. 15), and *Qeteb*, the " mid-day demon " (*Deut.* xxxii. 24; *Ps.* xci. 6); there is some uncertainty about this last, but in any case it was a recognized demon in later days. Satan, the " adversary ", mentioned in *Job* i. 6 ff., ii. 1 ff.; *i Chron.* xxi. 1; *Zech.* iii. 1, 2, does not come under the category of demons in the ordinary sense.[2]

Before we come to deal with the demonology as presented in the post-Biblical books, we shall give a brief outline of Persian demonology, to which, it is generally recognized, many writers of these books were, in certain particulars, indebted.

II

PERSIAN DEMONOLOGY

The *daēvas*, or demons, were created by Angra-Mainyu, the " Enemy-spirit " (*Bund.* i. 10, xxviii. 1–46). They were conceived of as spirits, and were, therefore, without bodies (*Yasht* x. 69, 97; *Vend.* viii. 31, 80). At times they appear in human form, the more easily to overcome their victims (*Yasht* ix. 15). They work best in the dark; they are called " the seed of darkness "; with the rising sun their power ceases, according to *Yasht* vi. 3, 4; the host of them is innumerable (*Yasht* iii. 10, iv. 2). At the head of this immense host is Angra-Mainyu; immediately under him are the six arch-fiends, of whom the most terrible is *Aeshma*; these six are the commanders of the demons (*Yasht* xix. 96; *Bund.* xxviii, xxx. 29; *Vend.* x. 9 ff., xix. 43). In a grade beneath these arch-fiends are over fifty demons who are personifications of vices: arrogance, lust, greed, pride, sloth, etc.; and then there are hordes of evil spirits under these fifty who bring trouble and misery to mortals.

Further, there is a " special cohort of demons (*drujes*) headed by *the Druj*, the feminine embodiment of deceit and

[1] Wellhausen, *op. cit.*, pp. 149 ff.
[2] Kaupel deals with the whole subject of Old Testament Demonology in his book *Die Dämonen im Alten Testament* (1930); but in many directions we find ourselves unable to agree with his views.

falsehood, who draws in her train a ribald crew of followers, corporeal and incorporeal ".[1]

Among others of what one might call the demon aristocracy there is the horrid monster, the " Serpent Dahaka "; he is in human form, but is called a serpent because " out of his shoulders grew two snakes from a kiss imprinted between them by Angra-Mainyu ".[2] Then there is the demon *Âz*, meaning " greediness "; this demon is he who swallows everything, and when, through famine and destitution, there is nothing more to devour, he eats himself ! (*Bund.* xxviii. 27). The demon *Aighash* is the malignant-eyed fiend who smites mankind with his eye (*Bund.* xxviii. 33). And, to mention but one other, *Kundak* is the demon who is a horse on whom wizards ride (*Bund.* xxviii. 42).

Now, according to ancient Persian belief, everything that is dirty or evil-smelling is the work of demons (*Vend.* xx. 3; *Yasht* x. 50, xii. 23). The demons themselves are filthy, they spread nasty smells about, and their *habitat* is always where there is something unclean (*Bund.* xxviii. 1). Among most uncultured peoples a distinction is made, in regard to both persons and things, between being in a state of ritual cleanness and uncleanness, and anything that is unclean is contagious and, if touched, communicates uncleanness. Attached to anything unclean there is a demonic essence, and anyone contaminated by this demonic essence must undergo lustrations; unless purified from this impure contagion no man may touch holy things, or enter a sanctuary, or approach the gods, otherwise he becomes guilty of heinous sin. This applies with special force to Persian Demonology. The true follower of Zoroaster must, therefore, wash not only his garments, but also his body, before approaching the deity, or before bringing before him an offering, lest, consciously or unconsciously, some uncleanness attaches to him. Even the place in which a sacrifice is offered must be scrupulously cleansed.

In accordance with this idea of the ever-possible danger of pollution owing to the ubiquity of demons, Parseeism enjoins the need of always keeping the hands clean, as well as every other part of the body; but inasmuch as the true follower of

[1] Hastings, *Dict. of Rel. and Eth.* iv. 620 *a* (Williams Jackson).
[2] *Ibid.*

Zoroaster was not allowed to use water, he performed his ablutions with fruit-juice, or even with dry soil; and (like the Jews) he cleansed himself both before and after eating food.

Due to the belief in demons is the idea that a dead body is unclean. According to ancient Persian belief, at the moment of death a female *Druj*, called *Nasûsh*, takes possession of the dead body; she is known as the corpse-demon (*Vend.* vii); the uncleanness of the body thus contracted communicates itself to anyone who comes in contact with it; and the uncleanness is of two degrees: the direct, whereby any person or thing which touches it becomes unclean; and the indirect, whereby anyone who touches a person or thing which has been in immediate contact with a corpse also becomes unclean (*Vend.* v. 27, 28, xix. 12). The uncleanness could only be obliterated by lustrations; and in these cases water (though this seems to contradict what was said just now), in addition to other means, might apparently be used. The laws of purity are more important than any others in the Persian religion (*Vend.* v. 23–25).[1]

To touch now upon another department of Persian Demonology. There are certain animals in the form of which demons are believed to appear. Lizards, tortoises, frogs, mice, rats, snakes, and ants are all demon-animals which should be destroyed. Of all these the serpents are the worst, and, as we have seen, *Dahaka*, the demon-serpent, was among the highest order of demons. In somewhat later times, Angra-Mainyu himself is represented as a snake. And as the wicked ones, i.e. the followers of Angra-Mainyu, were believed to become demons when they died, it was held that they became serpents. Of Persian origin probably is the belief which occurs in the Talmud (*Baba Kama* 16ª) that the backbone of a man who has never bowed in worship of God becomes a serpent seven years after his death. It stands to reason that no demon-animal was permitted to be eaten among the Persians; and it is evident that among the many animals mentioned in the Old Testament the eating of which is prohibited, there are a number which were originally regarded as demon-animals, hence the prohibition; others were, however, unclean, and might not

[1] Cp. Scheftelowitz, *op. cit.*, pp. 27 ff.

be eaten, because they were holy to some heathen god or goddess, e.g. the hare; the Persians, too, forbade the eating of a hare because it was holy to one of their deities.

A hen which crows like a cock should always be killed at once because it is obviously possessed by a demon, and will bring evil upon the neighbouring house. This superstition was prevalent not only among the ancient Persians, but is world-wide, and is met with even at the present day. The cat has had curious vicissitudes in this connexion: on the one hand, in ancient India the cat was to demons what a modern house-dog is (or ought to be) to burglars; in the olden days the cat was not known in Persia, but in the middle period, when it did appear it was looked upon as a demon-creature whose presence brought misfortune; and the same is true not only of India in later times, but also of most uncultured peoples, and even among some of a more advanced civilization.

What has been said, and of course it is a mere fraction of the available evidence, has had reference only to demons of a *materially* harmful character. That was quite bad enough when the belief was ingrained that at every turn you might meet some little devil who could make himself disagreeable. After all, there were means of counteracting its machinations; to these we shall refer presently. Vastly more serious, and here we begin to approach a fundamental problem, is the question of the belief in demons who kindle and inspire in men evil passions, such as anger, hate, envy, lust, falsehood, etc.; here we come to the moral, the ethical, side of Demonology, which leads to far-reaching questions.

In ancient Iran the idea that evil passions were prompted by an influence outside of man himself—that of demons— was very pronounced. Every kind of sin, slander, imputation of evil, lying, unjust action, unsatisfied passion, envy, anger, the annoying spirit of opposition, lustful acts, and every form of thought or action against what is right, was put down to the maleficent prompting of a demon—and this was not, be it emphasized, a pusillanimous shifting of the fault of the cause of wrong-doing on to someone else—it was a *bona fide* belief that when, e.g., a man lost his temper, this was not his fault, but it was the action of some wretched demon who gloried in making a man do that of which in his better moments he would be ashamed. It is a primitive belief, but it has insinuated itself into more developed religious systems.

An illuminating illustration of this Persian belief may be given (it belongs to the somewhat later phases of Persian religion): " Seek not to postpone till to-morrow what it is thy duty to do to-day; for Ahriman (Angra-Mainyu), the Evil One, has two demons who are entrusted with this matter. The first is called ' Sloth ', the other ' Later '. These two demons co-operate zealously in preventing a man from doing his duty; for whensoever a man is about to fulfil a duty or to do a good act, the demon ' Sloth ' says to him: ' Thou hast yet long to live, thou canst fulfil this duty at any time '. And the demon called ' Later ' adds: ' Put it off for the present, thou canst do it later '. Thus do these two demons co-operate in hindering a man from doing his duty until the end of his days draws near." [1] And then, of course, it is too late.

The terror of the belief in demons and their activity would indeed have been an awful thing for humanity had there not been among the Persians—and the same applies, of course, to other peoples—a large variety of means whereby demoniacal onslaughts could be checked.

Among the Persians the most efficacious way of keeping off demons was to light a fire. As is well known, fire was to the Persians a holy element; its protective quality was, therefore, infallible. For example, a newly born child and its mother were believed to be peculiarly menaced by the demons' onslaught; to counteract this a fire must be kept constantly burning in the house of a woman in child-birth; this would keep the demons away. A newly born child must be kept for three days in close proximity to a fire in order to ward off the approach of demons. In the case of a death—and we have seen how demons were believed to hover around a corpse—the house had to be fumigated by the smoke of a fire; and a fire was kept burning for three days for the benefit of the soul of the departed. [2]

But, clearly, in innumerable cases it was not possible to have the materials at hand to light a fire, especially in sudden emergencies; therefore other means had to be employed for protection; and these were multifarious.

[1] Scheftelowitz, *op. cit.*, p. 49.   [2] Scheftelowitz, *op. cit.*, pp. 66 ff.

In the *Vendîdâd* x. 16 it is said that certain words from the *Gathas*, uttered four times, " smite down Angra-Mainyu; these are the words which smite down Aêshma, the fiend of the murderous spear; these are the words that smite down the daēvas of Mazana (the land of fiends and sorcerers in popular tradition, it = Mâzamdarân ¹); these are the words which smite down all the daēvas."

The words referred to were thus a spell, the utterance of which rendered a demon harmless; and, after the fire, there is no doubt but that the spell was regarded as the most efficacious means of countering a demon's machinations. When a man was in a state of sin, or impurity, or ritual uncleanness, he would be regarded as possessed by a demon, and various purifications would be employed to expel the demon; but whatever ceremonies might be gone through, the really important part was the utterance of a spell. In the *Bundahish*, xxviii. 36, one of these is mentioned, a very short one: " In the name of God "; in saying this the demon is disarmed.²

A sick man is one possessed by a demon who has been sent by Angra-Mainyu; his sickness can be cured by washings and spells; and though more rational means were also used to cure him, they were not considered as efficacious as the spell.

A quaint idea (though the reason is clear enough) was that anything that came from a man, such as nail-parings, cuttings or shavings of hair, etc., was unclean, and became a weapon in the hands of demons unless they were protected by certain rites and spells. Thus, in the *Vendîdâd* xvii. 1–3 it is said: " Which is the most deadly deed whereby a man offers up a sacrifice to the Daēvas? Ahura-Mazda answered, ' It is when a man here below, combing his hair or shaving it off, or paring off his nails, drops them in a hole or in a crack. For by this transgression of the rites the Daēvas are produced upon the earth . . .'"; this last is a very strange doctrine which we cannot discuss now. But there was another way, in addition to spells, whereby the danger attaching to nail-parings and stray hairs could be dealt with; this was by drawing a circle, or

---

¹ A province on the southern shore of the Caspian sea.
² Cp. *Jude* 9: " But Michael the archangel, when contending with the devil he disputed about the body of Moses, durst not bring against him a railing judgement, but said, The Lord rebuke thee."

rather several circles, around them; thus it is said (*Vend.*
xvii. 6, 7; *Yasht* iv. 7) that around the spot where the faithful
Zoroaster-worshipper has buried his nail-parings or his hair-
cuttings, he takes a knife and describes three circles, better
still six or nine, uttering at the same time a spell, three, six or
nine times. If this is done it becomes quite impossible for the
demon to utilize the nail-parings and hair-cuttings for his
nefarious purposes.

One other point in connexion with the warding-off of demons
may be briefly referred to. We have seen that certain animals
were believed to be the incarnations of demons; certain
others were pointed to as warding them off. Thus, in *Bund.*
xxviii. 41 it is said that evil spirits remain at a distance if they
hear the crowing of a three-year-old cock, or even, it is added,
if they hear the braying of a donkey! The ancient Persians
held that the cock was created for the purpose of keeping
demons away. In *Bund.* xix. 33, xxviii. 41, it is recommended
to every true believer that he should have a cock at home,
because its crowing keeps misfortune away from the house.
If you want to do a really good work you cannot do better
than give a poor man, who is a believer, a cock and some hens.
Naturally enough, to kill a cock is sternly forbidden. Another
reason why a cock is such a safeguard against demons is because
of his red comb; demons cannot stand the colour, red being
reminiscent of fire; and we read that even a cock's comb,
apart from the animal itself, will keep demons at a distance.

Finally, one other animal may be mentioned who is a great
enemy to demons. In the *Vend.* xiii. 1, 2, it is said: " Which
is the good creature among the creatures of the Good Spirit
that from midnight till the sun is up goes and kills thousands
of the creatures of the Evil Spirit? Ahura-Mazda answered,
' The dog with the prickly back, with the long and thin muzzle,
the dog Vanghâpara '." The reference here is to the hedgehog; it was believed that the hedgehog ate vipers, and vipers
were, as we have seen, demon-animals. Plutarch (*Quæstiones
Conviviales* iv. 5, 2) counts the hedgehog amongst the animals
sacred to the Magi.

It is unnecessary to give further illustrations. There were
thus multifarious means whereby the harmful intentions of
demons were frustrated, and, to clinch the matter, there

was a grand annual ceremony whereby the whole innumerable army of demons was expelled, at any rate for a time. " For this purpose the Magi wrote certain words with saffron on a piece of parchment or paper, and then held the writing over a fire into which they threw cotton, garlic, grapes, wild rue, and the horn of an animal (probably a goat) that had been killed on the sixteenth of September. The spell thus prepared was nailed or glued inside of the door, and the door was painted red. Next, the priest took some sand and spread it out with a knife, while he muttered certain prayers. After that he strewed the sand on the floor, and the enchantment was complete. The demons now immediately vanished, or at least were deprived of all their malignant power." [1]

A periodic general expulsion of demons can be paralleled all the world over.

This concludes our general survey of Persian Demonology.

III

THE DEMONOLOGY OF POST-BIBLICAL JEWISH LITERATURE

We begin with the books of the Apocrypha. The comparatively rare mention of demons in this body of literature is to be accounted for owing to the subject-matter of the books in question. In most cases nothing calls for any reference to demons. An outstanding exception is the book of *Tobit*. Here Asmodæus, the evil demon, plays a prominent part (iii. 8, 9, vi. 15, 17, viii. 2, 3); he is the counterpart of the Persian Aeshma daēva, one of Angra-Mainyu's arch-fiends, mentioned above. In *Ecclus.* xxxix. 28–30 there is a striking passage; read in the light of Babylonian and Semitic demonology generally, there is no doubt that demons are referred to : " There are winds that are created for vengeance, and in their wrath lay on their scourges heavily ... fire and hail, famine and pestilence, these also are created for judgement; beasts of prey, scorpions and serpents, and the avenging sword to slay the wicked. All these are created for their uses." It is an important passage about which much could be said; but the main point is that the things mentioned are in part instruments

[1] Frazer, *The Golden Bough : The Scapegoat*, p. 145 (1913).

used by demons, and in part the incarnations of demons, according to the popular belief. Again, in *Baruch* iv. 35 vengeance on Babylon is predicted in the words: " For fire shall come upon her from the Everlasting, long to endure, and she shall be inhabited by demons for a great time."

Turning now to the Apocalyptic Literature, attention must be drawn first to the theory of the origin of demons contained in *i Enoch*. In chaps. vi–viii there is a much-elaborated account of the myth contained in *Gen.* vi. 1 ff. about the fallen angels who took wives of the daughters of men; their leader is called Semjaza, who is supported by " chiefs of tens "; Azazel is also mentioned as one of the leaders. Through these fallen angels " there arose much godlessness " among men, " and they were led astray, and became corrupt in all their ways " (viii. 2). The offspring of the unions between these fallen angels and the daughters of men were " great giants ". Then in xv. 8 ff. it goes on to say: " And now, the giants, who are produced from the spirits and flesh, shall be called evil spirits upon the earth, and on the earth shall be their dwelling. . . . And these spirits shall rise up against the children of men and against the women, because they have proceeded from them." This belief as to the origin of demons appears also in the book of *Jubilees* v. 1, 2, and elsewhere; similarly in *ii Enoch* xviii. 1–5, where they are called *Grigori*, i.e. " Watchers ", cp. *i Enoch* x. 7 ff. Erroneous as this belief is, it was held in later times (e.g. Josephus, *Antiq.* i. 73, *Jalkut Shimeoni*, Bereshith xliv).

Of the activity of demons among men a great deal is told; just a few illustrations will suffice. They are said to prompt men to idolatry, for " they lead them astray into sacrificing to demons as gods " (*i Enoch.* xix. 1, see also *Jub.* xi. 4 ff.). In *Test. XII Patr.*, *Reuben* iii. 3–6, all kinds of sin in men are said to be due to demons: impurity, greed, fighting, dissimulation, pride, lying, deceit, and injustice; similar demonic action is described in a number of other passages in this book. In the book of *Jubilees* xi. 4, 5, it is said that " malignant spirits assisted and seduced them into committing transgression and unclean-ness. And the prince Mastema (another leader of the demons) exerted himself to do all this, and sent forth other spirits, those which were put under his hand, to do all manner of wrong and sin, and all manner of transgression, to corrupt and to destroy, and to shed blood upon the earth." This prompting to evil goes on especially at nights, when the power of demons was supposed to be of particular virulence: " For even in sleep some malicious jealousy, deluding him, gnaweth, and with wicked spirits disturbeth his soul " (*Test. XII Patr.*, *Simeon* iv. 9). Evil thoughts as well as evil deeds are thus due to demons; this is again brought out clearly in the book of *Jubilees* xii. 20: " Deliver me from the hands of evil spirits who have dominion over the thoughts of men's hearts, and let them not lead me astray from thee, my God." Diseases of the body were likewise believed to be inflicted by demons (*Test. XII Patr.*, *Simeon* iv. 8; *Jub.* x. 10–13); in the latter passage it is told how the angels taught Noah " all the medicines for their diseases, together with their seductions, how he might heal them with herbs of the earth ". In contrast to this *naïve* idea, however, it is said in .*Test. XII Patr.*, *Simeon* iii. 5, that " if a man flee to the Lord, the evil spirit runneth away from him, and his mind is lightened."

Enough has now been said to illustrate the general belief in demons and their activity, as held during the Greek Period. Various matters in connexion with the subject have not been dealt with, such as the relationship between demons and the principle of evil, and as to whether it is not the outcome of antecedent dualistic beliefs; but our present object has been merely to point to the widespread belief in demons as the background of much that we read in the New Testament. A great deal of interesting information will be found in Julian Morgenstern's *The Mythological Background of Psalm 82*, off-print from " Hebrew Union College Annual ", vol. xiv (1939).

IV

BELIEF IN DEMONS IN THE NEW TESTAMENT

Here we are faced, it must be confessed, with a subject which has caused to many true believers searchings of heart. Most people nowadays find it difficult to believe that a deaf or a dumb person, or a paralytic, or an epileptic, or a lunatic, is the victim of a demoniacal onslaught. Medical science accounts for the existence of such physical defects on grounds far indeed removed

from the action of ill-disposed spiritual powers. This is not
to deny that in innumerable cases human suffering is due to
sin; but the sin lies with man, not with demons; and in
what numberless instances it is not due to sin at all! We recall
Jn. ix. 2, 3: " Rabbi, who did sin, this man, or his parents,
that he should be born blind? Jesus answered, Neither did
this man sin, nor his parents. . . ."

But if those are right who deny that sickness and infirmity
are to be traced to demoniacal activity, the question naturally
arises: How is the fact to be accounted for that, according to
the Gospel records, our Lord believed in demons and their
attacks on human beings? Let us consider a little what these
records say upon the subject, prefacing our remarks by re-
minding ourselves of the facts, referred to above, that the
popular belief in the activity of demons was universal, and had
been so for millenniums, and, on the other hand, that all
suffering and misfortune were regarded as marks of divine
punishment for sin;—the inherent incompatibility of these two
conceptions cannot be ignored.

First let us note that there are a certain number of passages
which record cases of the healing of sickness or other infirmity,
but in which there is no hint of these having been caused by
demons. Such are, for example, *Mk.* i. 29–31 (= *Matth.*
viii. 14–16, *Lk.* iv. 38–41); *Mk.* i. 40–45 (= *Matth.* viii. 2–4,
Lk. v. 12–16); *Mk.* ii. 1–12 (= *Matth.* ix. 1–8, *Lk.* v. 18–26);
Mk. v. 21–43 (= *Matth.* ix. 18–26, *Lk.* viii. 40–56); *Mk.* vii.
31–36 (cp. *Matth.* xv. 29–32); *Mk.* viii. 22–26 (no parallels);
Jn. iv. 46–54, v. 2–9, ix. 1–7 (no parallels). Passages such
as these are of interest since they suggest that sickness was not
necessarily ascribed to the malevolence of demons, nor as
inflicted because of sin.

Our next point worth consideration is this: There are some
passages recording cures in which it seems that the healed man
himself is his own victim quite apart from any demonic activity
(cp. *Jas.* i. 14, " Each man is tempted when he is drawn away
by his own lust and enticed "). When it is said that the demon
speaks, it is the man who utters the words; no doubt it is implied that the demon speaks through him; but it is difficult
for us in these days to interpret it thus. Passages like these give
the impression that our Lord did not Himself regard the sick

man as the victim of a demoniacal onslaught. They are not
many in number, it is true, but it is possible that they reflect
the actual facts of the case of other accounts of healing—
accounts which have been recorded by the evangelists in the
light of their own ingrained beliefs. The passages in question
must be studied with an open mind, they are: *Mk*. v. 1–20,
vii. 24–30, 31–37, ix. 14–29; *Matth*. ix. 32–34, xvii. 18;
Lk. vii. 1–10, xi. 14.

One other consideration; in view of the widespread popular
beliefs on the subject, it is significant to find how comparatively
few are the recorded cases in the Gospels in which there is a
definite recognition of the existence of demons on the part of
our Lord. Even assuming that the evangelists partaking of the
age-long beliefs about the activity of demons among men,
put into the mouth of our Lord words which they felt He must
have uttered under the conditions recounted, it is somewhat
remarkable that there are so comparatively few passages in
which our Lord is recorded as, in so many words, recognizing
the existence of demons. In the earliest Gospel, that of *Mark*,
there are four such passages; similarly in *Matthew* and *Luke*,
four in each; and in *John* only one. Some of these passages,
moreover, are parallels; they are as follows: *Mk*. i. 25 (= *Lk*.
iv. 35); v. 8 ff. (= *Matth*. viii. 28–34, *Lk*. viii. 26–40); but
the crucial words, " For he said unto him, Come forth, thou
unclean spirit, out of the man ", do not occur in *Matthew*
and *Luke*. Then there is *Mk*. vii. 29 (= *Matth*. xv. 28), but
here again there is a marked difference in phraseology in
these two concluding verses of the episode; in the former it
says: " And he said unto her, For this saying go thy way;
the demon is gone out of thy daughter "; but in *Matthew*
there is no mention of the demon: " Then Jesus answered and
said unto her, O woman, great is thy faith; be it done unto
thee even as thou wilt."

Next we have *Mk*. ix. 25 (= *Matth*. xvii. 18, *Lk*. ix. 42);
further, xvi. 17, here in the parallel passages containing our
Lord's final words to the disciples (*Matth*. xxviii. 16 ff., *Lk*.
xxiv. 44 ff.), there is nothing corresponding to the saying,
" In my name shall they cast out demons." We turn now to
Matthew, where, apart from the parallels already indicated,
only two passages come into consideration, namely, x. 8,

in neither of the parallels to which, *Mk*. vi. 7, *Lk*. ix. 1, are Christ's words about demons recorded. The other passage is xii. 27, 28; in the parallel passage, *Mk*. iii. 23–26, Satan is mentioned in place of demons, while in *Lk*. xi. 17–20 both Satan and demons are spoken of. Then as to the third Gospel, apart again from parallels already indicated, there is only one passage, xiii. 32, to be considered. Here it is once more definitely stated, " Behold, I cast out demons and perform cures . . . "; but there are no parallels in the other Gospels. Finally, in the fourth Gospel there is but a single instance of Christ, in His own words, making reference to the subject of demons: " I have not a demon " (viii. 49).

Thus, taking the four Gospels, and allowing for parallel passages, it is somewhat remarkable to find that there are so few instances of our Lord, in His own words, as distinct from words imputed to Him, making references to demons, and thus recognizing their existence.

In view, then, of what has been said, it cannot cause surprise that many scholars express doubts as to whether Christ really believed in the existence of demons. Thus, some maintain that the evangelists ascribe to our Lord popular views regarding demons which He did not Himself hold. Another opinion is that though Christ did not share the generally held belief in demons, He tolerated the popular conceptions for the people's sake in order to prevent their thinking that He was out of sympathy with them. This was part of the self-limitation involved in the Incarnation. Similarly, our Lord accepted the sacrificial system for the sake of the people, while not believing in the atoning efficacy of sacrifices as generally held. Once more, other authorities urge that although our Lord did not accept the popular views concerning demons, He would not divert attention from the deeper things He taught by raising discussion on side issues; He accepted the scientific premises of the people He addressed, just as He accepted their critical premises in dealing with the Scriptures.

We confess to a feeling of sympathy with these views; and, in conclusion, feel compelled to ask the two following questions: Does not Christ's whole conception of and teaching on Sin necessitate His repudiation of belief in demons? And, is not belief in demons the outcome of a dualistic conception which is ultimately a denial of true monotheism?

We have no wish to be dogmatic on this difficult subject; we only plead that, in a reverent spirit of enquiry, we should ask ourselves whether our Lord could really have shared the popular beliefs in demons of His day which subsequent ages have found impossible to accept as being in accordance with realities; and also whether, in a few passages, the evangelists may not have imputed to Christ the expression of ideas which to them were axiomatic, but which He Himself did not actually express.

As to the references to demons in the other books of the New Testament, there is but little to be said. The mention of them occurs only eight times. In three of the passages in question demons are identified with false gods (*Acts* xvii. 18; *i Cor.* x. 19–21; *Rev.* ix. 20); three others hardly come into consideration, namely, *i Tim.* iv. 1; *Jas.* iii. 15; *Rev.* xvi. 14; the really relevant passages are only two in number: *Jas.* ii. 19 and *Rev.* xviii. 2; these reflect the popular belief.

CHAPTER XXIV

RETROSPECTIVE SUMMARY

We have endeavoured to describe the religious beliefs of the Jews as these existed during the two or three centuries immediately preceding the beginning of the foundation of Christianity. Much that Judaism taught during this period contained truths which were accepted by the Founder of Christianity; in so far as these truths were accepted by Him, Judaism was a preparation for Christianity. In other respects Judaism presented inadequately developed truths; the full development of these was set forth in the teaching of Christ. But these, too, played their part in the gradual preparation of the Jewish people for Christianity. In a few instances Jewish teaching was definitely on the wrong lines; in these cases their repudiation by Christ was inevitable. Taken as a whole, however, Judaism must be regarded as constituting in a true sense the preparation for Christianity; this was recognized by our Lord Himself, in saying: " Salvation is of the Jews ", " Think not that I came to destroy the Law or the prophets. . . ."

As a preliminary study of Judaism during the Greek Period it was well that we should give a bird's-eye view of world-history from the time of Alexander the Great onwards, i.e. the Greek Period, up to the eve of the Christian era. To gain a general idea of the *milieu* in which the Jewish people found themselves during this period, a glance at world-history was called for on account of the various extraneous influences to which they were subjected. Although these did not affect the fundamental tenets of Judaism, contact with the world of thought in their surroundings, whether in the Dispersion or in Palestine, could not fail to leave its impress on the mental attitude of Jewish teachers and their followers. As this is seen in various ways in studying the history of the Jewish people during the period in question, it was necessary to deal in some detail with this special branch of history in addition to the general world-history.

Having then presented in outline the historical conditions, our next task was to enter upon the study of Judaism. It is obvious that we had to begin here with some reference to the ultimate sources from which we gain our knowledge of the various tenets of Judaism. The Old Testament Scriptures, it goes without saying, stand foremost, since they contain the traditional beliefs of the Hebrews handed down through the centuries.

There arises here the question, which had to be faced, as to how far these Scriptures were authoritative in the sense that what was written in them was to be accepted as binding. From the Exile onwards, and due in the first instance to the work of Ezra and his followers, the " Law of Moses " in its written (and later in its full oral) form assumed this position of authority. To this were added the prophetical books, and somewhat later the remaining books. Thus the Scriptures included the Law, the Prophets, and what are called the " Writings ". These constituted the primary source for the religion of the Jews. But it must be recognized that, while authoritative, these Scriptures were not yet what we understand by the term "canonical", i.e. writings of such a sacrosanct nature that no word might be added to, or taken from, them. This did not occur until the " Hebrew Canon " was officially fixed at the so-called council of Jabne, at the end of the first century A.D.

So far, then, our first source. The second source is the collection of books which now goes under the name of Apocrypha. These, though almost all included in the " Greek Canon " (the Septuagint), were never regarded as authoritative by the Palestinian Jewish religious leaders. They are, nevertheless, an important source for our knowledge of ortho-dox Jewish beliefs during the Greek Period.

The third source is the Apocalyptic Literature. The im-portance of these writings centres mainly in their eschatological teaching. For reasons which have been pointed out, this literature was not viewed with favour by the orthodox religious teachers. In some of the most important apocalypses a considerable amount of non-Jewish extraneous material has

U

41

been embodied. Herein lies a matter of profound interest and far-reaching importance. The influence of alien beliefs on the religion of the Hebrews goes back to early times. The Old Testament contains manifold marks of Babylonian mythology and legendary material. The influence of some Egyptian religious beliefs is also, in all probability, to be detected. But in the Apocalyptic Literature it is, above all, the influence of the religion of ancient Persia in the domain of eschatology which is to be discerned in many directions. The importance of this demanded some detailed account of Zoroastrian religion. Hellenistic influences also made themselves felt.

Our sources having thus been indicated, we were able to deal with the more outstanding tenets of Judaism as these existed during the Greek Period.

Since every dogma of Judaism was founded on the teaching of the Old Testament, it was demanded that in the discussion on each of these dogmas recourse should be had in the first instance to what is there taught on the subject. In some cases this involved rather fuller treatment than in others. This applies especially to monotheistic belief which constitutes the fundamental dogma of Judaism. It was not until the exilic period that monotheism, as distinct from monolatrous worship, was taught in its fullness. In the true sense monotheistic belief repudiates the possibility of the existence of any gods but One. During the Greek Period the evidence shows that among some Jewish circles the belief handed down since exilic times was not always strictly held; but orthodox Judaism strongly, and always, insisted upon a true monotheism; and this is fully illustrated in the Apocrypha and in the Apocalyptic Literature.

The worship of the One God brought with it rightly and necessarily an exalted conception of the Divine Transcendence. There arose, in consequence, the impulse to personify the divine attributes, whereby the will of God was fulfilled on earth without His direct action, which was thought to be derogatory to His majesty and glory. Thus we find already in the Old Testament indications in this direction: the spirit of God, the word of God, and Wisdom, are personified. In the later literature the word becomes identified with Wisdom. That the adumbration of eternal truths is to be discerned here must be recognized. The conception of the Divine Transcendence had the further effect of making men avoid the direct mention of the Name of God; the Almighty was spoken of in terms of circumlocution. It followed that the traditional name of the God of Israel, Yahweh, ceased to be uttered excepting on very special occasions.

Connected with belief in God, though in different ways, were the two mental attitudes of Universalism and Particularism; some consideration of these was, therefore, also demanded. Of greater importance, however, and belonging inseparably to monotheistic belief, is the subject of the Kingdom of Heaven; indeed, every dogma of Judaism is more or less directly connected with this. So much is involved in dealing with this stupendous subject that the only thing to be done was to take the various elements embraced within it one by one and examine them independently.

A preliminary consideration was the world-wide belief, in past ages, in the time of primeval happiness, a time which in due course would again be the lot of man on earth. The Hebrew conception of this was expressed by the term *Shūb Shebūth*, implying the bringing back of the primeval time of happiness; this was spoken of as the "Day of Yahweh". Here again it was called for that we should turn to the Old Testament and examine the teaching there contained concerning the Kingdom of Yahweh. This was conceived of as comprising the land of Israel; but, on the other hand, it was also spoken of as world-embracing. The two conceptions are incompatible, and can be accounted for only an the assumption that the latter was due to extraneous influence on Israel's religious thinkers. It receives full expression in some of the post-Biblical literature.

The subject of the Kingdom of Heaven embraces, as we have said, others which are among the most important in our study. First, the Messiah. Two stages of belief come before us here. Starting again, as we must, from the Old Testament, it had to be noted that certain passages which have been traditionally regarded as Messianic prophecies were not intended as such by the inspired writers. We have, therefore, applied the term "ideal figure" to him who is presented in these passages. He comes to inaugurate the return of the time of primeval happiness, spoken of above. In course of time the *rôle* of this " ideal figure " is transferred to a scion of the house of David. But in the reference to that happy time to come the Davidic ruler, now sometimes thought of as the Messiah, plays a quite subordinate part—it is Yahweh Who is spoken of as the Ruler. The examination of many passages in the post-Biblical writings in which the Kingdom is spoken of reveals a similar conception; the Messianic figure is presented, but he plays an insignificant part, and he appears as purely human. This all applies to the earlier stages of Messianic belief. In the second stage a great development is seen to have taken place; this development, it is true, does not appear in the teaching of orthodox Judaism, but it is put forth in some of the writings of the Apocalyptists whose presentation of the transcendental Messiah is that of the divine Judge who sits upon the throne of God, and who comes to inaugurate the Kingdom of Heaven. In this twofold conception of the Messiah, human and divine, incompatible as it appears, we are justified in perceiving the inspired efforts of men seeking after an eternal truth which was ultimately revealed in the Person of Jesus Christ.

Of the various other subjects which necessarily come into consideration in connexion with belief in the Kingdom to come, we dealt first with that which excludes men from the Kingdom, namely, Sin and its consequences. How Sin originated was a problem which exercised the minds of the devout and thoughtful. Our brief account of the theories propounded to account for the existence of Sin led to the contemplation of its prevalence, as illustrated in the writings of the period with which we are mainly concerned. Retribution as the result of Sin unrepented of was the lot of the sinner in this life, and also hereafter. But to the repentant there was the means of Sin being obliterated. Here we have, on the one hand, three highly significant indications, though quite exceptional, of the means of obliterating sin; they occur in the Old Testament: intercessory prayer, vicarious suffering, divine forgiveness freely accorded. But the normal means of ridding oneself of sins and their consequences was the offering of sacrifices; and this continued during the Greek Period.

Our thoughts then turned to the great subject of Immortality, indissolubly bound up with the Kingdom of Heaven.

How needful it is that in dealing with the Judaism of the Greek Period we should always primarily have recourse to the teaching of the Old Testament is pointedly illustrated when we come to speak of the belief in the life hereafter. For the normal undeveloped conceptions traditionally held persisted in spite of the fuller beliefs which were coming to the fore. What we learn here from the Old Testament is of the greatest interest; even the superstitious beliefs connected with necromancy were not without touches of the reality of things in so far as the continued existence of personality after death was believed in. But necromancy was incompatible with true religion; and the prophets, the champions of the worship of Yahweh, combatted the dangerous tendencies, and taught the doctrine of *Sheôl*. In a few passages in the Old Testament it is seen that with the gradually developing belief in Yahweh the conceptions regarding the life hereafter became more exalted; but they are exceptional. It was during the Greek Period, and, it must be recognized, owing to extra-Jewish belief, that the doctrine of Immortality in the fuller sense was held among the Jews.

It is, above all, in the Apocalyptic Literature that the developed belief in Immortality is set forth. Though in some details there is not always unanimity in what is described, in general, complete agreement reigns regarding the outstanding beliefs. First, it is taught that there will be the Judgement; the Almighty will sit upon His throne to judge all men; sometimes it is the Messiah who is thought of as the Judge. In some of the apocalypses the Resurrection is made to precede the Judgement. In others, again, it is said that the departed live in an intermediate state before their bodies rise to appear before the Judgement-seat. Difference of view appears again on the question as to whether all rise, the wicked as well as the righteous, or only the latter. And once more, while some teach the resurrection of the spirit, the more usual doctrine is that of the resurrection of the body. The final destiny of the righteous and the wicked, respectively, is very graphically described in the Apocalyptic Literature; the conceptions of Heaven and Hell are largely borrowed from extraneous sources.

This concluded our consideration of the doctrines of Judaism.

Attention was drawn next to the subject of Worship. Here, of course, the importance of the Temple in the national life of the Jews claimed notice, and what is said on this in the post-Biblical literature was examined; and some details regarding the conduct of worship received attention. The origin of the Synagogue and its worship followed, and it was pointed out that, so far as Palestine was concerned, there is no evidence of the existence of synagogues there prior to the Maccabæan struggle. In the lands of the Dispersion, on the other hand, it is certain that they existed in earlier times. Definite evidence of this is seen, for example, on an inscription found in a locality close to Alexandria belonging to the middle of the third century B.C. The account of public worship was supplemented by noting some of the many indications of the existence of private worship; personal religion was a more pronounced element than is often realized.

It was necessary that some attention should then be devoted to those who were teachers, using the word in a wide sense, among the people. The Scribes and the Wisdom teachers, taking priority chronologically, were first dealt with. The most important during the period with which we are mainly concerned were the Pharisees; something had also to be said about the Sadducees. Though not teachers in the ordinary sense, the Essenes and the Therapeutæ were emphatically such in their example of godly living. Both of these bodies must have exercised much influence for good; it was, therefore, fitting that something should be said about each of these.

Finally, the subjects of Angels and Demons were discussed; this was called for on account of the part they played in popular beliefs, quite apart from the underlying truths and realities regarding their existence.

. . . . .

We hope, then, that we have succeeded, at any rate to some extent, in showing how Judaism, as this existed during the Greek Period, was in many ways a preparation for Christianity. "Salvation is of the Jews." But, as we have seen, Judaism had absorbed much that was of non-Jewish origin. Thus, under God, through the medium of Judaism, Christianity accepted and brought to their fullness religious truths which had been the heritage of nations who had not acknowledged the God of Israel, but to whom divine revelation had been granted in accordance with their capacity for apprehension. The immeasurable significance of the Apostle's words to the Athenians it is impossible to exaggerate : " Whom ye ignorantly worship, him declare I unto you." In His mercy, God has never left Himself without witness among all the nations, " if haply they might feel after Him, and find Him, though He is not far from everyone of us." True, the Jews responded more fully to the witness which, in loving condescension, God had left of Himself among all nations, and they thus became, in due time, His specially chosen people. Yet, let us not forget the words of one of their inspired prophets : " Art not thou from everlasting, Yahweh, my holy God ! "

BIBLIOGRAPHY

ABBOTT, *The Message of the Son of Man* (1909).
APTOWITZER, *Parteipolitik der Hasmonäerzeit im rabbinischen und pseudoepigraphischen Schrifttum* (1927).
BERNARD, *The Odes of Solomon* (1912).
BEVAN, *Jerusalem under the High Priests* (1904).
BÖKLEN, *Die Verwandtschaft der jüdisch-christlichen mit der parsischen Eschatologie* (1902).
BONSIRVEN, *Le Judaïsme palestinien* (2 vols., 1934, 1935).
BOUSSET, *Die Religion des Judentums im späthellenistischen Zeitalter* (1926).
BOX, *The Ezra-Apocalypse* (1912).
BROWNE, *Early Judaism* (1920).
BUBER, *Königtum Gottes* (1936).
BÜCHLER, *Die Tobiaden und die Oniaden im ii Makkabäerbuche . . .* (1899).
—— *Der Galiläische 'Am-ha 'Areṣ des zweiten Jahrhunderts* (1906).
BURKITT, *Judaism and the Beginnings of Christianity* (1923).
BURY and Others, *The Hellenistic Age* (1923).
CHARLES, *The Apocalypse of Baruch* (1896).
—— *The Book of the Secrets of Enoch* (1896).
—— *The Ascension of Isaiah* (1900).
—— *The Testaments of the Twelve Patriarchs* (1908).
—— *The Book of Enoch* (1912).
—— *Eschatology, Hebrew, Jewish, and Christian* (1913).
—— ed., *The Apocrypha and Pseudepigrapha of the Old Testament* (1913).
—— *A critical and exegetical commentary on the Book of Daniel* (1929).
DALMAN, *Die Worte Jesu* (1898).
DARMSTETER, in *Sacred Books of the East*, vols. iv, xxiii (1880, 1883).
DEHN, *Der Gottessohn* (1932).
DODD, *The Bible and the Greeks* (1935).
ELBOGEN, *Der jüdische Gottesdienst in seiner geschichtlichen Entwickelung* (1913).
EMMET, *The eschatological question in the Gospels* (1911).
FERRAR, *From Daniel to St. John the Divine* (1930).
FRIEDLÄNDER, *Die religiösen Bewegungen innerhalb des Judentums im Zeitalter Jesu* (1905).
—— *Synagoge und Kirche in ihren Anfängen* (1908).
V. GALL, Βασιλεια του Θεου (1926).
GOODRICK, *The Book of Wisdom* (1913).
GRESSMANN, *Die orientalischen Religionen im hellenistischen-römischen Zeitalter* (1930).
GUIGNEBERT, *The Jewish World in the time of Jesus* (transl. Hooke, 1939).
HERFORD, *The Pharisees* (1924).
HÉRING, *Le royaume de Dieu et sa venue* (1927).
HUNTER, *After the Exile* (1890).
JAMES, *The Testament of Abraham* (1892).
KABISCH, *Das vierte Buch Esra auf seine Quellen untersucht* (1889).
KAUPEL, *Die Dämonen in Alten Testament* (1930).
KAUTZSCH, ed., *Die Apokryphen und Pseudepigraphen des Alten Testaments* (1900).
KITTEL, *Die Religionsgeschichte und das Urchristentum* (1931).
KOHUT, *Über die jüdische Angelologie und Dämonologie in ihrer Abhängigkeit vom Parsismus* (1866).

LAGRANGE, *Le Judaïsme avant Jésus-Christ* (1931).
LIGHTLEY, *Jewish Sects and Parties in the time of Jesus* (1925).
MACGREGOR and PURDY, *Jew and Greek : tutors unto Christ* (1936).
MESSEL, *Die Einheitlichkeit der jüdischen Eschatologie* (1915).
—— *Der Menschensohn in den Bilderreden des Henoch* (1922).
MOORE, *Judaism in the first centuries of the Christian era* (1927).
MOULTON, *Early Zoroastrianism* (1913).
—— *The Treasure of the Magi* (1917).
OTTO, *Gottheit und Gottheiten der Arier* (1932).
—— *Reich Gottes und Menschensohn* (1934).
REINACH, *Textes d'auteurs Grecs et Romains relatifs au Judaïsme* (1895).
RENDEL HARRIS, *The Odes and Psalms of Solomon published from the Syriac Version* (1911).
ROSS, *The Persians* (1913).
ROWLEY, *Darius the Mede and the four world empires in the Book of Daniel* (1935).
—— *Israel's Mission to the world* (1939).
RYLE and JAMES, *Psalms of the Pharisees* (1891).
SCHEFTELOWITZ, *Die altpersische Religion und das Judentum* (1920).
SCHLATTER, *Geschichte Israels von Alexander dem Grossen bis Hadrian* (1925).
—— *Die Theologie des Judentums nach dem Bericht des Josephus* (1932).
SCHÜRER, *Geschichte des jüdischen Volkes im Zeitalter Jesu Christi* (1901–1909).
SCHÜTZ, *Les idées eschatologiques du Livre de la Sagesse* (1935).
SMEND, *Die Weisheit des Jesus Sirach* (1906).
SUKENIK, *Ancient synagogues in Palestine and Greece* (1934).
TARN, *Hellenistic Civilization* (1930).
VOLZ, *Jüdische Eschatologie von Daniel bis Akiba* (1903).
—— *Die Eschatologie der jüdischen Gemeinde im neutestamentlichen Zeitalter* (1930).
WALKER, *The Teaching of Jesus and the Jewish Teaching of His age* (1923).
WATERHOUSE, *Zoroastrianism* (1934).
WEBER, *Jüdische Theologie auf Grund des Talmud und verwandter Schriften* (1897).
WENDLAND, *Die hellenistische-römische Kultur im ihren Beziehungen zu Judentum und Christentum* (1912).
WEST, in *Sacred Books of the East*, vols. v, xviii, xxiv (1880, 1882, 1885).
WILLIAMS JACKSON, *Zoroaster, the Prophet of Ancient Iran* (1889).
WILLRICH, *Das Haus des Herodes* (1929).
ZUNZ, *Die gottesdienstlichen Vorträge der Juden* (1892).

The S.P.C.K. has published the following handy volumes in the Series "Translations of Early Documents":

BATE, *The Sibylline Oracles*, Books iii–v (1918).
BOX, *The Apocalypse of Ezra* (1917).
—— *The Apocalypse of Abraham* (1918).
—— *The Testament of Abraham* (1927).
CHARLES, *The Ascension of Isaiah* (1917).
—— *The Book of Jubilees* (1917).
—— *The Testaments of the Twelve Patriarchs* (1917).
—— *The Book of Enoch* (1917).
—— *The Apocalypse of Baruch* (1917).
EMMET, *The 3rd and 4th Books of Maccabees* (1918).
FERRAR, *The Assumption of Moses* (1917).
OESTERLEY, *The Wisdom of Ben-Sira (Ecclesiasticus)* (1916).
—— *The Wisdom of Solomon* (1917).
THACKERAY, *The Letter of Aristeas* (1917).

INDEX

Printed and Bound in Great Britain by
Richard Clay and Company, Ltd.,
Bungay, Suffolk.